A WHITE SIDE OF BLACK BRITAIN

France Winddance Twine

A WHITE SIDE OF BLACK BRITAIN

INTERRACIAL INTIMACY
AND RACIAL LITERACY

Photographs by Michael Smyth

DUKE UNIVERSITY PRESS   DURHAM AND LONDON   2010

© 2010 Duke University Press

All rights reserved

Printed in the United States of America on acid-free paper ♾

Designed by Heather Hensley

Typeset in Monotype Bembo by Tseng Information Systems, Inc.

Library of Congress Cataloging-in-Publication Data appear on the last printed page of this book.

FOR *Allan, Nelista,*
and the antiracist community

CONTENTS

ILLUSTRATIONS

ACKNOWLEDGMENTS

A White Side of Black Britain is based on a long period of field research. Funding for that research was provided in the early stages by the Royalty Research Fund at the University of Washington (1996–97), the Dean's Office at the University of California, Santa Barbara (1998–2001), and the Sociology Department at Duke University (2003–4). The Rockefeller Foundation provided me with a one-month residency at the Bellagio Study and Conference Center in Bellagio, Italy, in July 2001, which enabled me to analyze data and complete drafts of two chapters. I am especially grateful for the friendships I developed there with Carol Wise (University of Southern California) and Wolfgang Mueller (University of Austria).

I am very grateful to the following chairs in the sociology departments at Duke University and the University of California, Santa Barbara, who provided me with generous research leaves or flexible teaching schedules which enabled me to continue my field research: William Bielby, Phil Morgan, Beth Schneider, Noah Friedkin, and Verta Taylor. I conducted much of the research for this book while teaching at the University of California, Santa Barbara and Duke University. I thank Kim Summerfield for her generosity, patience, and professionalism as she coordinated my teaching schedule. I completed the final chapters of this book while in residence at the London School of Economics and Political Science. I thank Paul Gilroy and Claire Alexander for their support of my residency.

This book would not have been possible without the support of the African Caribbean community in Leicester. Many people graciously welcomed me into their homes and their lives. They supported my research despite the emotional burdens that it placed on them and their families. Members of the community assisted me in various ways including providing me with crucial introductions to friends and family members, sharing their personal libraries with me, driving me to appointments, picking me up at the airport, inviting me to accompany them to black community events, sharing unpublished oral histories, and assisting me in identifying and obtaining published reports detailing the historical and contemporary experiences of the African, Caribbean, and Asian communities in Leicester. In this vein, I thank the following people for their support of my research: Bernice Bennett, Owen Brown, Jane Cole Brown, Gerry Burke, Mandy Burke, Jane Burke, Debbion Burkmar, James Burkmar, Rosemary Campbell, Mina Carter, George Andrew Carter, Caroline Churchill, Leticia Clarke, Charisa Clarke, Sue Cooper, Barbara Cover, Liz Cumberbatch, Aisha Dawkins, Imani Dawkins, Sharon Dawkins, Everal Dawkins, Eileen Louise Dawkins, Sherrill Dawkins, Rhea Dawkins, Tanika Dawkins, Maureen Dover, Jane Elliot, Mara Teresa Forana, Dane Farrell, Sue Farrell, Dawn Fletcher, Jennifer Finlayson, Dorothy Francis, Dudley George, Jackie George, Laura Jane Gordon, Jane Green, Melvin Green, Lisa Hackett, Kathleen Hackett, Ian Richard Hackett, Jackie Hall, Netifnet Arthur-Hawkes, Stephen Hawkes, Owen London, Kevin Hudson, Genette Hill, Lesley Morris, Derek Inham, Alexia Inham, Gillian Johnson, Leigh Pinsent, Elizabeth McCalla, Josephine McGinty, Marie Messiah, Helena Mitchell, Anita O'Reilly, Eshe Talibah Mitchell, Justine Moonen, Lesley Barbara Morris, Glenda Terry, Mark Littlewood, Fayann Clarke, Ann Lewis, Michael Lewis, Annette Piper, Brian Piper, Desmond Sands, Paul Simpson, Samantha Simpson, Chloe Talbot Kelly Smith, Jeffrey Smith, Alexander Smith, Marie Smith, Sheila Stabbaner, Danny Stabbaner, Paul Solomon, Zosha Solomon, Glenda Terry, Angelita Williams, Denise Williams, Max Williams, and Cheryl Weathers.

When I arrived in England in 1995 to conduct pilot research I was a recently hired assistant professor with no funding. Stephen Small of UC, Berkeley, Julia Sudbury, Julia O'Connell Davidson, and Jacqueline Sanchez-Taylor provided me with a bed to sleep on, meals, introductions to potential informants, rides to and from the airport, and other forms of assistance which helped me to launch my research in Leicester and London. Nelista Cuffy, a Leicester City Council employee when I began this research, became like a family member to me. She provided me with a place to sleep, picked me up from the airport, introduced me to key members of the African Caribbean community, drove me to interviews, taught me how to use the public transit system, and did everything she could to facilitate my research. I am forever indebted to Nelista; she became a dedicated friend and is one of the kindest women I have ever known.

Several families gave me forms of support that were crucial to launching and sustaining my field research. I can never repay their kindness. Mandy and Gerry Burke provided me with crucial contacts and introduced me to the Highfield Rangers club and took me to numerous black community events. Anita O'Riley gave me keys to her homes and allowed me to stay with her whenever I needed accommodations. Sharon and Everal Dawkins also graciously opened their home to me and invited me to spend many nights and eat many wonderful Sunday meals. Sharon Dawkins, Anita O'Riley, Helena Mitchell, and Netifnet Arthur-Hawkes did library research for me and sent me books and local reports that were unavailable or difficult to locate in the United States.

My collaborator and dear friend Michael Smyth, a distinguished Irish photographer and digital filmmaker, accompanied me on four research trips and was a joy to work with, and he patiently worked with me over a five-year period. His contribution to this book cannot be overstated. He created a visual archive and databank of more than 1,600 photographs. We have only been able to reproduce a small number for this book. I am very grateful to Michael for his hard work on this project and for accepting my invitation to collaborate with me—an unknown American—for a very modest amount.

I received invitations to participate in seminars and symposia, where I presented drafts of chapters of this book and received comments and criticism from the audiences. Along these lines, I thank the sociology departments at Cambridge University, Duke University, City University of London, Indiana University, Northwestern University, the Graduate Center at the City University of New York, the London School of Economics and Political Science, Stanford Humanities Center, UCLA, UC, Santa Cruz, University of British Columbia (Vancouver), University of Edinburgh, University of Iowa, University of Manchester, University of North Carolina at Chapel Hill, University of Surrey at Guildford, University of Toronto, and University of Wisconsin at Madison.

I participated in several organized workshops and mini-conferences that gave me feedback which assisted me in the conceptual framing of my book. Claire Alexander invited me to present a paper in the workshop she organized "Writing Race: Ethnography and Difference" (2004) at the London School of Economics. An earlier version of chapter 6 of this book was written for that conference. I thank Shelley Wong for her invitation to participate in the conference "Comparative Study of Race, Ethnicity and Indigeneity" (2004) at Cornell University. I thank Tina Campt, a historian, who organized "Remaking Black Europe: New Feminist Cartographies of Race, Gender and Nation" (2001). This interdisciplinary workshop was the only conference in which I have participated that brought together black feminist scholars across disciplines conducting original research on Europe. It was a transformative intellectual experience and mediated the isolation and loneliness of being a black American feminist writing on Europe. Finally, I thank Philip Kasinitz, John Mollenkopf, and Mary Waters for inviting me to participate in their Rockefeller Foundation conference held at the Bellagio Study Center (2003), "Second Generation Immigrants in Europe and North America." All of these workshops have left their intellectual imprint on my work and helped me to rethink sections of my book.

Jacqueline Nassy Brown was already a seasoned field researcher and theorist working in black Liverpool when I began my pilot research. I thank her for sharing the field with me and for her theoretical insights. Her friendship, support, and the outstanding theoretical contributions she has made to the scholarship on the African diaspora in Britain was a gift to me and other ethnographers conducting research on race in England. Several people held my hand throughout the final stages of preparing this book for publication. I completed the final editorial revisions while at the Center for Advanced Study in Behavioral Sciences at Stanford University. Bobbie Issaacman carefully read the entire manuscript with her keen editorial eyes, and it is a much better one for it. Steve Epstein gave me critical comments on the first chapters and helped me revise them. I am grateful to Christian Davenport, Lani Guinier, Cynthia Pilch, Susan Mattos, Rose McDermott, and Allen Issaacman for their friendship, laughter, and kindness. Anitra Grisales, a freelance editor, helped me prepare the manuscript for Duke University Press; her patience and humor guided me through the final revisions. Valerie Millholland, my editor at Duke University Press, has supported me and this book project during a series of traumas, including my mother's unexpected suicide in 2002, which delayed the completion of this book. Valerie continued to have faith in me and this book.

An earlier version of chapter 2 was published by Indiana University Press as "Transgressive Women and Transracial Mothers: White Women and Critical Race Theory" in *Meridians* 1, no. 2 (Spring 2001): 130–53. An earlier version of chapter 4 was published by Routledge (Taylor & Francis) as "A White Side of Black Britain: The Concept of Racial Literacy" in *Ethnic and Racial Studies* 27, no. 6 (November 2004): 1–30. An earlier version of chapter 6 was published as "Visual Ethnography and Racial Theory: Family Photographs as Archives of Interracial Intimacies" in *Ethnic and Racial Studies* 29, no. 3 (May 2006): 478–511. And an earlier version of chapter 7 was published by Sage as "White Like Who?: The Value of Whiteness in British Interracial Families" in *Ethnicities* 10, no. 3 (September 2010): 292–312.

I owe intellectual debts to the following friends and scholars, who support my intellectual life on a daily basis. In London I thank Claire Alexander, Les Back, Martin Bulmer, Michael Keith, Caroline Knowles, Miri Song, and John Solomos. In the United States I thank my friends and intellectual comrades Michelle Elam, Ingrid Banks, Kathleen Blee, Elizabeth Bernstein, Mitch Duneier, Charles Gallagher, Kathleen Gerson, Claudine Michel, William Darity Jr., Constance Penley, Gay Seidman, Darrick Hamilton, Maxine Leeds Craig, and Jack Sutton.

The following people have provided me with refuge during challenging times when I have been intellectually and emotionally exhausted. I thank them for the laughter, kindness, the great food, the camaraderie, and the many books they have brought to my life: Constance Penley, Richard Appelbaum, Siobhan Brooks, Joseph Jewell, Hilal Elver, Richard Falk, Lisa Hajjar, Arnell Hinkle, Jennifer Holt, Roger Friedland, Debra Friedland, Lisa Parks, Annette Ordas, Leila Rupp, Karen Shapiro, Prudence Carter, Verta Taylor, Howard Winant, Craig and Ann Addis, Dalton Conley, and John Wolfe.

My family members keep me grounded and help me stay focused on what really matters. I thank my Chicago relatives, especially Stacy Saxon, Marcia Berry, Michelle Reeves, Dominic Twine, and Daily Twine. My brother Steve Twine has been a source of inspiration for me. My "sisters" Irma McClaurin, Kathleen Blee, Debbie Rogow, and Evely Laser Shlensky are always there when I need them and have supported me in too many ways to count. Finally, I thank Allan Cronin and Paul Amar for all the things that they have done to sweeten my life.

FRANCE WINDDANCE TWINE
SAN FRANCISCO, CALIFORNIA

Introduction

~~~~~~~~~~

TERRITORIES OF WHITENESS IN BLACK BRITAIN

> The "matter of race" must include stories of whiteness.
> —JANE LAZARRE, *BEYOND THE WHITENESS OF WHITENESS*

> Whiteness changes over time and space and is in no way a
> transhistorical essence.—RUTH FRANKENBERG, *WHITE WOMEN, RACE MATTERS*

Diana Jeater, a white English woman, grew up in South London in the
1970s during a period when reggae music rather than roast beef characterized her cultural landscape. Jeater, who studied African history
and wrote a doctorate on the construction of moral discourse in white-
occupied Zimbabwe, designed a course on black history. Already immersed in black culture, she became politically allied with blacks through
music and her participation in the Anti-Nazi League. Jeater, who shares
her home and her romantic life with blacks and who, as a youth, was
allied with black political struggles against the racism of the British state,
has identified a need within black antiracist political discourses for language that can account for her experiences of whiteness in London. She
argues that there is no vocabulary or category within black political discourse to accommodate the "white hybrid identity" that she acquired as
a youth in multicultural London, a position on the "white spectrum" far
removed from her parents' and grandparents' generations:

> The issue of being white comes up for me every day. It's not a theo-
> retical pondering, it's a day-to-day struggle to make sense of who I
> am. . . . I live in Brixton . . . my lover is black; so is the woman I live
> with. I can cook sadza or curry at the drop of a hat, but I don't have a
> clue how to cook roast beef. Clearly my life is not entirely white. Yet

it is my lifestyle and I am a white person. I'm not trying to be anyone other than me. Nonetheless, I find that when people discover these things about me, they accuse me (and it is an accusation) of trying to be some kind of "honorary black." It seems to me that there isn't a category to describe people like me. (1992, 108–9)

As someone who grew up listening to reggae and eating Jamaican and Asian Indian food, Jeater is evidence that the experience of whiteness cannot be understood outside of its historical context. Her analysis of what her whiteness means and how she experiences it is generationally specific and historically bound, as the epigraph by Frankenberg reminds us. In Frankenberg's words, whiteness "is a complexly constructed product of local, regional, national, and global relations, past and present. Thus, the range of possible ways of living whiteness, for an individual white woman in a particular time and place, is delimited by the relations of racism at that moment and in that place" (1993, 236).

Writing in the 1990s Jeater argues for a new theoretical model, a vocabulary, a set of metaphors that creates sociopolitical spaces for white women who live *transracial* lives. She identifies one of the limitations of the research on the "new racism" that emerged out of the crisis of the 1970s:

When we did begin to question what it meant to be "white," we found that the reasons for asking the questions confined the scope of the answer. It was in the context of the "New Racism" that certain definitions of "whiteness" came under scrutiny. Although "race" was clearly vital to any understanding of what was happening to Britain from the mid-1970s, most white commentators did not really engage with the question of what "racial" identity might mean for them. This is not because white intellectuals were not aware that "race" was a very important part of what was going on, but they tended to concentrate on *racism*, which effectively meant a concentration of white constructions of black identity. . . . The focus on racism has meant that discussion of white interactions with black people have tended to supply only one symbol of whiteness; that of the racist. (1992, 122)

Jeater identifies a problem that continues to limit the theoretical utility of research on contemporary white identities. The experiences of white women like Jeater, who grew up sharing a cultural, ideological, political, leisure, and sexual life with black Britons, illustrate the need for a nuanced analysis of whiteness that includes the experiences of postcolonial whites who grew up in multiethnic areas of urban England. Although the voices of these white women have not been audible in the micro- and macrocultural analyses of black British communities, their experiences offer important theoretical insights into the varied ways that race, specifically whiteness, is lived in postcolonial Britain. Nevertheless white women like Jeater remain in the footnotes and endnotes of black British racial and cultural studies.

In 1991 an analysis of the U.K. census revealed that half of black men of Caribbean heritage born in the United Kingdom established domestic partnerships with white women (Modood et al. 1997). The increasing numbers of children of black Caribbean fathers and white mothers provides sociologists with a strategic empirical case to examine how white parents interpret, negotiate, and counter racial hierarchies. Despite this long history of interracial family formation, little analytical attention has been given to the ways that white parents conceptualize race and respond to racial hierarchies by training their children to align themselves with racial and ethnic minorities.[1]

White women like Diana Jeater who are members of transracial or interracial households and networks, regardless of their parental status, have been relatively invisible in British sociological analyses of families. When they have appeared, they have been presented as pathological, dysfunctional sexual dissidents incapable of sustaining a relationship with a white man (Banton 1955). In the work of scholars of mixed-race studies they tend to be treated as monocultural actors rather than the product of hybrid cultural traditions that can include African, American, and Caribbean influences as well as those of ethnic Europeans. White people are not culturally homogeneous. Although white English women like Jeater may have grown up in a monoracial white family, many attended multiethnic schools and participated in a multiracial youth culture. As such, they routinely traveled across and between ethnic interzones as they socialized and established relationships in pubs, dance clubs, play groups, and after-school youth clubs.

This book examines how white people (Irish and English) living in Britain who are parenting children of African descent negotiate race, racial logics, and everyday racism as the intimates of black men and women. I offer an analysis of the ways that white and black members of transracial families think about and transform the biological, social, and moral meanings of race and racism.[2] I employ the term *transracial* rather than interracial to signal the movements that members of multiracial families make between racialized bodies, social borders, ideological positions, and cultural practices. I am interested in how individuals produce and resist racial meanings as they position themselves and their children in postcolonial Britain.

The main goal of this study is to provide a theoretically grounded analysis of the ways that *white* members of transracial families negotiate race, racism, and racialization and acquire racial literacy. I focus primarily on white English and Irish women with children of African Caribbean descent. I also interviewed a group of white transracial fathers from the same communities. This enabled me to rigorously analyze the ways that gender hierarchies structure the experiences of white women and men in transracial families. I privilege the experiences and practices of white members of transracial families who have learned to recognize, name, and resist routine forms of white supremacy. By closely investigating the caretaking practices of white members of transracial families, we can gain theoretical insights into the conditions under which racial logics and racial consciousness can change.

In my earlier work, *Racism in a Racial Democracy: The Maintenance of White Supremacy in Brazil*, I analyzed the discursive and cultural practices employed by members of Brazilian interracial families to negotiate race and racism. I focused on the significance of the Brazilian state in shaping the racial logics, discourses, and racial grammar that upwardly mobile working-class Brazilians of African ancestry employed to manage white supremacy and racism (Twine 1997b). I introduced the concept of *white inflation* and drew on Bourdieu's theoretical work to analyze these Brazilians' discursive and material practices as they defended the national image of Brazil as a racial democracy. In *A White Side of Black Britain* I further develop this analytical strategy.

This book treats transracial families as micropolitical sites where race is produced and racial identities are created, contested, translated, and negotiated alongside black and mixed-race, biracial, and other hybrid identities. Like nation-states, families can be analyzed as micro-level sites where competing racial projects are negotiated (Omi and Winant 1986). The micro-level political projects that I analyze do not necessarily begin as political projects; nevertheless they can be a catalyst for shifts in the ability of family members to name, recognize, and analyze racism, racial boundaries, and racial hierarchies. Although I privilege the experiences of white birth mothers, I move between their analyses and that of their black family members. As such, this book can be read, in part, as a dialogue between black and white members of the same extended families. By including the analyses and insights of black family members, I am able to compare and contrast the ways race, class, gender, and political histories structure the interpretation, translation, negotiation, and production of racial logics and racialized identities in these families.[3]

How do white members of transracial families translate, transmit, and transform the meanings of race, racism, and their own whiteness in postcolonial Britain? This book recuperates the family as an empirical site to theorize how race and racial inequalities are managed and contested. My analysis begins with the racial experiences of white birth mothers and then shifts to the perspectives of their black family members, thus offering insights into a white side of the black British experience. Critics may argue that this presents a biased perspective and that the white parents whose voices are heard in this book do not reflect the typical experience of members of these families. My aim is not to present the typical experience, but to uncover mundane and quotidian parental practices that remain undertheorized and neglected in macro- and microsociological studies of race and racism in Britain.

This longitudinal ethnography of interracial intimacy and racial consciousness provides a micro-level cultural analysis of how white family members negotiate race and racism in a community in the East Midlands of England. It differs from earlier studies of interracial families, mixed-race identities, and whiteness in its multivocality and the careful attention given to the experiences and perspectives of white mothers, white fathers, black fathers, black mothers, and black sisters-in-law. By shifting the frame of analysis to the racial consciousness and practices of white birth parents, my aim is to provide an analysis of the relatively invisible caretaking practices used to counter racism—a form of racial labor that macro-level sociological studies of race and racism have not contemplated. Readers interested in a sociological exposé of the ways white members of interracial families recycle racism, engage in racist practices, and racially abuse their children will be disappointed.

Black British Race Studies

British scholars have produced a rich body of empirical research on race, racism, and race relations that provide trenchant analyses of the black British experience. These include studies of cultural identity, identity formation, migration, racism, and community responses to state racism by members of black British communities with origins in Africa, Asia, and the Caribbean (Alexander 1996, 2000; Gilroy 1987, 1990, 1992, 1993b; Centre for Contemporary Cultural Studies 1982; James and Lawrence 1993; Lawrence 1982; Solomos [1993] 2003; Hall, Gilroy 1987, 1993; Brown 2005; and Fisher 2009). A related body of research has focused on the experiences of interracial families and of mixed-race children raised in these families. This research has provided important insights into how members of these families negotiate racialization and racism and establish racialized identities (Benson 1981; A. Wilson 1989; Tizard and Phoenix 1993; Ifekwunigwe 1997; Ali 2003). The Centre for Contemporary Cultural Studies (1982) at the University of Birmingham generated a number of studies that analyzed the varieties of racism that members of racial and ethnic minorities face in Britain and their collective responses. I have been inspired by the research on race, racism, and racial identity among the African and Caribbean diasporic community in Britain, particularly the work of Paul Gilroy (1987), Stuart Hall (1991, 1992, 1994), John Solomos (1988, 1989, [1993] 2003), Les Back (Solomos and Back 1994, 1997), Claire Alexander (1996, 2000), Cashmore and McLaughlin (1991), and Barbara Tizard and Anne Phoenix (1993), Miri Song (1993) and Jacqueline Nassy Brown (2005). My goal is to contribute to this international and interdisciplinary dialogue on the ways ordinary people negotiate and respond to racism as members of interracial families.

British studies of race and racism have several limitations when viewed from the perspective of interracial families. First, earlier British studies have focused primarily on the mixed-race members of these families, particularly the children and young adults (Tizard and Phoenix 1993; Ali 2003; Ifekwunigwe 2003). Second, much of the research has focused on London, in the south, while neglecting multiracial families in other regions, such as the East and West Midlands, which also have significant concentrations of ethnic minorities and, by extension, multiracial families (Benson 1981; Tizard and Phoenix 1993; Ali 2003). The groundbreaking research of Jacquelyn Nassy Brown is an exception to this. Third, a sustained analysis of how gender intersects with class and race to structure the socioracial experiences of white members of interracial families has been missing from British studies of what I term *transracial motherhood* and of mixed-race children (Ifekwunigwe 2003; Wilson 1989). Fourth, although the voices of mothers have been represented in this literature, the voices and perspectives of fathers and black extended family members, including black sisters-in-law, have been notably absent. Finally, this book offers an innovative analysis of the ways whiteness is conceptualized by family members as a contingent form of capital (social, cultural, symbolic, and economic) and sometimes a liability, an element that has not received serious consideration in British sociological studies of the family.

Susan Benson, a British anthropologist, identified "a curious and striking imbalance" between anthropologists' and sociologists' objects of study and theoretical approaches: "[If] the researchers' interest is in political issues and responses to racism, or problems and social disadvantage (that's if s/he is a sociologist) she studies West Indians; and if s/he is interested in religion, ritual, culture and ethnicity (that is if s/he is an anthropologist), she studies Asians" (1996, 52). On the limitations of anthropological studies of ethnic minorities in Britain, Benson concludes:

> It must be acknowledged that the anthropological silence on questions of racism, power and domination had some uncomfortable resemblance to that earlier silence on questions of racism, power and domination in the colonial encounter. By adopting the single ethnic minority as a focus for study, or by seeing different ethnic minority communities side by side . . . structural patterns of disadvantage are reduced to external constraints . . . while considerations of race and racism become largely invisible. (50)

With some notable exceptions, such as the brilliant analysis of the meanings and negotiation of race and locality among the black community in Liverpool by Jacqueline Nassy Brown (2005) and the work of Claire Alexander (1996, 2000) on British black and Asian communities, this disciplinary imbalance on race, racism, and racial identity remains. One of my goals is to provide a theoretically informed feminist ethnographic study of British race relations that synthesizes the concerns of sociologists of race and racism with those of sociocultural anthropologists interested in the cultural production of ethnicity and ethnic boundaries.

Theoretical Frames: Racial Literacy and Ethnic Capital

I draw on critical race theory, feminist theory, and European social theory to support two theoretical concepts: racial literacy and ethnic capital. First, I introduce the concept of *racial literacy* to theorize a form of intellectual and antiracist labor that has not been analyzed in earlier studies of interracial families.[4] I define racial literacy as a reading practice, a way of perceiving and responding to the racial climate and racial structures that individuals encounter daily (see chapters 3 and 4). Racial literacy includes discursive, material, and cultural practices in which parents train themselves and their children to recognize, name, challenge, and manage various forms of everyday racism. My aim is to contribute a theoretically grounded empirical case study to the British and North American literature on "everyday racism" (Essed 1991, 1999; Feagin and Sikes 1994; Feagin and McKinney 2003; Solomos 1989; E. Lawrence 1982) and whiteness.

I argue that white women and men are positioned as both cultural insiders and racial outsiders, but their experience is mediated by the forms of capital that they possess, including their networks of support. I examine how they negotiate the instability and unpredictable value of their whiteness, which can be a resource, a cultural liability, or a source of injury to their families. How white members of transracial families negotiate the shifting means of their whiteness, and thus of race, has been undertheorized in the sociology of race and racism, and their daily cultural practices have been ignored by conventional analyses of social movements, racism, and antiracism.

Second, adding to the forms of capital that Bourdieu described (economic, cultural, social, and symbolic), I introduce the concept of *ethnic capital*, a variant of cultural capital that is highly valued by members of racial and ethnic minorities. I conceptualize ethnic capital as a form of currency, a resource rather than a liability, employed by members of ethnic minority communities to secure their belonging, while also reinforcing their cultural ties in the face of racism. Since countering racism, rather than assimilation, is the focus of my analysis, I sidestep debates presented by members of racially dominant groups about any presumed cultural deficiencies in black and ethnic communities in Britain. Instead I am interested in how ethnic minority communities serve as a resource for white members of transracial families (see chapters 4 and 5).

Among white members of transracial families invested in the inter-generational transmission of ethnic markers such as speech, style, cuisine, music, and generally taste, acquiring and transferring ethnic capital to their children enables them to gain respect in their families and local communities by promoting social cohesion and securing their children's cultural belonging. Ethnic capital is a resource that enables white transracial parents and their children of multiracial heritage to acquire, display, and transfer valued cultural skills that mark ethnic boundaries and thereby strengthen social relationships (social capital) with black family members and members of ethnic minorities.[5]

Whiteness Studies and Critical Race Studies

The interdisciplinary field of whiteness studies is the daughter of black studies; its origins can be found in the early scholarship of W. E. B. Du Bois. In *Black Reconstruction in America, 1860-1880* ([1935] 1976) Du Bois provided the theoretical foundations for what became critical white studies (Twine and Gallagher 2008). What could be called the second wave of this field includes the research of historians (Roediger 1991; Jacobson 1998), literary and cultural theorists (Morrison 1991; Lipsitz 1998), legal scholars (Clive Harris 1993; Lopez 1996), and film scholars (Dyer 1997). Until recently there has been an imbalance in this area, with much of the work focusing on the U.S. experience. A new body of research has expanded the national contexts and now includes a growing body of research on postapartheid South Africa (Durrheim 2005; Steyn and Foster 2008), Australia (Luke and Luke 1998), and expatriates in East Asia and South Asia (Knowles and Harper 2009).

Anthropologists, sociologists, and social psychologists working in the field of whiteness studies have provided innovative analyses of race and racialization, including research on poor and working-class whites (Hartigan 1997; Bonnett 1998a, 1998b; Weiss 2004; McDermott 2006), and racial consciousness and meanings of whiteness among white youth (Phoenix 1997; Cohen 1999; Kenny 2000; Perry 2002; Nayak 2003; McKinney 2005), white supremacists (Blee, 1991, 2002), and white mothers (Wilson 1981; Luke 1994; Byrne 2006). However, with few exceptions, little attention has been given to how whiteness and racism are managed by whites parenting children fathered by black men of African, African Caribbean, or African American parentage and who are engaged in transracial caretaking alliances.[6]

Caroline Knowles has argued, "In geopolitical terms, whiteness is insignificant. But if we are trying to understand the power geometries of globalization and in the operation of racism—then whiteness needs closer analysis" (2006, 90). From the perspective of the black British community, particularly those of African Caribbean heritage, whiteness is very significant in family formations. In 1995, when I began this ethnographic study, 50 percent of black men born in the United Kingdom had chosen a white partner (Modood et al. 1997). Thus the experiences of white women and men who are immersed in black British communities offer insights into the ways they conceptualize, negotiate, and counter race and racism as birth parents, children, wives and husbands, and in-laws.[7] British whites, like their North American counterparts, struggle with the unstable meaning and unpredictable value of their whiteness in a post-apartheid, postcolonial, and post–civil rights world. Two-thirds of the whites who participated in this study grew up in working-class families or families of mixed-class origins and spent part of their lives in multi-ethnic, poor, urban areas where whiteness was not associated with privilege, social status, or cultural superiority.

Sociologists of race are employing innovative research methods that offer more nuanced approaches to the analyses of white identities and whiteness. These studies include work on postcolonial whiteness (Knowles 2006), whiteness in postapartheid South Africa (Durrheim 2005; Steyn and Foster 2008), and whiteness in working-class communities (Hartigan 1999; Nayak 2003; Weiss 2004; McDermott 2006). Sociologists analyzing working-class whites in particular have provided exemplary models of how to capture the locality, mobility, and instability in the construction and performance of white working-class identities (Hartigan 1999; Weiss 2004; McDermott 2006).[8]

Theoretical insights and concepts developed by British and American feminist race scholars and critical race scholars are central to this book.[9] My analysis of whiteness (and blackness) utilizes concepts developed by feminist race theorists and race scholars in the fields of sociology, legal theory, and anthropology.[10] This book broadens and deepens the international contours of the theoretical analysis of British and American feminists by applying their work to the lives of white European women (Frankenberg 1993, 1997; Skeggs 1997; Crenshaw 1995; Collins 1986, 1990, 1994; Ware 1992, 1997; Phoenix 1997; Byrne 2006; Kenny 2000; McDermott 2006). It owes its greatest debt, however, to Ruth Frankenberg and Beverley Skeggs.

In 1993 Ruth Frankenberg, a British feminist race scholar trained in Britain and the United States, published *White Women, Race Matters: The Social Construction of Whiteness*, a groundbreaking study of white women in the United States. Unlike previous studies of race by white feminists, Frankenberg shifted the focus from ethnic minorities to white people and whiteness, asking the women how "race structured their lives." Arguing that whiteness has a "set of linked dimensions" and is a location of structural advantage or privilege, a standpoint, and a set of cultural practices, her goal was to "begin exploring, mapping and examining the terrain of whiteness" (1–2). I build upon the theoretical apparatus Frankenberg employed in her research on whiteness and shift the empirical focus to the United Kingdom, where she grew up.

In 1997 Beverley Skeggs, a British feminist theorist, published *Formations of Class and Gender*, a longitudinal study based on her research with working-class white women in northeast England, one of the most economically deprived regions of the country. Skeggs analyzed class as a "structuring absence" in the lives of these women, who were enrolled in an adult education course. One of her primary theoretical goals was to "reinstate class back into feminist theory by showing how class informs the production of subjectivity" (75). Skeggs expressed regret for neglecting the element of race in the lives of the white women she studied. Reflecting upon an otherwise brilliant analysis of how gender and class inequality operate in the lives of working-class white women, Skeggs argued, "One of the major failings of this research is my lack of responsibility for studying the category of race and paying it the same attention as I did class. . . . However, I established another research project on race in 1987 and 1989 which involved interviewing groups of young women (among others) in similar courses. This alerted me to similarities in the pathologization of Black and White working-class women" (36).

My longitudinal ethnography builds upon the research of Skeggs by examining a more economically diverse group of women from working-class, middle-class, and upper-middle-class backgrounds. While British historians have provided analyses of the ways that gender structured the racial experiences of white middle- and upper-middle-class women, particularly during the Victorian period (Ware 1992; Hall 1993; Tabili

1996), there remains a dearth of analysis of the period after the Second World War in terms of the shared struggles of black and white women who are raising children with black men. I synthesize the theoretical insights of British feminist scholars such as Beverley Skeggs, Ruth Frankenberg, and Vron Ware with those of U.S. black feminist race theorists. By bringing the work of British feminists into dialogue with the work of black American feminists, I offer an innovative and theoretically grounded case study that illuminates some of the ways black and white women encounter similar, although uneven, forms of gendered discipline, particularly when they are positioned as working class.

Leicester: The Research Context

Leicester, a hosiery-manufacturing city, is located ninety miles north of London in the East Midlands. Leicester's motto, *Semper Eadem* (Always the Same), refers to its political moderation and its position both geographically and politically in the middle of England. Formerly Britain's world center for the distribution of shoes and boots and the production of knitted goods, Leicester continues to be a principal supplier of the British knitwear industry, and textiles constitute a major segment of its economic base. According to a Leicester City Council report, Leicestershire "has the largest number of people employed in the manufacture of hosiery, knitwear and fabrics in the United Kingdom" (1993, 42). Thirty percent of the population works in this industry.

I chose Leicester as the field site for a study of transracial families because it is one of the most ethnically diverse cities in Britain, with one of the largest South Asian and black populations outside of London, Birmingham, and Manchester, the country's largest cities, and because it has been neglected in community studies of race and racism. In the 1970s it played a central role in the organized racism of the National Front, a neofascist group, and as a site for organized antiracism.

In 1997, after conducting pilot research in London and Leicester, I systematically reviewed the earlier anthropological and sociological literature on race, racism, and racial formations in ethnic and minority communities (Little 1948; Collins 1957: Banton 1955, 1960; Lawrence 1974; Glass 1961; Patterson 1963; Centre for Contemporary Cultural Studies 1982; Cashmore and McClaughin 1991; James and Harris 1993: Solomos and Back 1996; Back 1996). To my surprise I found no published

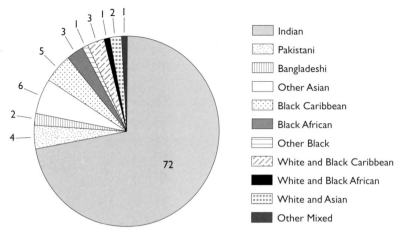

Indian
Pakistani
Bangladeshi
Other Asian
Black Caribbean
Black African
Other Black
White and Black Caribbean
White and Black African
White and Asian
Other Mixed

FIGURE I United Kingdom census, 2001: Asian, black, and mixed populations of Leicester. Office for National Statistics (2003, table KS06, p. 99). In 2001 Asian Indians constituted almost 72 percent of the ethnic minority community in Leicester. The combined mixed-race population was 8 percent of the minority population, which includes white and black Caribbean (3 percent), white and black African (2 percent), white and Asian (2 percent), and other mixed (I percent). The "other" category is equal in size to the black Caribbean and black African populations.

ethnographic or community study of race or racial formations based on data from Leicester. Because of Leicester's significance as a racial site, its unique relationship to East Africa, and its role during the 1970s as a central site of organized racism and antiracism, I decided to interview couples from Leicester who had formed their relationships during the politically volatile period following the 1958 and 1981 race riots.

In 1995, when I conducted the pilot research for this study, the total population of Leicester was 293,400, with whites constituting 71.5 percent and British Asians constituting 23.7 percent of the local population, making it one of the largest Asian communities in Europe.[11] In the 1991 census Leicester ranked second in terms of absolute numbers of South Asians and *first* for its population of Indian origin (Leicester City Council, 1996). The local black population, which is subdivided in the census into Caribbean, African, and black other, constituted 2.4 percent of the local population.[12] The African Caribbean population, a segment of the larger black population, comprised only 1.5 percent of the total population. The relatively small size of the black Caribbean population proved to be an advantage, for once I was introduced to several members of the

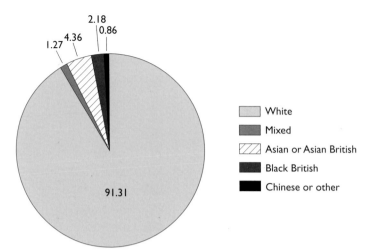

2.18
0.86
1.27
4.36

91.31

White
Mixed
Asian or Asian British
Black British
Chinese or other

FIGURE 2 United Kingdom census, 2001: percentage of national population by ethnic group. The white population is subdivided into British, Irish, and "other white." The mixed population category was added to the census in 2001 and is subdivided into white and black Caribbean (0.46 percent), white and black African (0.15 percent), white and Asian (0.36 percent), and other mixed (0.30 percent). The black or black British population is subdivided into Caribbean (1.08 percent), African (0.92 percent), and "other black" (0.18 percent). Chinese British are counted as a separate group and constitute 0.44 percent of the population.

leadership structure it was simple to identify and track down a network of black women who introduced me to their white sisters-in-law and who identified other transracial families in the community.

In 2001 the census reported that 330,573 whites were living in the city of Leicester (subdivided into British, Irish, and other white) and 441,213 in the larger Leicester urban area (which includes the surrounding rural and suburban villages). Whites constituted 67.86 percent of the Leicester population, and the Asian and British Asian populations (subdivided into Indian, Pakistani, Bangladeshi, and other Asian) comprised 26.63 percent. Almost all of these are Indians, which make up 22.98 percent of the population, while blacks and black British comprised 2.66 percent. People classified as mixed-race made up 1.69 percent of Leicester's population and 1.27 percent of the national population. At the national level the black and black British population comprised only 2.18 percent of the population, so the black and mixed-race populations of Leicester are slightly above the national percentages.

The census of 2001 reported that 91.31 percent of the population in England and Wales was white (subdivided into British, Irish, and "other white"), 4.36 percent was Asian or British Asian, 2.18 percent was black or black British (which includes black African, black Caribbean, and "other black"), and 1.27 percent was mixed (which includes white and black Caribbean, white and black African, and "other mixed").[13] The ethnic minority population, which is not evenly distributed across regions in England and Wales, is concentrated in the port cities of Bristol, Cardiff, London, and Liverpool and in the large urban centers in the East and West Midlands (Birmingham, Leicester, Manchester, and Nottingham). From the perspective of whites living in major urban areas in these regions, political and cultural life has been radically transformed by this post–Second World War ethnic diversity.

In an analysis of the 1991 census Tariq Modood and his associates found that half of all black men of Caribbean origin born in Britain had selected a white partner. In addition, they noted that "for two out of five (39 percent) children with a Black Caribbean mother or father the other parent was white. The white parent was typically a mother according to an analysis of out-marriage rates for ethnic minorities" (1997, 30). Thus interracial marriage between blacks of Caribbean heritage and white women has become normative in the black community.

As an urban center, Leicester is not distinctive in terms of the visibility of transracial families that include black men and white women. What distinguishes Leicester from other English cities is its strong ties to the Indian diasporic community in East Africa. During the period 1968–72 Leicester became a primary destination point for East African Asian refugees from Uganda and Kenya. In August 1972 Idi Amin expelled all Asians from Uganda, generating an influx of migrants holding British passports. The British government selected Leicester as one of three primary resettlement sites for these migrants because of the availability of cheap and low-standard housing, on the periphery of the central business district, that had been slated for slum clearance. Furthermore there was already a relatively small but established East African Asian community in Leicester. The arrival and subsequent integration of Ugandan Asians into Leicester's racial and ethnic structure generated a wave of intense anti-immigration debate and led to both organized racism and antiracism.

The size of Leicester's Asian Indian population is relevant to this study because in local political discourses Asians are simultaneously included and excluded in the black category. Indians constitute 78 percent of the

FIGURE 3 A Muslim couple walks by Starbucks, which opened in Leicester's city center in 2000. Behind them is the main entrance to the Leicester Outdoor Market, an open-air market that sells a variety of fresh produce, fish, meat, and cheese all year.

ethnic population; thus ethnics of Asian origin outnumber those of African Caribbean origin by nearly ten to one.[14] Religious, linguistic, and other cultural differences distinguish black Caribbean and Asian (Indian, Pakistani, Bangladeshi, and East African Asian) families. During my first months in residence in Leicester I quickly learned to ask who was included in the black category since this varied greatly by age, ethnicity, migration history, political affiliation, and national origin. I found that residents of all ethnic backgrounds, including whites, black or black British, Asians and Asian British, were provisional in their use of the term *black*. In one conversation they would shift from using it to encompass all former colonial subjects to limiting it to Africans and African Caribbeans. Although South Asians sometimes categorized themselves as black when applying for government grants, African Caribbean blacks argued that South Asians no longer embraced a black identity and used the term strategically to access state funds targeted at ethnic minorities.

This perception generated tensions between the black Caribbean and Asian ethnic communities over where blackness ends and begins. Several black Caribbeans who held leadership positions in the Leicester United Caribbean Community Association and other black voluntary organizations controlled by the African Caribbean community expressed resentment toward the local Asian community, whom they perceived as experiencing unearned rapid upward mobility; in their view, the Asian Indian community had secured control over much of the local state and county resources targeted for ethnic minorities.[15]

In her analysis of black and white women's experiences in interracial neighborhoods located in maritime communities, Laura Tabili writes:

> In Britain as in the colonies, the groups called "Black" and "white" were far from internally homogenous, mutually exclusive, or mutually hostile. The epithet "black" or the polite term "coloured" described Africans and West Indians, South Asians, Arabs and other colonized people. This diverse population shared neither physiognomy nor culture; they were united by a political and historical relationship of colonial subordination. Thus, "Black" was a political status rather than a physical description: the boundary between Black and white was structured not simply by natural attributes but by power relations, changing over time and continually contested. In the course of several decades this flexible category shifted and broadened to encompass

new groups. Racial definitions were further complicated by racially mixed children. (1996,168)

These local struggles over the meaning of blackness directly impact members of transracial families. Such contestations over blackness pose particular problems for the white working-class mothers of children of African Caribbean fathers who may reside in communities where the dominant ethnic minority population is South Asian, with origins in India or East Africa, because their children are sometimes mistaken for Asian and consequently discriminated against at one moment as Asian Hindus or Asian Muslims and in other contexts as black Christians.

Scholars analyzing the African diaspora in Europe have argued that, despite continuities such as the shared history of racism and colonialism, there are crucial differences that distinguish the black European experience from the black American experience (Campt 2004; Gilroy 1993a). Paul Gilroy writes:

> The bulk of the contemporary black population is the product of post-war settlements. This means that many of our racial problems stem from the brevity rather than the longevity of our stay in the overdeveloped world. There was no plantation slavery in Britain itself and it is therefore the experience of migration and our post-colonial position rather than the memory of slavery, which form the basic unifying experience for us. The oldest black population are found around the great ports of the eighteenth century—Liverpool, Cardiff, Bristol and London—but these older groups are different from post-war economic migrants. They may not, for example, have lines of descent from the Caribbean and intimate relationships with whites may be more common. (54–55)

In distinguishing between the "old" and the "new" forms of racism that blacks in contemporary Britain must negotiate, Gilroy identifies a central problem for interracial families in Britain: "Today's racist ideologies render blackness and Britishness mutually exclusive social and cultural categories" (58). For white parents of children fathered by men of African descent, this form of racism directly impacts their intimate lives.

In her analysis of the resettlement of Ugandan Asians after their expulsion from Africa, Valerie Marrett compares their motivation to migrate to Britain to that of Caribbean, Eastern European, and West Afri-

FIGURE 4 Three Asian women walking in the Leicester city center, past the Clock Tower, which is a popular meeting place on weekends. Bas-relief portraits of the earls of Leicester are carved into the base of this clock tower.

can migrants during the postwar period. She argues, "In the 1960s East African Asians came because of the 'push' factor from those newly independent African countries intent on Africanizing their economies—a process which coincided with the imposition of much tighter entry controls by successive British governments" (1989, 5).

The arrival of the Ugandan Asians generated panic in Leicester's white community. The white working class perceived this influx of educated entrepreneurs from East Africa as a threat both culturally and politically to their way of life. The National Front, a right-wing political party that unified the League of Empire Loyalists, the British National Party, and the Racial Preservation Society, decided to locate its national headquarters in Leicester. According to Marrett, "The main plank of the National Front's campaign was that one in five of all Ugandan Asians who came to Britain settled in Leicester" (1989, 59). John Solomos claims that the political aim of the National Front was "to provide a new arena for the far right activism, outside the Conservative Party and as an independent organization" ([1993] 2003).[16] As the site of an organized racist political party, Leicester also became a logical political organizing base for anti-racist organizers. Solomos notes, "Between 1977 and 1979 the activities of the National Front also became the focus for anti-racist political mobilization orchestrated by the Anti-Nazi League and Rock Against Racism" (190). In the aftermath of the race riots in 1981, Leicester became a national testing ground for racist and antiracist political organizing.[17]

This moment in Leicester's history marked a turning point in the city's race relations because most of the Ugandan Asians were middle-class entrepreneurs who brought capital with them. Thus the white working classes, formerly part of the "Labour aristocracy," encountered a financially privileged economic class of migrants during a period when the British economy was in a postindustrial and postimperial decline. In the neofascist political discourses of the National Front the migration of Ugandan Asians became a symbol of the postcolonial threat to the white English way of life. Whiteness was marked as a position of cultural and economic vulnerability.

This is significant because half of the white women and men who participated in this study grew up and lived in communities that were resettlement sites for these East African Asians as well as Asians from the Indian subcontinent. Consequently, like the working-class whites in Detroit that John Hartigan Jr. (1999) studied, the lived experience of

FIGURE 5 The Central Mosque of Leicester, in Highfields, as seen through a British Telecom phone booth.

FIGURE 6 An Asian woman walks past a sari shop on Belgrave Road, also known as the "Golden Mile" because of the parade of jewelry shops, sari palaces, and Indian restaurants that line its streets. East Asian Africans transformed this once derelict strip into a residential and commercial hub that is the cultural heart of the Hindu community and the site of the Diwali festival.

whiteness was altered for these white English of working-class origin who came of age in Leicester's inner city or on its housing estates.

On 1 January 2001, *The Guardian* published a story titled "Side by Side" in which the reporter described "a revolution" that had occurred in Leicester, a modest and moderate-size city in the East Midlands of England. Esther Addley reported, "Steadily, and almost entirely without fanfare, Leicester seems to have become Britain's most ethnically harmonious city. . . . If this story of unalloyed harmony sounds improbable, it is difficult to find anyone on the streets of Leicester who will disagree with it."[18] An analysis of the U.K. census predicts that within the next decade Leicester will become "Britain's first black majority city" with a white minority.[19]

In three decades Leicester had transformed itself from a site of organized racism and neofascism in the early 1970s to a model of racial harmony. One month after the *Guardian* article, the *New York Times* ran a front-page story noting, "Government figures have just projected that Leicester will become, in a decade, the first British city with a nonwhite majority."[20] This article was accompanied by a photograph of a class that appeared to consist entirely of Asian students, taken at Moat Community College, a school in Highfields that I visited on several occasions, which is located in a poor, inner-city area of Leicester on the periphery of the central business district.[21] This is the same school that virtually all of the black men who participated in my study had attended as children in the 1970s.

Research Methods

This book is based on data collected over ten years in Leicester and London between April 1995 and June 2005 during eight periods of residential field research. In 1995 I conducted a pilot study in London and Leicester in which I interviewed twenty-five transracial mothers.[22] My first set of interviews helped me to focus and refine the interview schedule for the biographical data on racial consciousness I later collected. The second period of my field research began in January 1997; I moved to an urban neighborhood located about one mile from the Leicester city center and resided there for eight consecutive months.

My research used a multimethodological approach: racial consciousness interviews, participant observation, shadowing, archival research, media analysis, and photo-elicitation interviews. During the first stage of research I conducted life history interviews primarily with white birth mothers of African-descent children. Between 1995 and 2000 I collected what I call *racial consciousness biographies* with the same people each year while living in their communities and participating in their daily lives. I employed four avenues to locate and recruit white birth mothers from diverse age and socioeconomic backgrounds. First, with the assistance of Nelista Cuffy, who was employed by the Leicester City Council, I identified and contacted black British youth workers who ran after-school programs and other community events. Virtually every black male youth worker I contacted had a white partner who was the birth mother of his children. They gave me referrals to their childhood friends who had established families with white partners and their family members. Several of the families that appear in this book, including Sharon and Everal Dawkins (see chapters 2, 6, and 7) and Sue Farrell (see chapter 2), were introduced to me by black youth workers. These men provided me with roughly one-third of my referrals, which became the basis for my snowball sampling.

Second, in addition to structured interviews and photo-elicitation interviews, I conducted participant observation. This included direct observations of family members in their homes, at public meetings, at grocery stores, and at community events. I also received permission from five families to shadow them for periods ranging from twelve hours to four days. Shadowing included staying overnight in their home. Third, I conducted three focus groups with black women. Finally, I carried out archival research and media analysis.

In 1998 I returned to Leicester; for the next ten years I met with white transracial mothers and selected family members to discuss how they negotiated racism and racial and ethnic boundaries. This enabled me to focus on shifts in racial logics, strategies, and practices and to identify how white members of black-white transracial families responded to the racial climate and racial structures they encountered. The women and men who graciously agreed to share aspects of their lives with me, who invited me into their homes and to their children's birthday parties, who cooked dinners for me, picked me up at the airport, drove me to late-night appointments, and tolerated my unending questions, constitute neither an ideologically nor culturally homogeneous group. They varied in their attitudes, education, occupational experiences, political activism, marital life, and religious beliefs.

Another avenue that I employed to identify and recruit members of transracial families involved contacting local housing associations which are private charities that provided housing for poor and low-income families receiving state support or who resided in the inner city. This generated referrals to families that included single or unmarried white mothers and their birth children. I also attended black community events such as the annual awards ceremony organized by the group African Caribbean Education, as well as annual business meetings and other events organized by the African Caribbean leadership. Through these venues I met a number of black professionals, primarily women, who had white sisters-in-law they arranged for me to meet. A third avenue was media appearances on radio programs that targeted the local black community; I used my guest appearances to publicize my research and to recruit more transracial families into my study.[23] Finally, I asked everyone I interviewed for referrals, and this produced a snowball sample.

Visual ethnographic methods were also central to my research. The significance of the visual in terms of how bodies are racialized and how members of transracial families manage the gap between their social experiences and the ways their bodies are racialized cannot be easily conveyed in words. In 2000 I hired Michael Smyth, an Irish photographer and digital filmmaker based in Dublin, to accompany me to Leicester to shoot black-and-white photographs of family members who had given their permission to be photographed. Smyth shot photographs of places in their neighborhoods that they identified as meaningful or significant to them in their daily lives. Between 2000 and 2005 he created a visual data bank for my research. He shot 1,650 black-and-white photographs of family members, home interiors, public streets, buildings, and important community institutions and accompanied me to the homes of twenty-five families. As I continued to revisit and re-interview family members and to conduct participant observation at black community events, Smyth accompanied me on four research trips to photograph these events.[24]

During the final phase of my research I interviewed my participants' former husbands, black sisters-in-law, and black mothers-in-law and one set of white grandparents. These interviews supplemented my participant observation and field research among white mothers and offered a different perspective on the ways that race was managed in these fami-

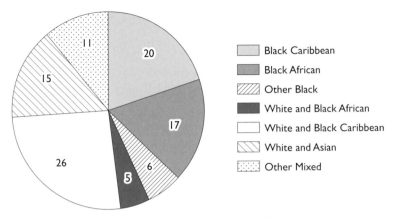

FIGURE 7 Ethnicity of dependent children in British households.

lies. I was interested in examining how family members' gender, generation, and race shaped the *racial logics* they employed. This was one of the most difficult phases of research. I first obtained permission from the white birth mothers (the former wives, domestic partners, or sisters-in-law) before contacting or having private conversations with their family members, particularly in cases where there had been family tensions, disagreements, and ambivalence about the issues raised in this book. In the families that I followed for a decade, I interviewed between two and five family members who occupied a different racial, gender, or generational position in the family and thus offered unique insights into their experiences of race and racialization.

The Families

This study includes women and men from a wide range of class backgrounds, as defined by their education, occupation, income, cultural training, and inherited material wealth. Its longitudinal nature enabled me to revisit themes annually, learn about new strategies, recruit additional family members, and track down divorced or estranged family members (with the permission of their former partners). The women and men who form the core of this study were employed, semi-employed, or retired; they were artists, art dealers, clerical workers, dancers, hosiery factory workers, fitness instructors, forklift operators, graphic designers, hairstylists, homemakers, librarians, magistrates, musicians, police officers, probation officers, adult education teachers, primary school teachers, social workers, solicitors (lawyers), retail sales clerks, store managers, taxi drivers, telephone operators, welfare rights consultants, and youth workers.

The white birth mothers who participated gave birth to their first child between 1959 and 2004. As the century turned and the euro currency was born, they translated, negotiated, and revised the meanings of race, racism, and antiracism in their domestic lives, their local communities, and their relationships in the context of heterosexual marriage, divorce, deaths, and aging. When I began the pilot study for this research in 1995, the participants ranged in age from nineteen to sixty. They were the parents, aunts, uncles, and grandparents of children between the ages of six months and thirty-seven years. Their partners were blacks of British, (West) African, and Anglophone Caribbean origin, and in three cases, black Americans who were retired from the U.S. Air Force. Twelve percent of the white mothers in this ethnography study were Irish; the remainder were of English or Scottish ancestry.

Of the eighty-five members of the interracial families I interviewed during the period 1995–97, I selected one-third to re-interview each year.[25] During the following eight years (1998–2005) I conducted a series of follow-up interviews on the same themes and topics and gave participants an opportunity to update me on their experiences of race and racism as well as other events in their lives.[26] Between 1998 and 2005 I spent periods ranging from two weeks to twelve weeks each year conducting participant observation with the mothers, attending black community events, interviewing extended family members, and reading internal reports of black voluntary organizations and county reports. I also continued to expand my sample by recruiting black sisters-in-law, former and current black male partners, white friends, and business associates. I continued to maintain contact with twenty-five of the original sixty-five families that I had recruited into the pilot study.

A longitudinal ethnography offers several theoretical advantages. By returning to the field every year, I was able to develop long-term relationships with family members that allowed me to revisit the same themes and to observe changes in practices and attitudes. For example, some black family members, particularly sisters-in-law, who were initially strongly opposed to interracial relationships nevertheless were able to develop emotionally close and supportive relationships with their white sisters-in-law (see chapter 7). Following participants over time allowed me to better track the dynamic nature of their relationships and changes in their racial grammar, racial discourses, and strategies for countering racism, instead of presenting a snapshot portrait that reflected one particular moment in the life cycle of the marriage. I directly observed how parents resisted, recycled, or revised the way they talked about race at home.

Among the subset of forty-two families that I followed over the decade I witnessed shifts in their racial logics. During the course of this study black and white members of working-class families typically changed the terminology they used to describe themselves and their family members of multiracial heritage. This was sometimes in response to school forms that involved the use of British ethnic monitoring schemes used to identify and track the number of racial and ethnic minorities. A typical experience among the families studied was that children of multiracial heritage who self-identified and were described to me by their parents and extended family as "half-caste" in 1997 became "mixed-race" by 2000 and then either "African Caribbean" or "black British" or remained "mixed-race" by 2004. I would not have observed these changes in language and self-identification if I had not conducted a longitudinal study. Black and white family members modified their positions in interracial marriage over the years. I saw white grandparents who had initially rejected their daughters, black sons-in-law, and grandchildren of African Caribbean heritage alter their behavior and embrace their interracial family, although not necessarily changing their overall ideologies about racial difference. As families acquired new members, experienced illness, death, divorce, or separation, had new experiences, and managed crises, I observed the instability and unpredictability of racial meanings and racial discourses.

Organization of the Book

In chapter 1, "A Class Analysis of Interracial Intimacy," I ask how black postwar immigration and forms of capital structured the experiences of interracial intimacy and transracial family formation among white women after the Second World War. This question is answered by following the lives of three white women who established relationships with black immigrant men between 1960 and 1970. A comparative analysis of the intersecting forms of capital (economic, cultural, social, and symbolic) they possessed allowed me to disentangle the ways that class hierarchies, heterosexual gender regimes, and capital influenced how these women negotiated race, racism, and respectability.

In chapter 2, "Disciplining Racial Dissidents," I draw on the narrative accounts of eight white transracial mothers to show how they may become "unwhitened" when their peers, family members, and associates learn of their romantic relationships and sexual intimacies with black men. As white women engaged in stigmatized sexual relationships, they learned that their violation of racialized gender codes prohibiting "respectable" white women from engaging in premarital and interracial sex repositioned them outside of normative whiteness and made them lose their place on the white spectrum. Thereafter they became symbolically reconstituted as "honorary blacks."

In chapter 3, "The Concept of Racial Literacy," I introduce a theoretical concept that describes a form of invisible parental labor which has not been considered in conventional sociological analyses of racism and antiracism.[27] I analyze several dimensions of racial literacy and provide a theoretical framework for examining how white parents respond to racial hierarchies. I argue that having intimate relationships with blacks neither guarantees nor is a sufficient condition for acquiring racial literacy. I profile white parents who do acquire racial literacy, which allows them to equip their children with conceptual tools and practices to counter everyday racism.

Chapter 4, "Racial Literacy in Practice," continues to map out the dimensions of racial literacy. In this chapter I focus on the specific conceptual tools and social networks that white parents provide their children in their efforts to assist them in negotiating racism and racial hierarchies. They engage in practices that reinforce their children's social and political connections to black communities. The sociology of race and racism literature has not carefully examined the practices of white parents who embrace an antiracist position and are training their children to strongly identify with the black community.[28]

In chapter 5, "Written on the Body," I examine hair care and heritage cooking, two consumption projects in which white transracial mothers engage. These projects are used by these mothers to reposition themselves as the "ethnic equivalents" of their black sisters-in-law and mothers-in-law. By adopting the grooming and cooking practices of their black in-laws they transfer a form of ethnic capital to their children. This chapter expands upon the sociological theory of Pierre Bourdieu by introducing a form of capital that Bourdieu never theorized. By purchasing consumer products targeted to an "ethnic market" and by adopting the consumption regime of their black relatives, these white women asserted a *black signature* in a multiracial household. This signature, or cultural style, distinguishes them from white transracial mothers who neither embraced a black aesthetic nor believed that they needed to adopt an African or black-centered cultural profile. I discovered that one-fifth of the white transracial mothers I interviewed perceived black mothers as their reference group and labored to become an ethnic equivalent or cultural clone of their black sisters-in-law and close black friends. These same white mothers expressed a strong identification with their black relatives as they struggled to become an ethnic resource for their families, particularly their children.

In chapter 6, "Archives of Interracial Intimacies," I analyze the use of family photographs and visual culture as it is employed by transracial families to project a profile of respectability. In photo-elicitation interviews white mothers reviewed family photographs that they selected. Interviewing the mothers *after* I had established a relationship with them enabled me to revisit themes that we had already discussed. Photo-elicitation interviews allowed me to introduce reflexivity into my research and to identify contradictions, shifts, and tensions between my analyses of the ways that racism and racial profiles were managed over time by the white members of the transracial families I studied. Focusing on one family, I analyze my employment of family photograph albums as a reflexive methodological strategy and as evidence for theory on race and intimacy.

In chapter 7, "White Like Who?," I analyze the discourses of black men and women as they present their views on the social, cultural, and symbolic meanings and value of the whiteness of their wives and sisters-in-law. Although competing racial narratives and representations of whiteness circulated among all of the transracial families I studied, black family members adhered to a strict gender regime that placed accountability for race training on the shoulders of mothers—regardless of these mothers' racial or ethnic identity. This contradicted the assumption held by some of these same family members, that white people are culturally unqualified to prepare children of African Caribbean ancestry to cope with racism. The discursive and ideological terrain within these families illuminates how white people get symbolically positioned in a hierarchical system of class inequality, heterosexual gender regimes, and cultural norms that privilege specific performances of femininity.

Black women and their white husbands have been neglected in analyses of race and racism in Britain. In chapter 8, "Gender Gaps in the Experience of Interracial Intimacy," I examine the experiential and perceptual differences between black women and their white husbands as they frame and analyze their experiences of race and racism. I show how race intersects with gender to shape the responses of members of the black and white communities to interracial intimacy. I focus on four white men born between 1936 and 1964 who formed relationships with black women who became their wives between 1972 and 1984. Their experiences, when compared to that of their wives (and the white women who appeared earlier in this book), show how interracial intimacy and the racism that accompanies it is a gendered experience. White men who interracially married and grew up in the same working-class communities as the white women in this study provide a strategic comparative case that facilitates a rigorous analysis of the role of gender in interracial intimacy. I also provide a contrast with the white transracial mothers, who experienced forms of discipline and punishment that distinguished their experiences from that of their white male peers who interracially married.[29]

In the epilogue I revisit the major findings and detail patterned differences I uncovered between white members of transracial families who possess racial literacy and those who do not. I also detail how class and capital intersect with gender to structure the experience of interracial intimacy.

I

~~~

A CLASS ANALYSIS OF INTERRACIAL INTIMACY

> Whiteness as a site of privilege is not absolute but rather crosscut by
> a range of other axes of relative advantage and subordination; these
> do not erase or render irrelevant race privilege, but rather inflect or
> modify it.—RUTH FRANKENBERG, "ON UNSTEADY GROUND: CRAFTING AND
> ENGAGING IN THE CRITICAL STUDY OF WHITENESS"

> Taboos on sexual activity have been fundamental to state formation
> and to social stratification. In the 1920s, 30s and 40s, at the height of
> Britain's imperial power, interracial marriage was deplored as a threat
> to racial boundaries and as a catalyst for racial conflict.—LAURA TABILI,
> "WOMEN OF A VERY LOW TYPE: CROSSING RACIAL BOUNDARIES IN LATE IM-
> PERIAL BRITAIN"

On 17 July 1943 the *Picture Post* published an article titled "Inside London's Coloured Clubs," which was accompanied by a photograph of black
American servicemen dancing with white English women (Nava 2007,
76). According to Mica Nava's analysis, this photograph was a catalyst for
censorship in the U.S. military: "After the publication in the American
press in 1943 of black American servicemen dancing with white English
women, the army command went to extraordinary lengths of impos-
ing military censorship on all photographs portraying interracial dancing
and social mixing. It also did its best to discourage such behavior in the
flesh, though with only limited success, given its lack of authority over
English women" (76). Nava, a cultural theorist, traces the emergence in
urban London of "visceral cosmopolitanism," which she defines as "the
partly unconscious . . . in play in feelings of desire, sympathy and hospi-
tality towards cultural and racial others and the foreign" (63). Focusing on

urban commercial cultures during the interwar period, she offers a critique of earlier postcolonial and race literatures and also identifies gaps in the psychoanalytic literature which has provided little insight into the attraction of racial others:

> Very little work has been done on the *attraction* of otherness. The empathetic identification of white women with black men and the construction of black men by white women as desirable has also been neglected by postcolonial critics and historians of race, for whom the focus has justifiably been on the most injurious legacies of difference. Yet the psychic and political forces at work in these relationships have had wide-ranging as well as contradictory repercussions. In the domain of sexual politics and everyday life, a romance with an excluded other man may enable the white women to diminish her own social marginality—but only in the context of the relationship itself. (92)

Drawing on diverse archival sources, including department store campaigns, dance, theater, and Hollywood films, Nava is careful to distinguish between the meaning of "the Negro" in Britain and the United States. She argues that although American commercial culture had an impact on British concepts of race and modernity, it produced "contradictory logics" in the meaning of racial difference. She also notes, "Women played a central part in the social reconfigurations of the period. The cultural response of English women to racial others which emerged during this conjuncture was ultimately both a product of Americanisation and a critical repudiation of it" (94).

On the other side of the Atlantic, in 1989, Ruth Frankenberg, a British-born feminist and antiracist scholar, examined the ways that race structured the lives of white women, in particular "white women's places in the racial structures of the United States at the end of the twentieth century." In *White Women, Race Matters* Frankenberg begins with the premise that white women's lives are "sites both for the reproduction of racism and for challenges to it" (1993, 1). Using a concept she terms "the social geography of race," Frankenberg details the ways that the "racial and ethnic mapping of environments in physical and social terms" structures the types of social relationships possible for the white women she interviewed. She argues, "There is no way for white women to step outside of the reach of racism's impact on the material environment. . . . White women can and do challenge racist discourses" (71). Her aim is to "defamiliarize the white experience," thus providing theoretical insights into the ways that whiteness, in this case white femininity, is a gendered, material, spatial, and sociopolitical experience always mediated by constructions of race and masculinity. The opening epigraph to this chapter reflects the careful attention that Frankenberg gives to the multiple and intersecting conditions (historical, material, political, social, and ideological) that structure the lives of white women and men.

At the end of the Second World War there were close to 130,000 black American GIs stationed in Britain.[1] Their presence generated anxieties and ambivalence. Although the labor of black men was needed to support the war effort, interracial relationships between black American soldiers and white English women, both sexual and social, were defined as a problem by the British and the Americans. The British government feared what the press referred to as a "brown baby" crisis: an increase in the birth of children of interracial parentage. The British War Office established a series of policies designed to minimize interracial social contact and discipline the *white women* involved, all the while maintaining the appearance of tolerance and avoiding the vulgar forms of Jim Crow segregation common in the United States.

The British government worked in concert with the U.S. military to establish military and state policies that would ideally restrict black American men's social and sexual access to white English women while maintaining "tacit racial segregation." During a period when interracial marriages were illegal in thirty of the forty-eight states, black GIs socialized, romanced, and established relationships with white English women whom they met in cinemas, pubs, and dance halls. David Reynolds, a historian, details the forms of discipline employed in efforts to discreetly constrain and control the sexual activities of white women, while not appearing to participate in a British version of Jim Crow segregation:

> Local police forces routinely reported women soldiers found in the company of black GIs. . . . Most common was the vigorous use of the wartime Defence Regulations, especially for prosecutions for trespass against women found with black GIs on U.S. military premises. Five, who were caught . . . in Leicestershire, were each sentenced to one month's imprisonment in June 1943. In Leicester the following January, two factory workers from Preston, aged twenty and twenty-two,

were found sleeping in a hut where black GIs were stationed. They were prosecuted under the Defence Regulations for trespass on a military camp and given three months hard labour. (1995, 229)[2]

These punitive policies aimed at women did not prevent these relationships from occurring with regularity. Reynolds describes the conflicts between white and black men that ensued:

There were some particularly serious clashes in 1944 in Leicester between Black GIs and white paratroopers from the 82nd Airborne Division, veterans of the Sicily campaign. Relations with local women were the prime cause. . . . One Unionist MP in County Londonderry complained that the girls going out with black GIs were "mostly of the lowest type and belong to our 'minority.'" (228)

What stands out in these descriptions is the assumption that only women of working-class or impoverished backgrounds would voluntarily engage in relationships with black men. This reflects an attempt to position these women as outside of middle-class norms and to establish a symbolic and class-inflected boundary between "respectable" middle-class women and hypersexual, irrational, working-class women.

While the British government cooperated with the U.S. government and set up socially segregated social events, it is important not to blur the distinctions between the American and the British response to race and racism. The refusal of white American troops to accept the fact that white English women did not reject black GIs was a catalyst for the segregation policies put in place by the British. The establishment of separate social events was a compromise imposed by the U.S. military on the British government. As Nava notes, "The indignation and aggression of many white troops about this state of affairs eventually led to the establishment of separate social events and dancing clubs for black servicemen, which white women could attend without fear of conflict. These were endorsed by the British government under pressure from the United States' army command" (2007, 76).

After the war racial discourses among British politicians and the press about the impact on British society of black immigration and the assimilation of black colonial settlers centered on black poverty and interracial sexuality. In his analysis of the changes in British racial discourses and representations of blacks, Paul Gilroy argues that in the pre-Thatcher era

(Thatcher served as primer minister in 1979–91) blacks were not yet represented as primarily a criminal class: "Miscegenation, which captured the descent of white womanhood and recast it as a signifier of the social problems associated with the black presence, emerged ahead of crime as a theme in the popular politics of immigration control" (1987, 79–80).

The Race Riots of 1958: White Racism and
Interracial Intimacy in Postwar Britain

In the late summer of 1958 riots broke out in Notting Hill (London) and Nottingham (a city in the East Midlands), where white youth formed "lynch mobs" and attacked "coloured" men. Describing the events that led to the riots in Nottingham, Edward Pilkington writes:

> It all started one Saturday night, 23rd August 1958, in the Chase Tavern in Nottingham, one of the only pubs in St. Ann's where West Indians could drink. A Jamaican man was talking to a white woman next to the bar. This was clearly an impropriety in the eyes of a white man standing close by who shouted "Lay off that woman." The Jamaican did not take kindly to this suggestion. . . . Who punched whom first is not known. But a scuffle ensued, provoking other scuffles, which in turn broke into a larger fight, spilling out of the pub onto the St Ann's Well Road. . . . What had begun as a pub brawl turned suddenly into a major race riot. West Indians were ambushed down back-alleys and severely beaten and other black men jumped into cars and drove at high speeds at the crowd. According to Nottingham's police chief Athelstan Popkess the row consisted almost entirely of whites hostile towards blacks. (1988, 106–7)

According to Pilkington, the Notting Hill riots were also sparked by the threat of interracial sexuality. Pilkington notes that in Gallup surveys taken at that time, this issue outweighed all other concerns:

> But all of these prejudices looked tame in comparison with the one burning hate that consumed the passions of so many young white men in the 1950s—sexual relations between white women and black men. A Gallup poll conducted shortly after the race riots found that the most common resentments expressed by whites were that blacks should not be allowed to compete equally for jobs (37 per cent) and that blacks should not be able to enter housing lists on the same con-

ditions (54 per cent). But these were dwarfed by a startling 71 per cent of respondents who were opposed to racial intermarriage. (92–93)

As Gilroy argues in his analysis of the profound changes in linguistic racism between the late 1940s and 1968, "Though the riots of 1958 may have marked a turning point in the history of modern racism, press coverage of the conflict in Notting Hill and Nottingham is notable for the degree to which the crime theme, though present, is again subordinate to other images and anxieties. . . . Black crime was not frequently cited as being a contributory factor" (1987, 79). The "other images and anxieties" on which the press focused had to do with sexuality and miscegenation.

The Notting Hill and Nottingham race riots generated vigorous debates about the "coloured problem." Britain was shocked when reports of these racial conflicts were published, revealing that the youth employed language familiar in the United States, such as shouting "Lynch him." Anthropologists and sociologists were hired to undertake community studies as part of a larger five-year study of race and racism. Some analysts argued that one cause of the riots was the growth of the minority population, especially of "undesirable coloured immigrants" (Glass 1961, 151).[3] In the absence of any systematic data on racism in the public sphere, the Institute on Race Relations commissioned surveys of boroughs throughout the country that had significant coloured populations (Banton 1960, Glass 1961, Daniel 1968).

The postwar racial disturbances and racialized conflicts highlight the gendered nature of the struggle over the ways that racial privileges were intertwined and in tension with gender subordination. After the race riots vigorous debates raged in the media, Parliament, and pubs about how to assimilate immigrants into British society. Policy initiatives to manage race and racism were put into place and the government began to monitor, document, and try to prevent racial discrimination.

In the decades following the riots several groundbreaking studies were published on racism and racial discrimination (Daniel 1968). In 1966 the think tank Political and Economic Planning (PEP) designed a research study to determine how extensive racial discrimination was in Britain in fields not covered by the Race Relations Act of 1965. To answer these questions researchers interviewed immigrants about their experiences, spoke with white Britons who were in a position to discriminate (employers, landlords, mortgage lenders, and service providers), and conducted validating situation tests in which individuals of different ethnic backgrounds who possessed equal qualifications were sent to apply for jobs, housing, and services. The PEP survey concluded:

> There is racial discrimination varying in extent from the massive to the substantial. The experiences of white immigrants, such as Hungarians and Cypriots, compared to black or brown immigrants, such as West Indians and Asians, leave no doubt that the major component in the discrimination is colour. . . . It is moreover impossible to escape the conclusion that the more different a person is in his physical characteristics, in his features, in the texture of his hair and in the colour of his skin, the more discrimination he will face. Of all groups the experience of the West Indians was consequently the worst, not only because their expectations were highest, so that they found themselves more often in situations where discrimination can occur, but also because prejudice against Negroes is most deep-rooted and widespread. (Daniel 1968, 209)

In this and subsequent government reports, however, white members of multiracial households were completely overlooked. Multiracial households were essentially treated as black households and their white members ignored despite how central they may have been to the economic and emotional life of the black members. It is in this context of racial discrimination, ambiguity, and ambivalence about blacks that white women established relationships with black men, bringing different forms of social, economic, and cultural capital to their relationships.

Bourdieu: Forms of Capital and Social Inequality

In his analysis of the reproduction of social and status inequality in French universities, Pierre Bourdieu (1994) identified four distinct types of capital that structure fields of power, social and class relations, and the distribution of resources in modern capitalist societies: economic capital, cultural capital, social capital, and symbolic capital. In Bourdieu's schema, individuals operate in a social universe in which they struggle to accumulate and then convert into power the forms of capital they possess.[4]

Applying Bourdieu's schema to postwar Britain illuminates that whiteness was a *contingent* form of capital for women socially classified as white. Postwar Britain remained a highly class-stratified society in which the meaning and value of whiteness was contingent upon intersecting forms of capital. These forms of capital structured how white women and men negotiated their relationships with black men and the degree to which they were disciplined, exiled, or repositioned as outside of respectability. Although I treat whiteness as a form of capital, the value of whiteness is provisional and interpreted within the context of class inequalities, gender hierarchies, marital status, migrant status, education, age, and national origin. An analysis of the various forms of capital illuminates how racism rebounds onto white women engaged in interracial relationships.

In the following section, I provide a comparative analysis of the way capital was strategically employed (or not) by three white women who established families with black men between 1960 and 1975, a period when neofascist and right-wing parties emerged and the British state began to allocate resources for the police to target and contain urban black populations (see Cashmore and McLaughlin 1991).

Chloe Talbot Kelly: Portrait of an Artist with Cultural Capital

Sociological portraits of interracial families during the postwar period typically focused on poor and working- and lower-middle-class families. The experiences of women like Chloe Talbot Kelly, who is from an upper-middle-class background, fill gaps in the sociological literature on race and illuminate our understanding of how white women negotiated racial and ethnic boundaries during the last gasp of the British Empire, a period of increased racial violence toward "black colonials" in England. It is in this context of profound public anxiety, economic decline, and ambivalence about race and white masculinity that Chloe returned to London in 1960 and began dating black men.

In May 1997 Herdle White, the producer of *Talking Blues*, a weekly BBC radio program broadcast on Saturday afternoons in Leicester, the only program that targets the African Caribbean community, invited me to appear as a guest on his show. I discussed my recently published book on race relations in Brazil and advertised my new research project. After the show his wife, Frances, graciously invited me to their home, a beautiful detached house in the suburb of Wigston, for tea and scones. When I asked her if she would introduce me to other white women who have married and established families with black men, she gave me the name of her closest friend, Chloe Talbot Kelly Smith. Both had married child-

FIGURE 8 A formal portrait of Chloe Talbot Kelly taken in the 1960s in London.

hood friends, black Jamaican men of middle-class origin who had migrated to England together in the late 1950s.

When I was introduced to Chloe in 1995 she had been married to Jeffrey Smith for thirty-four years. She lived with her husband in a spacious four-bedroom house in Stoneygate, a fashionable middle-class neighborhood in Leicester that has become a magnet for upwardly mobile and middle-class South Asians.[5] Chloe is a charismatic and sharp-witted, petite woman, with short brown hair and striking blue eyes. Barely five feet tall, she has a wicked wit and a sense of humor that captivated me. Every afternoon she can be found working on her bird illustrations in her art studio, a converted garage attached to the house. Born in 1929 in Hampstead, an upper-middle-class section of London, Chloe is a fourth-generation artist on her father's side and third-generation on her mother's side.[6] She belongs to the last generation of English colonial elites to grow up during the age of empire.[7] Her family can best be characterized as a constellation of upper-class artists, professional soldiers, and cotton traders who were socially and economically integrated into the British colonial structure, with ties to imperial governments in what had been British West Africa and North Africa during the height of the British Empire. In fact her father was a Member of the British Empire, an honorific title bestowed by the queen.

Chloe returned to London from Sierra Leone in 1960 after ending a six-year marriage to a white English man after having, in her words "fallen in love with Africa." She bought a flat in London and quickly reestablished her career as a self-employed bird illustrator. In October 1963, when Chloe was thirty-four years old and five months pregnant, she married the father of her child, thirteen years her junior, at a registry office in London. Her parents met her husband, Jeffrey Smith, a Jamaican British man, for the first time on her wedding day. Their only child, Alexander, was born in 1964 at the Mothers' Hospital, a Salvation Army charity hospital in London. They had an after-birth party in their Islington apartment, the flat that Chloe had purchased when she returned from Sierra Leone.

It is 8 o'clock on a rainy spring morning in Leicester. Chloe has already made tea and toast for me. She has been up since 6 and has finished reading all of the daily newspapers—the tabloids and the broadsheets. She reads everything—*The Manchester Guardian, The Times, The Leicester Mercury*. The sun peaks out briefly. We are looking at a painting of a land-

FIGURE 9 Chloe Talbot Kelly in 2001, age sixty-six.

scape in Sierra Leone she did in 1958, when she lived there with her first husband. Pictures of her family members line the walls, a painting of her mother as a child and portraits of her father, accompanied by Chloe's landscapes illustrating her life in West Africa. The walls of the reception room facing the garden are lined with paintings by Chloe and her father, and a catalogue for a retrospective of her father's paintings is on the chair in this same reception room.

There are two reception rooms on the first floor of Chloe's three-bedroom home. The first, which is used as a living room and in which the television is located, is to the right after you enter the front door. A black leather couch and two black leather chairs, original Barcelona chairs designed in 1929 by Ludwig Mies van der Rohe for the German Pavilion of the International Exhibition, dominate the room. They reflect the cultural, social, and economic capital that her parents gave her. Two bookcases line the walls, and there is a table strewn with books on architecture, the history of London, modernism, and art history. Chloe points to a painting—a detailed New Zealand bird—which she describes as her best bird illustration. This illustration is so exquisite that it looks like a photograph and was subsequently reproduced on a New Zealand postage stamp in the early 1960s.

From Chloe's living-room window the Masjid Umar, a visually stunning mosque built in 1999, can be seen. One of Leicester's twenty-two mosques, it sits on the corner adjacent to the Old Presbyterian Church and serves a growing Muslim population in the city. One block away from the mosque is a madrassa, a Muslim religious school, where girls and boys are taught to memorize the Quran and receive religious instruction in the afternoon. At sunset, after the early evening prayers, the doors of the madrassa open and hordes of girls wearing long black gowns and white veils are collected in white vans, provided without charge by a privately owned transportation service organized by the Muslim community.

In Chloe's narrative of her life, she did not recall experiencing any racial harassment in public. Her class privilege, her profession, and her immersion in friendship networks of West Indian and West African friends were forms of social capital that shielded her from vulgar forms of racial abuse and feelings of social marginalization. Although she gave birth to her son in a Salvation Army charity hospital and was not wealthy in monetary terms, she possessed valuable forms of social capital (networks of relationships), cultural capital (a prestigious job), and symbolic capital (a boarding school accent and posture that signaled upper-class status) that were common among women of upper-class London backgrounds. In her son's words, his mother belonged to the "nether reaches of the aristocracy."

Chloe's experiences illustrate some of the complex ways that respectability is negotiated and forms of capital retained, despite her out-of-wedlock pregnancy by a black man. She not only made use of her social capital, but also possessed forms of economic capital that enabled her to avoid and minimize the rebound racism that less privileged white women reported encountering as wives of black men. For example, she used the social networks she inherited from her father and mother to secure a mortgage loan, which protected her from dealing with landlords who might discriminate against her because of her black husband and mixed-race child. The combination of Chloe's ability to convert her social capital into economic capital, her parents' continued support, and her husband's job as a postal worker enabled her to sustain a middle-class, if not an upper-middle-class life in London and later in Leicester.

Examining the forms of capital that Chloe possessed demonstrates how she was able to transgress gender and racial conventions while retaining her *respectability* and financial stability. First, Chloe inherited her father's *social capital*, his social relationships with elite white men in London. Her father's prominent position and social connections as a former master at Rugby enabled her to secure a professional apprenticeship in the Bird Room of the British History Museum, which led to her first paid illustration commissions and secured her income, or *economic capital*. The third form of capital that Chloe possessed was *cultural capital*. This included her boarding school education in Scotland and her apprenticeship at the British Museum, her accent, her posture, and the way she socially interacted. Finally, she possessed *symbolic capital*, which includes the accumulated weight of the other forms of capital such as her whiteness, femininity, and social relationships in London.

Examining Chloe's life history from this perspective illustrates the significant role that various forms of capital played in her negotiation of her intimate life. They enabled her to dissolve an unsatisfying marriage and return to London, where she established a financially stable career as a bird illustrator. Because she was a member of the upper-middle class, her status as a recently divorced woman with an unpredictable income did

FIGURE 10 Chloe Talbot Kelly putting on her coat as her son Alex frames a painting in their framing shop, a business that they jointly manage in the city center.

not prevent her from securing approval for a bank loan. This distinguishes her from less-privileged working- and middle-class women at that time, as she was able to counter and more easily navigate the gender discrimination that unmarried and divorced women routinely faced in London in the 1960s. It is during this period that Chloe began actively dating black African men. Describing her relationship with the black community, Chloe explains her method for meeting black men and women during the early 1960s in multicultural London:

> I met quite a few Africans and a lot of Nigerians, one or two Ghanaians. . . . I put a little—got a friend to put an advertisement in the paper for me. I wanted to meet more [African men]. I wanted to see more what they were like. . . . I met quite a few of them. I think they were probably all looking for white wives. . . . I only met them *privately*. . . . I was also thinking it might be quite nice to meet an educated black man and go back and live in Africa. I loved Africa.

The fact that Chloe met these men privately in the homes of black friends suggests that she was very conscious of the stigma that attached to white women who voluntarily pursued black men. Furthermore, by meeting black men in this way she avoided the routine forms of racism and racial abuse that working-class white women who met black men in public spaces such as pubs or clubs may have encountered. She shielded herself from such abuse by placing ads in the names of friends. In this way Chloe's African and Caribbean friendship networks constituted an important form of social capital that enabled her to arrange private meetings and thus remain in the racial closet until her pregnancy and subsequent marriage brought her relationships into public view. Chloe summed up the social trajectory that led to her relationships and subsequent marriage in these words: "I mean, it's very difficult to describe how we met, [we were] not in the same social circles at all. Not really. [My husband] was working in the post office. I did everything that my circle wouldn't have done. I married somebody younger than myself, in a manual occupation, and black to boot."

An analysis of photographs in Chloe's private collection from that period show her in various situations with her son, Alex: standing next to him, laughing with him, walking in the garden at her father's house at Rugby. These photos were all taken when Alex was between three and six years old (1967–71). In several photographs taken in her London apart-

FIGURE 11 Chloe Talbot Kelly in her studio, a converted garage attached to her house.

ment, she is shown holding Alex and talking to a dark-skinned man of either West African or South Asian heritage. Alex told me that these were close friends of his mother. Chloe seemed to have a number of African male friends. These photographs document her immersion in an African and African Caribbean social network, which, along with her class privileges, further shielded her from vulgar forms of racial abuse that her contemporaries—other white women involved with black men—reported as routine.

Chloe violated one of the most powerful taboos that structured gender relations, racial regimes, and status hierarchies among upper-middle-class white English women: interracial marriage and sexual relations. She divorced a white man, established a sexual and marital relationship with a Jamaican immigrant, became pregnant, married, and gave birth to a child fathered by a black man who was her junior by more than a decade. Even artists of her social background did not typically violate these prohibitions. For white women who did not have an independent source of income or a wealthy lover, a premarital interracial sexual relationship that resulted in a pregnancy would have typically had devastating social and economic costs.

The racial rules were different for Chloe's white male peers, who could take a mistress and in some cases even a wife of ambiguous, mixed, or "impure" racial origins without being cast out into the racial borderlands. Although white English men might establish casual relationships or even long-term relationships with black or Asian women, in 1963 it was rare for a respectable upper-middle-class white woman to live with and marry a black man from a lower-class background. When asked how her parents reacted to her pregnancy and relationship with a Jamaican man younger than herself, Chloe replied, "I have never given a damn what people think. . . . I think possibly I take that from my father. My mother was disapproving. She said, 'You'll have to work really hard all your life.' And she also had seen that terrible Griffith film *Birth of a Nation*. . . . It's a film that's guaranteed to stir up prejudice, and my mother had a sort of fear of black people."[8]

Chloe minimized the racism that she may have encountered and emphasized *her* decisions and *her* choices. She strategically employed her economic, social, and cultural capital to mediate any racism that was directed at her or her husband. As an internationally recognized artist and the mother of a son she adores, Chloe seemed relatively content with the life she had created for herself.

I now turn to a woman of middle-class origin, who, like Chloe, established a relationship with a black Jamaican man twenty years her senior to provide a comparative case that further illustrates the role of capital in negotiating the transition to transracial motherhood. In contrast to Chloe, Sonya had a very different set of expectations and maternal experiences. The differences in her age, marital status, and educational experiences illuminate why she was not able to convert the educational, social, and cultural capital that she possessed into equivalent forms of power (Bourdieu 1984). Thus, although she operated in a similar racial field and discursive community that opposed interracial relationships, her age, lack of education, and marital status positioned her in ways that catapulted her into downward mobility.

Sonya Smyth: A Portrait of Downward Mobility

Sonya Smyth, the daughter of a pub owner and homemaker, grew up in a middle-class family in Blackpool. Born in 1956, she came of age during the postwar era. Sonya moved to Leicester in the late 1970s to attend the local university. Her brother was already a student there. One year later she became pregnant with her first child.

In 1976 Sonya gave birth to her first child, a daughter. She moved to Highfields, where she initially shared a kitchen and bathroom with several other families. Sonya described their extreme poverty; they had no radio, no television, and no books, basically no form of entertainment. By 1990 she was the mother of four children.

Both Sonya and Chloe possessed similar forms of capital, such as white femininity, an education, and employment. They both had relationships with black men who migrated from Jamaica in the 1960s and became pregnant prior to marriage. But unlike Chloe, Sonya gave birth to all four of her children outside of marriage and with little, if any, financial support from her parents or the fathers of her children. Chloe lives in a solidly middle-class neighborhood in Leicester, while Sonya lives in an impoverished community where drugs, prostitution, and gang activity pose daily challenges.

Chloe was an employed artist in her late thirties and already divorced from her first husband when she gave birth to her son. She and her husband both agreed that it was her choice to become pregnant, and since she had an established career she was prepared for the economic consequences of her decision to become a mother. Her pregnancy was neither an accident nor a source of financial trauma; her pregnancy and subsequent marriage did not alter her *material* lifestyle. She continued to live in the London apartment that she had purchased in 1960, continued to draw illustrations on commission at the British Museum of Natural History, and continued to receive support from her parents and friends. Her pregnancy and the subsequent birth of her son did not catapult her into downward mobility because she did not lose any of the benefits of her *class* privileges as the daughter and granddaughter of prominent and established London-based artists.

Although Sonya had access to supportive services for unmarried, pregnant women, she nevertheless suffered economically and remained vulnerable upon becoming a mother. Moreover, as a woman who strongly identified with her father's Irish heritage and consequently an ethnic minority in England, she may have faced additional forms of discrimination. Mary Hickman has analyzed anti-Irish racism in England and the ways the Irish were "rendered invisible as a minority":

> In Britain the inclusion of the Irish within the category White European does not protect them from various forms of racist discrimination and prejudice. Contemporary racist portrayal of the Irish focuses on various aspects of the Irish experience, culture and Irish politics. The racial stereotypes most commonly utilized depict the Irish as all: terrorists and inherently prone to violence, stupid, welfare scroungers, non-human (pigs), untrustworthy, unreliable, feckless, religious fanatics, culturally backward and drunken. (1996, 31)

Sonya undoubtedly faced some racism both as a woman of Irish parentage (her father) and as the domestic partner of a black man.

Sonya's family did not support her relationship, and she did not have the same organic support system that Chloe could access. Without family, childhood friends, or a husband who would share in child care, Sonya was unable to remain in the paid labor force. Eleven years after Chloe gave birth to Alex, Sonya had her eldest son. By 1990 she had given birth to four children and was an unemployed homemaker.

Sonya did not acquire professional training or educational credentials that could provide her with the social, economic, and cultural capital that shielded Chloe. Like her contemporaries, Sonya did not deviate from the heterosexual gender regimes of that era, which placed the responsibility of child rearing primarily on the shoulders of women, and thus she did not reenter the paid labor force after giving birth. Thus, as for other unmarried women in her community, parenting children for her required the economic support of the British State. Although she reported that the fathers of her children periodically offered forms of support, it was not enough to move her out of poverty and restore her to a middle-class lifestyle.

As a woman who grew up in what she describes as a "a middle-class family" and who, as a young woman, had access to cultural and educational capital, Sonya did not retain in Leicester the support system and resources she had possessed in Blackpool. Giving birth to four children as an unmarried woman transformed her into an overworked mother and homemaker. Living in an impoverished inner-city district of Leicester with significant African, Bangladeshi, black Caribbean, Irish, and Polish populations called attention to Sonya's whiteness and made her hypervisible as a transracial mother with children of color. As such she became a target of what Frankenberg refers to as "rebound racism" as her children encountered discrimination in the school system.

Although Sonya and Chloe had both become pregnant prior to their marriage to black immigrants, the balance of power in their relationships differed radically. In striking contrast to Chloe, Sonya was twenty years younger than the father of her first child, while Chloe was thirteen years older than her son's father. Chloe maintained more power in her relationship as a wife and mother due to the stable profession that she had developed prior to her pregnancy and subsequent marriage. Her self-employment as an artist and husband's stable income protected her from downward mobility. Thus she neither experienced significant changes in her economic situation nor lost the emotional support of her parents. Sonya's transition to motherhood was more stressful due to her status as an unmarried mother who lacked the emotional and financial support that a husband could provide as well as a satisfying job. She was forced to apply for income support from the British government. Chloe, on the other hand, remained employed. As a homeowner, a self-employed professional artist, and a cosmopolitan woman who chose to become pregnant, Chloe was more prepared for the transition to motherhood.

Jane Green: The Value of an American Passport

Jane Green is a petite white woman who wears her auburn hair cut very short in a fashionable pixie style. Fifty-six years old and the mother of three children, she has been married for thirty-three years to Melvin Green, a black American. The fifth of six children of working-class parents, she was born five years after the end of the Second World War. She remains very close to her parents: "They never disowned me. I was always welcome in their home." Jane lives a short walk from one of her sisters in a predominantly white suburban community. She is currently employed as a manager for a fashion retail store on High Street.

On the wall above the couch in the living room there are three maps and two photographs. One of the maps, dating back to 1826, depicts the City of Leicester Abbey, with the eight coats of arms of the families that held titles as earls, including DeMontfort. The second map, located below the map of Leicester, is of Warwickshire, the county next door, which is Shakespeare country. In the very center of the wall hangs her parents' wedding photograph, taken in 1940. Below that hangs her husband's high school graduation photo. I commented on the maps and Jane walked over to the bureau in the living room, from which she pulled out a copy of the Magna Carta of 1215, of which she is very proud. There is also a three-foot-tall, dark-skinned black doll wearing a bandana and a cook's outfit that sits prominently on the mantel of the fireplace to the left side of the couch. She bears a resemblance to the black mammy figures in old Hollywood films.

Jane belongs to a very close-knit family and visits her mother weekly. The centrality of her parents in her life is symbolized, in part, by the presence of their wedding photograph. Jane is very proud of her English heritage and feels a strong connection to her community, as reflected in her ability to describe the origins of the ruling families of Leicester. In contrast to other white working-class mothers in this ethnographic study, Jane was not punished or disciplined by her parents for forming a family with a black man. The material culture of her living room reflects both her nationality and her husband's cultural heritage as an American.

It was at her older sister's wedding to an American who was honorably discharged from the U.S. Air Force that Jane was introduced to Melvin, whom she married a year later. Melvin, a native of Ohio, grew

FIGURE 12 Jane and Melvin Green at her fiftieth birthday party in their living room.

up in a working-class family in Lorain and was the former roommate of the groom. Jane was eighteen years old when they began dating. Within a year she became pregnant, and eight months later they married, in July 1970 in a civil ceremony, shortly before he was honorably discharged from the U.S. Air Force. Her eldest daughter was born one month later.

All her children's births were registered in London at the U.S. embassy, which classifies them as "overseas births" and entitles the children to a U.S. passport. Jane's two daughters are very light-skinned, attractive girls who, according to Jane, did not encounter any racism at school. One daughter could easily be assumed to be a white English girl. Like Sonya, Jane emphasized the gender conflicts over domestic work and her husband's intense criticism of her domestic skills early in her marriage. She identified conflicts within the home over different cultural styles, rather than racism outside of the home, as the central terrain of struggle in their marriage.

Jane believes she had access to experiences and resources, such as the ability to live and work in the United States, and other forms of symbolic capital that marriage to a white English man of her class background would not have provided. In contrast to Sonya and Chloe, her marriage to an American provided her with a source of symbolic capital that women who married Jamaican British and Bajans (Barbadian British) did not acquire. Thus her husband's nationality compensated for his blackness and mediated the stigma that typically attached itself to white women of working-class backgrounds who married black men.

Jane and Melvin have lived in the United States on three occasions. In 1972 they and their two daughters moved to Ohio, where her sister lived, so that her husband could acquire the training to become a certified professional barber. Jane spent several months working as a counter clerk at McDonald's and then started a house-cleaning business, primarily for Oberlin College faculty. During her second stay in the United States, in 1989–90, Jane established another successful house-cleaning business. She described this as a very happy period in her life: "I used to clean houses. I fitted in there. It was a very mixed community. . . . I think all of our neighbors were black but I never felt out of place. I never felt any threat or anything against me. I used to ride around in town on my bike. And it was just a free and easy time. Hard work but I enjoyed it."

Although Jane did not possess Chloe's economic, cultural, and symbolic capital as an employed artist, she retained close emotional ties to her

FIGURE 13 Jane Green, holding her husband's high school graduation portrait, taken in Lorraine, Ohio. Behind her on the wall is a map of Leicester.

FIGURE 14 Melvin Green.

family (particularly her mother and sisters). Although her parents had assumed that she was going to establish a family with a white English man, they did not reject her, punish her, or reposition her outside of the borders of respectability and of family. Instead she continued to see her parents on a weekly basis. Thus, in contrast to Sonya, she not only retained the emotional support of her family, but she also acquired new forms of social and cultural capital from her marriage, while Sonya lost capital. Except for her residences in the United States, Jane has always lived very close to her family and sees them on a weekly basis. The support of her sisters and her mother and their proximity have been a continual source of emotional and social support for Jane. Thus, in some ways, she did not radically alter her lifestyle when she married her husband. She continued to live near her family, and when she did move to the United States she lived near her sister and worked while her husband acquired the vocational training, skills, and credentials that he needed to secure a better job when they returned to England.

When Jane went to the United States, she did so as the mother and legal wife of a U.S. citizen, which gave her the legal right to work. This status provided her with access to economic and social capital. In contrast to Sonya, Jane continued to work in the paid workforce after the birth of her children and always had an independent source of income. This not only reinforced her self-esteem but also provided her family with the additional income needed to purchase a semidetached house in a predominantly white middle-class suburb, a sign of upward mobility and economic security. Sonya, on the other hand, lives in an economically impoverished section of the inner city adjacent to a vice district associated with poverty, prostitution, and cheap housing that is an interzone for interracial sexual liaisons. Due to its affordable housing, it has served as a magnet for immigrants from Bangladesh, Pakistan, East Africa, West Africa, and Eastern Europe. It is a transition zone from which upwardly mobile families typically migrate when they have accumulated sufficient capital.

Jane's entry into marriage and motherhood, although it had its challenges, gave her forms of symbolic, social, and economic capital that women who married unskilled or semiskilled black men from the Caribbean did not possess. Jane perceived her children's dual nationality as Americans and British as a "flexible resource" and a source of capital because it gave her access to a residency permit. The right to live and work in the United States is a resource Jane has utilized on three extended occasions when her husband was changing careers. Although she worked in unskilled and semiskilled occupations, she exercised control over her labor and worked at her convenience, while enjoying the benefits of being English in the States.

Conclusion

After the Second World War Britain experienced profound demographic, economic, political, and social change that generated anxieties about the racial future of the nation. The racial and ethnic structure of Britain's largest cities was changing as British passport holders from Ireland, the Caribbean, Africa, and Asia immigrated. These migrants varied not only in the cultural capital that they possessed, but also in their deployment of it. Nava argues:

> During this period English women were not only more likely than English men to socialize with the newcomers; they were also more likely to identify with the migrants, who like themselves were often marginalized and denied power in the overlapping regimes of white and male supremacy. So the alliances of white women with racial others and the socially repudiated can be understood . . . as a form of proto-feminism; interracial relations constituted a revolt against the constraints of docile "femininity" as well as parental culture, and in this way anticipate the political critique that was to emerge more clearly at the end of the decade with the women's movement. (2007, 99)

White women who formed interracial relationships with black men traded on their white femininity and brought different forms of social, economic, and cultural capital to their relationships. Their transition to marriage and motherhood cannot be understood outside of the larger structural changes occurring in Britain during this historical moment. Their age, sexual experiences, social networks, and nationality and their family's reactions to their marriage structured the way they managed the capital that they possessed.

In this chapter I analyzed the forms of capital possessed by three white women with different levels of education who married black men of different national origins. Chloe, Sonya, and Jane all became pregnant between 1960 and 1970 and prior to their marriages. Chloe married in 1963, and Jane in 1970.[9] Sonya never married. A comparative analysis of the forms of capital they leveraged demonstrates how the specific capital they brought with them or generated thereafter significantly shaped the degree to which they were able to retain social and economic capital which enabled them to retain their respectability. Chloe married a Jamaican man of middle class origins in the last months of her pregnancy. Her first marriage of six years to a white English man ended in divorce. Sonya did not marry the two Jamaican men who fathered her children. Jane married a man from Ohio who was on active duty in the U.S. military when they met. Chloe and Jane both married the fathers of their children prior to giving birth. They also retained the ongoing emotional and financial support of their parents after their marriage, while Sonya temporarily lost the support of her relatives. Although Jane possessed neither the educational nor cultural capital that Chloe had, her active participation in the paid labor force enabled her and her husband to achieve a middle-class lifestyle and purchase a home in a predominantly white, prosperous, and politically conservative suburb of Leicester.

The capital these white women possessed structured their transracial family formations. White women who established relationships with black men during the postwar period, as Britain was losing its empire, can be thought of as "ethnic settlers," to use Joanne Nagel's term, on a new frontier of interracial relationships during a time of demographic, cultural, economic, and social transformation in Britain. Although Chloe and Jane established settled lives with black men, both retained their social and cultural connections with their parents and extended families. Chloe also maintained the professional contacts she inherited from her father. Thus the value of their whiteness was not diminished like Sonya's, who remained an unmarried mother and experienced downward economic and social mobility. Furthermore, Sonya's lifestyle was radically altered upon becoming a mother, while Chloe and Jane retained their familial, and social networks of support.

In the next chapter I shift the analysis to the *gendered* forms of discipline and punishment that white women reported across diverse age and class positions. I focus on nine white women who established relationships with black men and became transracial mothers as unmarried teenagers, university students, employed married women, and community activists. Applying the theoretical insights of black feminist race scholars who analyzed the situation of black women and other women of color in the United States to the lives of these nine women will illuminate the ways white women who are defined as transgressive can be temporarily "unwhitened" and disciplined in ways similar to the way women of color are disciplined.

2

DISCIPLINING RACIAL DISSIDENTS

Transgressive Women, Transracial Mothers

> You go beyond being a white person and you become the figure of hatred as well. That's how I feel. You become the black person that they're calling [a derogatory name], in a sense. I become less white. I'm a traitor, if you like, to the white cause—whatever the white cause is.—ALLESANDRA RICHARDS, THE WHITE BIRTH MOTHER OF A BLACK TEENAGE DAUGHTER

> Is there not something unseemly in our society, about the spectacle of a white woman mothering a black child? A white woman giving totally to a black child; a black child totally and demandingly dependent for everything, sustenance itself from a white woman.—PATRICIA WILLIAMS, THE ROOSTER'S EGG

The meaning of *transgression* and the process by which certain categories of women are defined as transgressive remain central to feminist analyses of race, racism, and reproduction. When considering how women are disempowered, feminist theorists have analyzed the intersections of race, class, marital status, immigrant status, and sexuality to illuminate women's experiences and practices of motherhood. White women who become *transracial mothers*, that is, mothers who are socially classified as belonging to a racial group considered distinct from that of their birth children, may be subjected to forms of surveillance, discipline, and moral censure usually restricted to women of color. Although transracial mothers are one of the fastest growing groups in Britain's major cities, they remain marginalized in feminist analyses of race and racism.

In this chapter I draw on American black feminist race theorists to analyze the maternal struggles and forms of punishment that white trans-racial mothers encounter. My goal is to illuminate how white women who bear children of color can become socially reconstituted in their families and communities as the cultural equivalents of black women or women of color and thus subjected to similar forms of surveillance, social ostracism, and discipline by members of the white community.

Critical race theorists have analyzed poor, unmarried, abused, and immigrant women who are subjected to forms of social control. These women pose a threat because they challenge idealized notions of mother-hood through their inability or refusal to marry and establish two-parent, middle-class, nuclear families. In a discussion of what she calls "living room political discourse," Lisa Ikemoto, who is concerned with the par-ticular vulnerabilities of women of color to forms of social control in the United States, argues:

> The mother, in a wide range of race- and class-specific forms, has served as a cultural reference point or framework for particular sets of norms. These norms operate on three overlapping levels. At each level, patriarchy, white supremacy, white nativism and middle-class privi-lege interlock into a matrix of standards and presumptions that appear to be part of the "natural order." . . . At one level, there are norms that operate directly on women by expressing assumptions, expectations, and standards for women who are pregnant or who have children. . . . Racism and class bias also mediate the assumptions, expectations and standards set for pregnant women and women with children. (1999, 159–60)

Ruth Frankenberg (1993) argues that white women can become "unwhit-ened" by their heterosexual alliances with men of color. Applying the insights of critical race scholars such as Ikemoto and Frankenberg and those of American black feminists who have illuminated the experiences of ethnic minority women, to the experiences of white mothers engaged in transracial caretaking alliances, we can theorize about how "political intersectionality" works in the lives of a group of British white mothers (Collins 1957; Roberts 1995, 1997, 1999).

It is clear from the experiences of these women and their relatives that white transracial mothers are perceived as transgressive in contempo-rary Britain. They are transgressive because they challenge gender hierarchies and notions of racial difference that threaten to transform the racial status of their natal family. As such, white mothers who violate racial and gender conventions encounter forms of punishment similar to those experienced by mothers of color (Romano 1998).

Black Feminist Theory and White Mothers' Vulnerabilities

Black feminist theorists offer a number of theoretical frameworks that can be employed to examine the forms of discipline encountered by white women who violate racial and gender conventions. Patricia Hill Collins, a black American feminist theorist, has innovated feminist analyses of motherhood by placing women of color at the center. Collins poses the question, "What themes might emerge if issues of race and class generally, and understanding racial and ethnic women's motherwork specifically, become central to feminist theorizing about motherhood?" In her typology Collins delineates several dimensions of struggle:

> Racial ethnic women's struggles for maternal empowerment have revolved around three main themes. First, the struggle for control over their own bodies in order to preserve choices over whether to become mothers at all is one fundamental theme. The ambiguous politics of caring for unplanned children has long shaped African-American women's motherwork. . . . A second dimension of racial ethnic women's struggles for maternal empowerment concerns getting to keep the children that are wanted, whether they were planned for or not. (1994, 52–54)

Several of the dimensions of struggle identified by Collins as specific to women from racial and ethnic minorities in the United States can be applied to the struggles of white transracial mothers in Britain. The two most prominent issues raised by the women I interviewed are their struggle to control their own reproductive labor and their struggle to retain their children.

There are parallels between society's perception of poor and working-class white unmarried mothers in Britain and poor black women in the United States. The Jim Crow segregation that kept American blacks impoverished and the control of unmarried women's sexuality have been central themes in the public policy debates about poverty, immorality, and state welfare on both sides of the Atlantic. Once white mothers are

FIGURE 15 Casey Clarke and her daughters.

constructed as transgressive and are publicly recognized as members of multiracial or black families, their risk of being subjected to what they call "racial abuse" increases. This abuse includes how they are treated in hospitals, schools, and police stations; the assumptions made by others about their maternity, morality, sexuality, and respectability; their subjection to verbal and physical abuse; and the denial or withdrawal of social courtesies typically extended to white people by other white people. The analytical framework Collins developed to theorize about the lives of American women of color can be deployed to illuminate some of the ways that white transracial mothers are policed and controlled as a group of transgressive mothers.

Dorothy Roberts, a black American feminist legal theorist, has argued that any mother who does not conform to "an idealized and racialized standard of selfless motherhood" is likely to be punished by the courts in domestic violence cases. While recognizing that there are differences between mothers, Roberts argues, "All mothers struggle to various degrees against oppressive social circumstances. The dominant culture and legal system places the bulk of childcaring on the mother's shoulders without the compensation, power, support they need and deserve" (1999, 45–46).

Sites of Surveillance: Hospitals and Unwed Mothers' Homes

Ricki Solinger (1992) studied the social and medical treatment of unmarried teenage mothers in the United States prior to the legalization of abortion in 1973 and developed a cogent comparative analysis of different forms of treatment and discipline offered to black and white unmarried pregnant women. In England, as well as in the United States, it was not uncommon for unmarried white women to be sent away to institutions where they could give birth and undergo reeducation.

Feminist analyses of unmarried *white* mothers in the United States and England stress the similarities between unwed mothers' homes and prisons. Feminists on both sides of the Atlantic have argued that in addition to providing material support for women who had "sinned," the primary ideological function of these homes was to discipline and punish those who had transgressed Victorian gender codes that precluded "respectable" women from engaging in premarital sex. According to Martine Spensky, who analyzed the changes in British welfare policy that occurred when the Poor Laws were repealed and new welfare policies introduced after the Second World War:

> Throughout the [nineteenth] century, working-class women, who were under the moralizing influence of upper-middle-class women philanthropists, came to judge unmarried motherhood through the eyes of the latter. . . . When respectability became the newly acquired wealth of the labouring classes, their attitude towards "sexual deviance" hardened and no one remained to identify with unmarried mothers who were left to the Poor Law whenever they were considered "undeserving" or to philanthropy whenever considered "deserving." (1992, 105)

Quoting an issue of the *Church of England Monthly Review* from 1858, Spensky describes the Christian origins of these homes:

> Special homes for unmarried mothers and their illegitimate offspring were opened by different missions towards the end of the nineteenth century. They were created on the model of the penitentiary: the mother had to repent of her sin. She stayed in the home with her child for a year while she was taught a trade, usually that of a domestic servant. When she came out, she was sent into service so that she could pay for the upkeep of her child who was sent to a foster mother. . . . Only the mother of a first illegitimate child was considered as "deserving" of a treatment better than that of the workhouse where other lone mothers were received, because there, she might be "contaminated by tougher women," "fail to repent," and become a prostitute. The homes were opened because of the increase of poor mothers. . . . They served also as a means of regulating women's sexuality and way of life. The woman who came out of the home was supposed to be very different from the one who entered it: amended, "respectable," employed and a "good" mother (i.e. one who provided for her child). (109–10)

As this description makes clear, in addition to being socially ostracized from their families and friends, these women were subjected to discipline and domesticity training within these institutions in exchange for limited material and medical support during their pregnancies. Peggy Hamilton, a fifty-six-year-old widow of a black American serviceman and the mother of five adult children, described her experiences in 1960, when, as an unmarried pregnant teenager, she entered an unwed mothers' home in the Midlands of England:

> I went in there the day that he was born. And they threw me out three weeks later. They told me to leave because I was discussing the fact that you paid to stay in this place. My mother had paid for me to stay in this place, and yet from half past seven in the morning, you were working. You were working right up until you were actually in labor. . . . You'd be scrubbing the floor, doing the washing. It was very, very degrading. And I kicked up such a fuss. I said, "You know, I don't really see why I should be doing this work when my mum's paying for me to be staying here." And basically they said, "Do you want to go home?" And I said, "Definitely." And I left and came home. But people [in my village] were having bets on each other, with each other, as to whether I would have the nerve to bring this baby back to [town] . . . because, remember, I was . . . the first young girl to be having a baby for a black man. The first in this region.

Hospitals, like homes for unwed mothers, are another institution in which women can be surveyed and disciplined. Poor women of color are regularly subjected to drug testing and other forms of surveillance in public hospitals, while middle-class women can avoid such surveillance and purchase privacy by entering private hospitals. The result, according to critical legal theorists such as Laura Gomez (1997) and Dorothy Roberts (1995), is that poor women are unable to restrict access to their test results, which increases their risk of being charged with criminal neglect of their fetus or infant. Like women of color, the white transracial mothers in my study reported that hospital staff assumed they were abusive or negligent mothers and treated them accordingly. Sharon Dawkins, a thirty-three-year-old mother of four daughters, describes what happened when she took her youngest daughter to the hospital for medical treatment in 1995:

> She'd had an accident and cut her head, and previously two weeks before I'd had to go down because she'd cut herself on her mouth. [So it was] the second time I took [my daughter] down to hospital. And I don't know if it was because they were stereotyping me, but they kept me waiting there. They made me take off all of her clothes. It was a

FIGURE 16 Sharon Dawkins and her daughters, Aisha, Tanika, Rhea, and Imani (on her lap).

head injury. It didn't even kick into my mind initially what they were trying to insinuate. And they left me sitting there for an hour with this two-year-old with no clothes on, and in the end I said, "Look, you know, she's crying. She wants her clothes back on. Can somebody give me her clothes?" And the nurse said to me, "Not until the doctor's examined her." I said, "Well, it's a head injury." "Yes, but the doctor wants to check for anything else." And I said, "For anything else, like what?" The nurse said, "Well, like bruises." And then it clicked that they were insinuating that this was an abused child.

Sharon's experiences were not uncommon; according to other mothers in her situation, the treatment she reported was routine and part of a pattern. This suggests that white transracial mothers are more likely than monoracial mothers to be suspected by hospital staff and social service agencies of being abusive because of their *presumed* marital status (unmarried) and the racial status of their children. Assumptions routinely made about white mothers whose children are visibly of African ancestry are that they are unmarried, unemployed, and receiving government assistance. This is apparent from Sharon's description of another incident that occurred in the same hospital waiting room on a different occasion:

A [white] lady was sitting next to me . . . and she was definitely staring at Tanya, and she was saying, "Oh, does she go to nursery?" And I said, "No." And she said, "Well, haven't you got her in a social services nursery?" And I said, "No." "Well, I thought you single-parent people could get your children into social service nurseries." And I just said to her, "Excuse me, but I'm not a single parent. I'm married. And I go to work. And I've no need for a social service nursery." But she sort of assumed that I was on my own and that I wasn't working.

When white women refuse to sever their ties to their black male partners and instead establish transracial caretaking alliances with them, their children's symbolic racial status can be temporarily transferred to them. The assumptions made about Sharon's marital and economic status parallel the controlling images and ideologies employed to justify the racial oppression of black women in the United States (Gomez 1997; Solinger 1992; Roberts 1997; Romano 1998; P. H. Collins 1990).[1] While there are differences in the history of welfare in Britain and the United States, what is significant here is that Sharon, like many American black women, is continually confronted with negative assumptions about her sexuality and her reproductive history.

Disappearing Acts: Tales of Abortion and Expulsion at the Racial Borders

White mothers and their birth children of African ancestry have been pathologized and their behavior described as evidence of moral decline in Britain.[2] These themes are evident in such distinguished films as *Brothers in Trouble* (1996) and *Secrets and Lies* (1995), which recycle images of hypersexualized working-class white women (typically Irish) and prostitutes, whose lack of sexual restraint causes them to produce children of visible African ancestry. These films, along with the long-running television show *EastEnders*, circulate the myth of the working-class white mother who has an African-descent child as a consequence of commercial sex, coercive sex, sexual misadventure, or an immoral lifestyle.

Four forms of discipline that are described by white transracial mothers in this study place them in this flawed moral category akin to that of the black welfare mother in the United States. The first two forms of discipline involve their social treatment as "honorary blacks." When these women refuse to abort their child and then retain custody after birth, they can be temporarily or permanently unwhitened by their association with black men. These mothers are then subjected to social ostracism and exiled from their families.

In the mothers' narrative accounts of their pregnancies and birth experiences, they described how family members attempted to reestablish the racial borders of the family by expelling them when their actions threatened to bring black men and the children they fathered into the family circle. The themes of sexual agency and anguish over the question of abortion emerged as these women of diverse reproductive and ethnic histories, who range from semiskilled manual laborers to university-educated professionals, described negotiating conflicts with families, boyfriends, and peers when they became pregnant. Resonating across the interviews are their struggles to exercise what Roberts calls their "reproductive liberty" (Roberts 1997). These women all faced opposition as they asserted their right to carry to term their often unplanned pregnancies and to retain custody of their children in circumstances of economic impoverishment or instability.

Virtually all of the women who were living with their parents at the time of their first pregnancy reported being strongly advised to abort their child and were either expelled or threatened with expulsion from their parents' home. It was at this moment when some of them became honorary blacks in their natal white families. The punitive sanctions imposed on three young unmarried white women who became pregnant while living with their parents on working-class housing estates in the late 1970s and early 1980s are representative of what I was told by one-third of the women I interviewed.

Katrina Nash is a forty-five-year-old mother of three daughters. In 1970, when she was an unmarried sixteen-year-old living at home with her parents, she became pregnant. Her parents responded to this news as follows:

> This was 1969 and it was the time of Enoch Powell. You know he made the Rivers of Blood speech then and so there was a lot of hatred towards black people at that particular time. So there I was, sixteen, pregnant to a black man. . . . We caught the bus back to my parents' house. And my mother was there, of course. As soon as we walked into the door, you know, she knew. And she said, "You're pregnant, aren't you?" I said, "Yes." And she just went mad. She didn't speak to him, didn't acknowledge that [he] was there—screaming and shouting at me. . . . I was told to leave [the house] at that moment. Within an hour of going into the house, I'd left.

Katrina moved in with her boyfriend's family and was supported by his mother, a black immigrant from Jamaica, until she was able to get council housing. At the age of seventeen Katrina gave birth to her first child, a daughter, and became an unmarried mother in need of government assistance.

In 1997, when I first met Katrina, she told me that she had not spoken to her parents or brother for eighteen years, even though they lived within walking distance of her home. An incident that occurred that year, when she encountered one of her father's friends in the city center, led her to reevaluate her relationship with her family and to sever all ties with her parents and her brother:

> After I'd left home and been excluded from the family home, my father told his friends that I'd been killed in a car accident. Rather than tell people the truth, he was prepared to go to these extremes. . . . My dad's friend was [shocked] when he saw me [downtown], he thought

he'd seen a ghost. And I said, "What? What's the matter?" And then it was just an incredible exchange because he couldn't believe that my dad had done this.

What Katrina describes here is her own social death. Her account illustrates the intensity of some parental reactions and their investment in patrolling the racial borders of their families. Katrina's parents were so invested in denying their relationship to their daughter and, by extension, to their grandchildren of African Caribbean heritage that they falsely declared to the world that their daughter was dead.

Sharon Dawkins, whose children range in age from six to sixteen, grew up in North Braunstone, a white working-class housing estate on the west side of Leicester that is ranked the most deprived area in the East Midlands and the fifth most deprived in England.[3] According to the Braunstone Household Survey of 1999, 51 percent of residents leave school before the age of sixteen, and 11.8 percent of the population are single parents (compared with the national figure of 4.2 percent). This housing estate, in which whites are 96.6 percent of the population and blacks only 1.7 percent, is known for its antiblack racism.

Sharon told a story similar to Katrina's about her parents' reaction when they learned that their teenage daughter was dating a black man:

I just couldn't believe it. . . . It was unbelievable. It was the beginning of the end really for my relationship with them and living at home, because when I was sixteen they just threw me out anyway. Because they just couldn't stand the thought of me being with a black man. It wasn't natural. It wasn't natural to mix bloods, you know. . . . I got called all the "dirty whores" under the sun. What is wrong with me? Why can't I be normal and go out with a white man. . . .

The first time I got pregnant I had an abortion. . . . [The decision] was influenced a lot by his mother. . . . It wasn't a planned pregnancy. . . . My mum and dad weren't very happy either. And it was, well, [my boyfriend's mother and my parents] came down for a family discussion. Everybody thought I should get rid of this baby. And they were like discussing me like I wasn't there, you know.

In a relatively new relationship that had not yet stabilized, Sharon described the fears that, in part, motivated her to accept her mother's and future mother-in-law's instructions to abort her child:

I don't want to be classed as one of these, another white woman with a half-caste child and no father around. That's how I felt. And it took me—what, at least a couple of months, to make up my mind. It was all, "Shall I? No, I can't do it. Yes, I've got to do it," you know. "Well, if he's not going to be around, I don't want to have the baby. At least if he comes back, he will have come back for me and not just because I've got a child for him." . . . I went and had this abortion done and I regretted it as soon as I did it. . . . Everybody heaved a sigh of relief. . . . Well, that's out of the way now. . . . There was no concern [for my feelings]. My dad just didn't want a half-caste grandchild because he always said to me "If you ever marry one, I'll never come to your wedding. And if you have children by one, I don't want them on my doorstep."

What stands out in Sharon's explanation for her actions is that she carefully considered the controlling ideologies about racial and sexual transgression in her community as she contemplated her possible future as an unmarried mother of a multiracial child.

Simone, a thirty-five-year-old mother of three sons, is married to her childhood sweetheart; they began dating when she was fourteen and became engaged when she was eighteen. Her brother's response to her dating a black man was to withdraw all affection and emotional support:

He came up to me and said to me, "You are no longer my sister. I will never ever speak to you again." I went, "Fine because it's your problem. Not mine." And he didn't speak to me. . . . And it was two years of pure hell. It really did hurt because my parents are a lot older. My brother was the closest one to me. . . . I've not spoken to my brother properly now since I was fourteen and I will be thirty-three years old this year. My brother didn't come to my wedding and my older brother didn't come to my wedding either.

Simone, like Katrina, has had no subsequent social contact with her brother, and on the rare occasion when she sees him at family events he does not acknowledge her presence. This type of rejection by family members is one of the most common forms of discipline reported by white transracial mothers and further illustrates how white women can become socially constructed as honorary blacks and exiled from their families. The material, psychological, and social consequences of expulsion from one's natal family can be devastating for women from working-class backgrounds, particularly if they lose the financial and emotional support of their children's father. For working-class mothers this often leads to increased economic vulnerability and increased dependence on the state in times of crisis. Ostracism from the family can also result in these women's children being deprived of the opportunity to establish bonds with their first cousins in their age cohort. It thus also imposes a transgenerational price.

Even if white women are not rejected by their families their parents may refuse to express affection or concern for their grandchildren of African Caribbean heritage. Half of the white and black family members in this study reported that their children had been rejected, socially ostracized, or subjected to forms of racist verbal abuse by white grandparents, aunts, uncles, or cousins. This form of discipline, aimed at transracial mothers, positions their children as ineligible for the affection, courtesies, and respect extended to the white children in the family.

Valerie Wellington, the mother of five children, has been married to Conrad, the British-born son of Antiguans, since 1983.[4] The daughter of a hosiery worker and a bus driver, Valerie worked from home as a hosiery mender when her children were young. She grew up in an area of the city she described as "very white." Conrad's parents immigrated from Antigua in the 1960s and, like most of the black Caribbean population in Leicester, settled in Highfields, where Conrad and Valerie met as teenagers. Four years after terminating her first pregnancy she and Conrad married. The first of their five children was born two years later.

In 1995, when I was first introduced to Valerie, she was receiving therapy for clinical depression, obesity, and her feelings about having had an abortion. Although she now has a husband who adores her and their five children, Valerie continues to struggle with depression because of her family's racism and her inability to protect her children from it. The following description is typical of the routine forms of intrafamilial racism that occurred in her mother's home:

> [My daughter] was trying to play a game with [my nephew] across the table with a little ball, quite friendly and quite innocently. . . . My sister's son told this to [my daughter]. "Oh, give me the ball back, you nigger." And this was in my mum's house. My mum never done a thing [to intervene]. My sister laughed it off like it was a big joke. I just went

FIGURE 17 Mandy and Gerry Burke, friends of Sharon and Everal Dawkins.

and hit the roof. I know they've got to face racism but not in their family. Racism shouldn't be in their family.

After this incident Valerie stopped taking her children to visit their white grandparents.

The incident that Valerie described is one example of the forms of discipline encountered by white women who establish families with black men and bring children of multiracial heritage into the family. White grandparents routinely allow other white family members to use their grandchildren's color and African Caribbean heritage as a weapon against them. Valerie expressed frustration not only that her parents were not central in the emotional and social life of her children, but that her children learned to perceive whites as a source of danger and injury to them. This issue is discussed fully in chapter 7. The point here is that Valerie's mother's refusal to intervene when witnessing her white grandchildren racially abusing her grandchildren of color is a way to continue punishing Valerie for establishing a family with a black man.

Valerie's inability to protect her children from the racism of their white maternal relatives challenged her sense of maternal competence. In addition, it brought into stark relief her personal ties to white racism and her fear that her children would begin to perceive *all* white people, including her, as racists:

> I don't want them to feel that because I'm white [racist thoughts] are going through my mind. And I'm their mother. . . . I get upset sometimes because I feel like, yeah, I'm white. I'm not happy with the way things have served them . . . like from my family. And I'm not very happy about the things I can't change, but I wouldn't like them to see me in the same way [as they view my parents]—as racist. I wouldn't like them to see all white people in the same sort of way . . . as my family's been with them.

Valerie's feelings are representative of the fears expressed by white mothers who were unable to alter the racist practices of their parents and their siblings but wanted to sustain cordial relations with them. For mothers such as Valerie the dilemma is how to convince their children that white people are not all racists when they have consistently been rejected and subjected to racism by their white grandparents, uncles, aunts, and cousins.

When I interviewed Valerie two years later she was a different person. After several years of therapy she had lost close to 90 pounds and was no longer suffering from clinical depression. Moreover, with the support of her husband, close friends, and family, she had learned to cope with the fact that her children had established close emotional bonds with their black extended family but spent little time with the white side of their family.

Irrationality and Hypersexuality

A third form of discipline described by transracial mothers is the radical shift in their status, from respectable to sexually immoral. A number of mothers reported that their friends no longer saw them as respectable in racial or sexual terms. When women who were either university students or employed full time, and thus financially independent, informed their parents that they were seriously dating black men, they encountered strong disapproval and intervention. Parents and friends strongly discouraged them from remaining in such interracial relationships. This was true for women across diverse class backgrounds. Women who married before they had children reported the same levels of disapproval and opposition from friends and family as those women who became pregnant and gave birth as unmarried teenagers. Thus, with few exceptions, neither professional status nor marital status seemed to significantly alter the reactions of friends and family to the women's alliances with black men.

Sue Farrell, who was born in 1961, is a self-employed aerobics instructor and the mother of three children. In 1995, when I met Sue, she had been married for ten years. She met her husband, Dane, the son of Jamaican immigrants, at a local gym where he worked. Dane went on to train officers at the policy academy and has since become a very successful physical trainer for a Premier League football team in England. Nevertheless Sue experienced the discipline described earlier:

> My so-called friends at the time, they disowned me really. If I was going to do something as silly as that [marry a black man] then they really didn't want to know me. Someone took me to the side and said, "I don't think you realize what you're doing. This is a mistake—a terrible mistake of your life. And if you don't sort of forget him then I'm afraid you'll have to forget us." I got a lot of lectures from people tell-

FIGURE 18 In the nineteenth century the Victorian houses that line Highfield Street were the single-family homes of the upper middle class. In the 1950s and 1960s they were subdivided and became multifamily housing for large numbers of poor families.

ing me how stupid I was and [who] couldn't understand the reason [I would marry a black man]. It's just a fact now, get over it, and don't I realize I'm lowering myself and degrading myself. . . . My mum hit the roof. Well, I think "whore" would be too strong a word, but that's generally what—from a mother to daughter—she was implying, that I was a whore and a slut for going with this [black] person. I mean I was twenty-one years old. And my mother is very reserved. And she felt if I were sleeping with anybody it would be a terrible thing. She just felt it would be *twice* as bad to sleep with a black man than a white person, I suppose.

Sue's comments reflect a theme that was consistent across my discussions with women, regardless of their class background and their parents' level of education. Sue's close friends and family members questioned her *rationality* and her *sexuality*: dating and then marrying a black man made her both irrational and sexually suspect. She was also accused of "degrading" her entire family. Within a year of this confrontation she moved out of her parents' home and purchased a house with her partner. They later married in a church ceremony and established a family.

In contrast to women who became pregnant as teenagers prior to marriage, Sue's marriage and maternity were carefully planned. Her husband has always worked full time as a successful trainer, and they bought their first home as soon as they decided to live together. Compared to poorer couples, they appear to have suffered few emotional and economic problems. Nevertheless Sue faced the same strong opposition from her parents and peers as unwed mothers in transracial relationships.

Andrea MacKenzie is a forty-three year-old solicitor employed by the Leicester City Council and the mother of two children. A widow since 1991, she was married for fourteen years to a native of Jamaica. Educated from the age of eleven at a boarding school, Andrea reported having had no social contact with black people prior to attending university. While doing voluntary work at a home for the elderly she met her husband, who was assigned there as part of his training as a psychiatrist. They began dating and quickly fell in love. She was shocked by her parents' response to her interracial relationship:

I'd been brought up to respect everybody, and therefore I naively assumed that [he was different] but that it shouldn't be a problem. I wrote to [my parents] and told them about [my black boyfriend]. . . .

FIGURE 19 Sue and Dane Farrell.

It was made very clear to me that it was not acceptable. I don't know whether my father said it to me, or my mother said it to me on my father's behalf, but I can remember having a discussion with him and . . . he used the word, he felt "humiliated." So I questioned that—said that I didn't understand that. And he said, well, you know, if he told people—if he told his friends that his daughter was going out with someone who was black, "What would they think?" So I said, "Well, you wouldn't tell someone your daughter was going out with someone white, so why do you have to go around telling them that your daughter is going out with someone black? You know, you don't go around talking about it in those terms." But he made it very clear to me that he wasn't at all happy. And he didn't meet [my husband] for quite some time—another sort of six to nine months . . . and we had the most appalling, awkward, difficult meeting.

Her father refused to attend their wedding, which took place after Andrea completed her studies at the College of Law. She described his reaction when he learned of the upcoming wedding: "[He] was appalled and said he'd have nothing to do with me. . . . I think it pushed [my mother] near to the edge of a nervous breakdown. . . . He lost me as a daughter." Andrea never saw him again.

In 1997, when I was introduced to Chelsea Carrington, she was the forty-six-year-old mother of a preteen daughter and had been actively involved in human rights, immigrant rights, and other forms of social justice work for two decades. In the 1980s she had established strong ties with black, Asian Indian, and white women activists who were working on behalf of ethnic minority youth in inner-city communities. This work socially integrated her into multiethnic communities and led to her involvement with a black man. As a university student in 1981 she learned Urdu and worked as a volunteer tutor in English for Asian Indian immigrant families. This work radically shifted her awareness of the historical legacies of colonialism, racism, and politics:

> I was doing community work. . . . I also started to be a tutor of English and going into people's homes to visit . . . and then I started to read black history. . . . I started to read a lot. I got involved in a lot of community, political things like the Law Centre. I got the experience as well, learning about what [Asian Indian and African Caribbean] children were experiencing in school. . . . I started to read a lot of Carib-

bean literature. It made me sort of think a lot more about what the political issues were. What [black] people's experiences were. . . . That was the first time that I'd actually started to seek out books by black people—to read about black people's experiences . . . in this country and in . . . America, I suppose, as well.

Unlike women who did not engage in political work prior to their pregnancies, Chelsea had already acquired some understanding of Britain's colonial history and knew firsthand about the experiences of African Caribbean and South Asian communities. In fact, like a number of the unmarried black women in the black voluntary sector with whom I developed friendships, she had volunteered a lot of time to projects designed specifically to empower black and South Asian girls living in inner-city communities. Chelsea also coauthored a report for the Imani Center, which was established to provide support for girls from ethnic and minority communities.[5]

When Chelsea got pregnant she was thirty-eight, a financially independent professional who had moved out of her parents' home a decade earlier. Nevertheless her parents' response to her pregnancy bears a striking resemblance to the responses of parents of women who became pregnant as teenagers living at home:

> Well, I think they were quite shocked, would be to put it mildly, really. I think they were very upset—both at the thought that I was going to be, in their terms, "an unmarried mother," and their very, fairly traditional views. I mean, [they were] very much of the views that you shouldn't even be having sex with someone unless you're married. I mean, I think, although they never articulated it—the thought that she was going to be racially mixed—it was a shock to them really. They felt quite sort of *betrayed*, I suppose. I mean—I think that's probably not too strong a word. . . . We didn't actually see them for a long time. My daughter is seven years old now. It's probably been nearly seven years before I can say that my mother would ring and she would come over [to visit], and it's only really in the last eighteen months I think that [my daughter] has actually gone and seen the house where I grew up.

It is not coincidental that the language Chelsea used to describe her mothers' reaction echoes Sue Farrell's language. Their pregnancies,

FIGURE 20 Children playing in front of their home on the Braunstone Housing Estate, the poorest housing estate in the East Midlands. Sharon Dawkins grew up on this estate.

whether in or out of wedlock, called their parents' attention to their intimate *sexual* involvement with black men. Women who were not racially literate (see chapter 4) tended to interpret this primarily as gender oppression, explaining that their parents embraced a sexual code that oppressed women while allowing men to engage in sexual adventure. White women were required to remain asexual or discrete in their sexual relations until they were married or engaged to white men. Chelsea's experiences as a university-educated professional were very similar to Andrea's and Sue's. Respectability was lost regardless of marital status.

Racial Abuse on Housing Estates

Transracial mothers, particularly working-class women who live on housing estates and possess neither academic nor economic resources, described a fourth form of discipline that they termed "racial abuse." A number described having to adjust to patterns of racial abuse in public when they first began dating black men, and later as young mothers. The forms of abuse they reported closely resemble the abuse encountered by blacks and South Asian immigrants on housing estates (see Commission for Racial Equality 1986). Virtually all of the women who gave birth to their first child during the period 1960–85 reported this pattern of racial abuse. By the late 1980s this type of abuse was more muted.

Sonya Smyth, the forty-one-year-old mother of four children born between 1976 and 1990, was introduced in chapter one. Born in 1956 in Blackpool, she is the daughter of an Irish man and a woman of English heritage. Shortly after moving to Leicester, where her brother was enrolled at the local polytechnic, she gave birth to her first child at the age of twenty, the result of her first sexual experience with a Jamaican man twenty years her senior. She did not inform her parents of her pregnancy until her fifth month so that they could not pressure her into aborting her child.

In 1997 Sonya received a monthly child benefit payment for each child and £105 per week in income support from the government. A former resident of Braunstone, a white working-class estate and one of the most economically deprived areas in Leicester, Sonya now lives in Highfields, in a neighborhood characterized by poverty, high levels of street prostitution, and drug trafficking. She lives in a four-bedroom terraced home with her four children on a street where the majority of the residents are

Bangladeshi. When I went to visit her at home, her neighbors—women wearing black veils—observed me from their windows as I knocked at the front door.

As the unmarried mother of four children of African Caribbean ancestry living on a street where all of her neighbors are married, religious, and in monoethnic families, Sonya believes that she is treated as if she were a commercial or casual sex worker. She is unhappy in Highfields, where she does not feel safe, and is trying to move back to Braunstone, the white working-class area that she had fled six years earlier. Poor unmarried women in Sonya's situation have very restricted housing options, however. They can live in housing provided by the city council, or they can rent housing operated by a housing association, a private charity that rents homes below the market value. The only other white woman residing on her street is a known prostitute who also has mixed-race children, which reinforces the stigma and social isolation Sonya experiences. Sonya claims that her neighbors cannot distinguish between her and other white women who occupy the same economic position; both depend on the state for support and neither one is married.

Sonya is very conscious of the stigma attached to unmarried white women who are parenting birth children of visible multiracial heritage, and she resents being lumped into the same category as other white single mothers. The social and symbolic distinctions that she draws between herself and the white prostitute who lives on her street are not recognized by her Asian neighbors. Since Sonya self-identifies as a homemaker and did not become pregnant while engaged in commercial sex work, this presents a status dilemma; she is unable to control the perception that she is a hypersexual and amoral woman who routinely sleeps with black men, bears their children, and then relies on the government for support while the fathers move on.

In my study half of the white women who live on working-class housing estates and receive income support reported experiencing racial abuse from South Asian and white neighbors. Their struggles to get relocated to another estate, however, often resulted in their moving to an equally bad or worse situation. During her last pregnancy, in 1990, Rita and her children were subjected to daily forms of verbal abuse: "Well, we were living on a white [housing] estate. . . . He was just a baby in a pushchair . . . and [he] was getting stones thrown in his face and stuff when he was one year old . . . gravel off the road. Groups of young white lads would throw it." To protect herself and her children from this form of routine racial abuse Sonya fought for nearly a year to get out of Braunstone and eventually moved to Highfields, where they encountered different problems.

In seeking to relocate, Sonya drew a territorial link between white supremacy and racial violence against her children. The problem for Sonya, however, was that moving out of a predominantly white estate to a place where she was a minority did not provide the safety she had hoped for. Instead she continued to be positioned by her neighbors as someone living outside the borders of respectability. In her view her new, South Asian neighbors embrace the same racist discourses and engage in the same patterns of verbal abuse as did her former white supremacist, working-class neighbors. Wherever she lives, her unmarried status, the racial status of her children, and her poverty combine to stigmatize her and turn her into an iconic symbol of degraded white femininity.

Two-thirds of the white women living on predominantly white housing estates with their children of African heritage described a pattern of routine racial abuse that sometimes led to physical assaults.[6] Although families have a legal right to be moved if they can prove that they are being abused or targeted by neighbors as a result of race, women reported that they often had to wait months, sometimes even a year before the city council found appropriate and acceptable housing. In the meantime their families continued to endure daily verbal abuse, racist graffiti, threats of physical violence, and other forms of provocation.

Peggy Hamilton, who was kicked out of the unmarried women's home after she gave birth to her first child, whose father was a black American serviceman, described her experiences as a young mother residing on a newly built housing estate on the outskirts of Leicester in the early 1960s:

> I've walked down the street with my son [in a stroller] and [white] people have spat in my face—because you were classed then, well, you were classed as a whore. I went to live with my sister and . . . this was a new housing estate that they had built. There was a [white] family that used to live across the street from us. And they would, at every opportunity, say racist things about my son. . . . He was sitting outside and the children, youth would be coming home from school and they'd be saying, "Oh, look, the little *wog* is sitting outside in his pram."[7]

It was an expression that came through from the war—the soldiers being abroad and everything—very derogatory—very.

And then when he started to walk and the children were coming home from school. The daughters said "Oh, look, the little wog's learned to walk."

I was really, really furious. I really was. I went over to their house and I rang the doorbell. And the mother and father came to the door and I said, "I think you should talk to your daughter. You know, she's just called my little boy a wog. There's no need to be calling him that."

So the father said, "Why? He is a wog."

I said, "How can you? He's just a child. He's just a baby."

Their in-laws lived in the house next door to them as well, which brought their mother-in-law and the father-in-law out. And they started saying [racist] things. And there was a really low wall and the mother-in-law was standing in front of this low wall and she said something to me. I can't remember what it was, but it was really nasty. And I pushed her. And she fell over the wall. So they called the police, and I was charged with assault. They took me to court and I was fined ten shilling and fifty pence. But ten shilling then was an awful lot of money.

Peggy's story is representative of the daily abuse experienced by other white working-class mothers who are raising their African-descent children in predominantly white rural communities or on exclusively white housing estates in urban areas. Unlike the other mothers raising children in white working-class communities, however, Peggy had social and economic resources available to her that mitigated and softened the blows of racism. First, she married an American, and although he was black she had the support of the U.S. military base community and access to resources that women who married black British men or Caribbean heritage lacked.[8] Second, despite her family's initial shock at her pregnancy they never disowned her, and she continued to receive their emotional and financial support.

Because the government did not keep official statistics on racial abuse during this period, however, it is impossible to know how often Peggy's experiences were repeated in multiracial families. In the 1960s the verbal abuse to which Peggy's neighbors daily subjected her and her son was not identified as a problem worthy of government intervention. Racial harassment was an invisible problem that mothers such as Peggy endured without state support. *Living in Terror: A Report on Racial Violence and Harassment in Housing*, published by the Commission for Racial Equality in 1987, eight years prior to my interview with Peggy, summarized the lack of support that women in Peggy's situation would have encountered in the two decades prior to 1987:

> Six years ago, when the Commission published its report on racial harassment on local authority estates, violence stemming from racism was not seen as an important issue by most housing institutions. In particular public sector landlords generally did not envisage a role for themselves in helping support victims of racial harassment or in implementing strategies to combat it. The climate has changed in recent years and this use of racial violence has become far more public, both in terms of the response of institutions and the attention given to it by the media. 97)

The Home Office Report *Racial Attack* (1981) contained the first official estimates of racially motivated offenses. It found that "Asians were fifty times more likely than whites to be victims of racially motivated crimes and West Indians thirty-six times more likely" (7). In the late 1980s the government began to collect national and local data. According to its report, "Racial harassment is a serious and increasing phenomenon."

Questions remain about how multiracial families were counted in these reports. Were they classified on the basis of the mother's racial origins or the father's? Another related problem for white transracial mothers is that even in the mid-1990s, when I began my research, government reports on racial harassment tended to focus on Asian and black families that were monoracial or monoethnic, and separate statistics were not kept on multiracial families. As a consequence, white women parenting as either single mothers or as the domestic partners of black men living in multiracial family units often disappeared into the endnotes of official statistics.

Conclusion

Whether they established interracial relationships and became transracial mothers as unmarried teenagers, as university students, as employed married women, or as unmarried community activists, the nine transracial mothers introduced in this chapter all reported encountering forms of *gendered* discipline that repositioned them at the racial borders of their families and communities. Some members of their families and communities perceived their heterosexual liaisons with black men as a transgressive act that threatened to alter the racial profile of their natal family. The forms of social rejection, ostracism, and disapproval that these women reported demonstrate that transracial motherhood is still considered a deviation from the idealized monoracial norm and may racialize and reposition white transracial mothers in ways that distance them symbolically and socially from the white mothers of presumably monoracial white children.

How do white women and men who become members of interracial families learn to recognize and negotiate racism? In the next chapter I discuss a set of conceptual tools and analytical skills that I call *racial literacy*. Racial literacy enables white transracial parents to identify, translate, negotiate, and counter everyday racism and forms of discrimination that may have been previously invisible to them. As such it helps whites to navigate racial logics, racial hierarchies, and everyday forms of racism.

3

THE CONCEPT OF RACIAL LITERACY

> I was not a white mother when they were born, when they began to smile, speak, walk on their own. Nor were they "Black" nor even primarily sons when they first walked to school alone, wept at a failure or a prize denied, when one of them was called fat by another kid in the second grade. They were simply my children.—JANE LAZARRE, *BEYOND THE WHITENESS OF WHITENESS*

> But the Black people I encountered seemed to know as many versions of whiteness as Eskimos developed words for snow, and my place on the white spectrum seemed recognizable immediately in my inflection, body language, and especially deeds.—MAB SEGREST, *MEMOIR OF A RACE TRAITOR*

During the 1990s a number of memoirs were published in the United States by middle-class white mothers that inaugurated a new literary genre: the memoir of a white mother of black children. These memoirs are exemplary instances of a genre that combines feminist autobiography with novellas of racial consciousness and are part of a tradition of literary writings by white southern feminists, both lesbian and heterosexual, analyzing racism and their "place on the white spectrum" (Segrest 1994, 19; see also Pratt 1984; Jones 1990; Lazarre 1996; Reddy 1994).[1] In these memoirs white mothers analyze their growing awareness of the way their whiteness shapes their experiences and is implicated in larger structures of racism. This awareness shifts their sociopolitical vision, and they begin to perceive forms of everyday racism directed against their children and husbands, while also experiencing what Frankenberg terms "rebound racism."

Drawing upon rhetorical tools employed by nineteenth-century abolitionists such as Harriet Beecher Stowe (the author of *Uncle Tom's Cabin*), Lazarre (1996) and Reddy (1994), as respectable and educated wives and mothers, argue that racism is a white problem and one that impinges directly on families. As both insiders and outsiders, Lazarre and Reddy bear witness to everyday white racism.

When her memoir was published in 1996 Jane Lazarre had been married to an African American for twenty-seven years and they had raised two sons who self-identified as black. With the skill and poetry of a novelist, she takes us on a tour of the intellectual, emotional, and ultimately transformative journey through the territories of her whiteness. Describing her racial consciousness as a member of the Jewish left in the late 1960s, when she was a young and inexperienced teacher in the New York City high schools, she writes, "I still believed that claiming blindness to color could actually make you blind, that if people only treated each other as equals, centuries of history could be dismissed, even erased" (30).

Three decades later, having witnessed the everyday racism that her husband and sons encounter and learning from her black relatives, Lazarre's vision shifted: "Like any black person I have ever known, I now perceive obvious and subtle racism in the immediate world around me every single day." She describes how routine and mundane experiences as a teacher, a mother, a wife, and a relative forced her to confront what she calls "the blindness of whiteness," which is shorthand for the forms of privilege that enabled her, as a white person, not to see the racial structure of the United States (49).

These memoirs are the American cousins of a literary form that emerged in postwar British cultural studies. In *The Uses of Literacy* (1958), for example, Richard Hoggart draws on his childhood experiences to provide a comparative analysis of two periods in working-class life. He analyzes his life as a text, thus blurring the distinctions between sociology, literary criticism, and political theory. Lazarre too analyzes her life as a text and provides critical readings of her experiences as a mother, museum exhibits she attended, and her interactions with black students and her black family members.

It is in the autobiographical writings of white feminists that I first acquired sociological insights into the conditions under which whites can experience transformational shifts and realignments in their racial self-consciousness. White lesbian feminists who established families have described shifts similar to those experienced by heterosexual women married to black men. In *Memoir of a Race Traitor* (1994), for example, Mab Segrest, a white lesbian antiracist activist, describes organizing against white supremacy with blacks in North Carolina during the 1990s. Writing as an activist rather than an academic and literary scholar, Segrest describes shifts in her perception of the meaning and value of whiteness that resemble those of Lazarre. She describes how, as a white woman, she began to feel "irregularly white":

> I was in daily intimate exposure to the cruel, killing effects of racism, which my Black friends spoke of in the same way as they commented on the weather. . . . I often found myself hating all white people, including myself. As I took on racism I also found its effects could be turned on me. The possibility of overt violence or the reality of subtle ostracism gave me a sense of shared risk, not the same as the dangers faced by my friends of color, but close enough. (80)

Segrest put her life in danger by working closely with black antiracist organizers who trained her to take their messages into white Christian communities in order to mobilize support against the Ku Klux Klan. She asserts:

> White folks have a habit of listening to white folks with different ears. . . . I learned how to repeat the message heard from Reverend Lee or Chris to white audiences, sensing that my words would be heard differently, as if my vocal cords were turned more to the frequency of white ears. . . . At first I was surprised when Black folks let me in the doors of their homes and meetings given the disaster racism was inflicting on their lives. But the Black people I encountered seemed to know as many versions of white people as Eskimos developed words for snow, and my place on the white spectrum seemed recognizable immediately in my inflection. (1994, 19)

The shifts in racial awareness and in vision that Segrest, Lazarre, and Reddy have mapped in elegant detail highlight an area that remains undertheorized in the otherwise theoretically innovative and ethnographically rich literature on whiteness that has been published during the past two decades.[2] Feminist sociologists and feminist race theorists have offered few insights into how white women in situations similar to Lazarre's and Segrest's acquire forms of consciousness that enable them to embrace an antiracist white identity and to identify strongly with blacks.[3]

In this chapter I respond to these gaps and silences in the sociology of race and racism literature by introducing the concept of *racial literacy*, an analytical orientation and a set of practices that reflect shifts in perceptions of race, racism and whiteness. It is a way of perceiving and responding to racism that generates a repertoire of discursive and material practices. The components of racial literacy include the following: (1) the definition of racism as a contemporary problem rather than a historical legacy; (2) an understanding of the ways that experiences of racism and racialization are mediated by class, gender inequality, and heterosexuality; (3) a recognition of the cultural and symbolic value of whiteness; (4) an understanding that racial identities are learned and an outcome of social practices; (5) the possession of a racial grammar and vocabulary to discuss race, racism, and antiracism; and (6) the ability to interpret racial codes and racialized practices.

This chapter introduces the first three components of racial literacy; the remaining three components are addressed in chapter 4, when I examine how parents transfer racial literacy to their children. These two chapters demonstrate that white women and men involved in intimate interracial relationships can acquire racial literacy and develop a form of consciousness that enables them to perceive routine and subtle forms of everyday racism that were not previously visible to them.

The acquisition of racial literacy demands an ongoing set of negotiations in which the white members of interracial families choose to immerse themselves in a transracial world that demands an emotional, cultural, or political investment. In other words, acquiring a critical awareness of the ways that racism and racial ideologies might structure one's intimate life is not an automatic consequence of living a transracial life nor of establishing an intimate relationship with someone who is black. Indeed those partners who developed racial literacy were in the minority of white respondents in my longitudinal study.

Racial literacy provides members of transracial families with the tools to analyze the contradictory ways that racial logics and racial hierarchies structure their private and public lives. It enables them to critically evaluate and negotiate the racism that they and black members of their family encounter. As the intimates of blacks, they can be characterized as "honorary blacks" or "insider-outsiders" because they regularly witness the harmful social and material consequences of everyday racism; as individuals who are socially classified as white, they may also access resources that are channeled toward people who assert a white identity and are then rewarded for their whiteness. However, their whiteness is always mediated by their class position, marital status, occupation, sexuality, gender, and immersion in specific local, national, and familial communities.

Several dimensions of racial literacy emerged in my research, along with the practices that enable white members of interracial families to develop a critical racial frame: (1) identifying routine or everyday forms of racism, (2) evaluating how gender and class hierarchies intersect to shape the localized experience of race and racism, (3) identifying and evaluating the meaning of whiteness, and (4) negotiating local geographies of race and racism.

Danielle Johnson: Identifying Everyday Racism

Born in 1972, Danielle Johnson is blonde with hazel eyes and a cherubic face. The daughter of a man employed by the British military, she grew up in Cyprus, Northern Ireland, and Spain. She earned her university degree with a major in women's studies in 1994. I was first introduced to Danielle by one of her colleagues in 1998, one year after her marriage to Adam Williams. She met her husband, a second-generation black British man and native of Leicester, at a children's residential home that he managed while she was completing her internship as a social work student. Their first child was born one year after their marriage.

It is a spring morning in 2003. Danielle had given birth to her second child, also a son, six months earlier. I meet Danielle in front of the Phoenix movie theater in the city center of Leicester. Zuri, her younger son, is strapped to her chest, while Eli rides a red bicycle in circles around her legs. *Real Women Have Curves*, an American film about a Mexican American girl in Los Angeles, is advertised on the theater's billboard. Danielle and her family had recently moved into a two-bedroom flat one block away in a new red brick building located behind the Phoenix Art Center. We enter a locked gate and took the elevator up to the second floor. After giving me a brief tour of her home, we sit down on the living-room couch to catch up on events.

After her son's birth in December 2002, Danielle decided not to return to her old position and instead took an on-call position that allows

FIGURE 21 Lisa Hackett (on right) and her mother-in-law at a Sunday family meal.

her to work from home and provide social work services in the evenings. Adam takes care of the children after he returns from his day job. As she described to me the adjustments she had made in her career and her schedule, Danielle detailed the various forms of everyday racism she routinely encountered as the mother of two sons of obvious African ancestry. She described a conversation that she had recently had with her black mother-in-law, who was vacationing in Guyana when I visited:

> The other day [my son] was asking me what color he was. We got to talking and in the end I was saying different people might say he was mixed parentage or different terms. Other people might [refer to him] as black.
>
> And he said to me, "Well, I'm black like Papa."
>
> I said, "Yes, that's right." So that's how he sees himself. Well, [my mother-in-law] had said something to me about this conversation because he had obviously said to [his grandmother], "I'm black. I'm like you."
>
> Her and Joyce [Danielle's sister-in-law] were saying to me, "Well, that's okay. He can think that *now* . . . because he doesn't understand the complexities of [race]—but as he gets older you're going to have to explain to him that he's *not* black.
>
> It never occurred to me [prior to this conversation], but they don't actually perceive him as black like them.

This conversation demonstrates Danielle's recognition of intrafamilial differences between her black husband, his sister, and their mother, and shows that she has acquired the ability to detect competing racial logics and forms of racial thinking among her black family members. Danielle identified differences between how she and her mother-in-law racially define her son, whom she consistently referred to as black in her conversations with me. Danielle has learned that a perceptual and interpretive gap exists between herself and her black in-laws. She and her husband consider her son black because in their view his multiracial parentage will not protect him from racism. They believe that he will still be exposed to and vulnerable to similar, if not the same forms of racism as darker-skinned children of visible African ancestry. Her son's black Guyanese grandmother and his black British aunt, by contrast, employ a different calculus of racial belonging that positions her son as mixed-race rather than black because his birth mother is white. Danielle now understands that among her black relatives her whiteness influences their calculation of her son's position on the spectrum of blackness. This divergence in racial calculations and racial logics is something that white mothers must recognize and negotiate.

Danielle's ability to perceive and negotiate competing intrafamilial interpretations and meanings attached to her son's physical body, including his skin color, hair texture, and other markers of his white European ancestry, is one form of racial literacy. Danielle has learned to negotiate the fact that her black in-laws differentiate between her children and those of her black sister-in-law, while also accounting for the forms of everyday racism that she believes children of all degrees of visible African ancestry encounter, particularly once they enter the school system. In her view, white teachers, service providers, and police and the white public do not distinguish between children of African descent who have two black birth parents and those who have only one black parent.

In our discussions I observed Danielle grappling with the contradictory, contested, and complex meanings of race that position her son on the margins of his black extended family. She consistently described her sons as black in our conversations, and she has taught her parents to refer to them as black rather than half-caste, a term that continues to be in common use in this community.[4]

Another example of racial literacy involves understanding how one's whiteness shapes the public's interpretation of one's familial and intimate relationships. Half of the racially literate white transracial mothers I studied repeatedly cited the public's assumption that they were not biologically related to their birth children. One woman described this experience as "my secondhand racism." Danielle described a routine interaction at the bank:

> [The bank teller] said to me, "Let me see your baby." She must have been about nineteen or twenty. "Let me see your baby." I was carrying him in this thing. "Oh, he's so cute. He's so cute. What's his name?"
> "Zuri."
> "Oh, that's unusual. That's so unusual. Where's it from?"
> I said, "Oh, it's an African name."
> She says, "Oh, right. That's a really nice name." She carried on. She was sorting my money out.
> And then she said to me. "You must have really wanted him."

And I said, "Yeah."

And then she said, "To go all the way to Africa and get him."

Francine, she was so sincere. And I just sort of looked at her. And then she clicked. And then she was really embarrassed. . . .

"Oh my God," she said. "Is he yours?"

And I said, "Yeah, he is."

What distinguishes Danielle from white women who described similar situations but who are *not* racially literate is that Danielle analyzed and understood this interaction to be a form of everyday racism. The bank teller assumed that only a certain type of working-class white women, such as uneducated women who engage in casual or commercial sex, would have sexual relations with a black man; that a respectable and presumably middle-class, university-educated woman like Danielle is neither of working-class origins nor is she a former sex worker; and that she therefore must have acquired her son through international adoption.

Danielle is the primary caretaker of her two sons. She carried them in her womb for nine months, feeds them, takes them to play groups, takes her older son to and from school daily, and spends all day with her younger son. Nevertheless she is often not recognized as their biological mother in public spaces. As such, she is not seen as belonging to a natural family unit, and she must regularly defend her biological relatedness. Her struggles illuminate one dimension of racial literacy: the recognition that racism is subtle assumes many different forms. Another dimension is her ability to translate racial codes and racial logics that link class position, respectability, gender, and whiteness. In Danielle's analysis, her whiteness is read as a "sign" of her respectability by the bank teller, who then draws conclusions that deny Danielle's biological relatedness and distance her from her black birth son.

Allesandra Richards: Gender, Class, and Locality

Born in 1960 to white working-class parents in Leicester, Allesandra Richards is the thirty-four-year-old single mother of a teenage daughter. Her daughter's father, with whom she has no contact, is a black man of Caribbean origin with whom Allesandra had a six-month relationship when she was eighteen. She lives with her daughter in a spacious two-bedroom home that she rents from the city council on an inner-city public housing estate that she describes as "very Asian." Her home is a short walk from the commercial strip of Belgrave, an Asian neighborhood that hosts the largest city festival and parade for Diwali, a Hindu holiday.

In explaining why she left school at sixteen, without academic qualifications, Allesandra located herself within the class structure: "I went to a very working-class school where the children were seen as factory fodder. . . . You wasn't allowed to aspire to anything high and nothing was expected of you." When Allesandra was thirty she enrolled in Leicester University and earned her degree in sociology when she was thirty-four; she acquired the tools to analyze class inequality and racism, resulting in her acute racial literacy.

She described to me how she became the teenage parent of a daughter of black Caribbean ancestry: "I used to go to nightclubs with my friends in town. It was a black nightclub. . . . You see the thing about the race division in England, I suppose that there are specific white places and black places. And you get a few people that cross that division—that dividing line. . . . I would say they do tend to be women." What Allesandra had uncovered was similar to the "color line" in the pre–civil rights era in the United States, although it was not state-sanctioned in the East Midlands of England. Furthermore, as she and the black women and men I interviewed recognized, this was a *gendered* line that white women were more likely to cross than white men.

Another example of Allesandra's racial literacy is her analysis of her family's response to her pregnancy:

> I would probably have had an abortion if the circumstances were different, but I daren't tell me mum because of what was going on at home with my brother. . . . The district nurses were coming around and giving him shots of morphine. I think if my dad had had his way, I would have been gone. Because my dad is very racist—and *still is* to this day. I love my dad and my daughter loves her grandfather but [his racism] is something that we haven't hid from her.

Allesandra's younger brother was dying of cancer when she learned that she was pregnant, and her mother was nursing him twenty-four hours a day. His death left a void in the family when she was seven months pregnant, which the birth of her daughter filled. As a way of coping with her grief, her mother developed an intense emotional attachment to her granddaughter. Initially Allesandra's father would neither look at nor engage in any physical contact with his grandchild. Allesandra analyzed the racial ideologies of her parents and how these were mediated by her brother's death and the subsequent grief and loss. It was her brother's death that saved her from being expelled from her home like other teenage mothers (see chapter 2). In her view, her father was and remains a racist, although he changed his position over the years and now genuinely loves his granddaughter and is protective of her. This is another example of racial literacy.

Allesandra's ability to analyze and distinguish between her father's treatment of her daughter as an individual and family member and his racist attitudes toward blacks as a group is another form of racial literacy. Five years later, when I interviewed Allesandra and her daughter, who is now herself the mother of two sons, her daughter agreed with Allesandra's analysis that, although her white grandfather loved her and would do anything for her, he remained a racist.

Allesandra is immersed in a black social and friendship network. Her black female friends provide her with valuable forms of social capital, cultural knowledge, and support, which, along with her formal education, has helped her to develop racial literacy. Two of her three closest friends are African Caribbean, and she has relied on their support to raise her daughter. She describes the forms of emotional, material, and social support she has received: "My daughter will sleep at my best friend's home if I need to go out. Her children will sleep at my house. She'll feed them. I'll feed her children. . . . It's reciprocal. . . . I just know that [my black friend] will always do it. She'll never say no." The caretaking alliances that Allesandra formed with her black female friends are a form of comothering.

Because she has developed racial literacy skills, Allesandra now maintains a critical social distance from the white working-class community in which she was raised:

> Being the mother of a black daughter has affected me a lot because I feel ostracized from the [white community] and I've ostracized myself from it. I've excluded myself from [the white community] and I have also been excluded by whites because I can't sit in a pub or anything and listen to all the [racist] crap they come out with. . . . There's a lot of white people that I feel I have nothing in common with, only color, and color's not enough to bind us.

In the white community it is only with her natal family that she maintains a very close relationship.

Another dimension of racial literacy Allesandra has acquired is her ability to recognize that her social acceptance in the white community is contingent upon her conforming to and endorsing specific racial and ethnic boundaries between herself and black men. This can be seen in her description of an incident that occurred years ago when she worked part time in a fish-and-chips shop. A white customer with whom she had a collegial relationship discovered her transracial maternal status:

> I used to work in a little chip shop . . . and you would build up a relationship with people, them coming every week with the same orders, right? And there is an incident that sticks out. There was a white guy—I have to say he's white, it's relevant to the story. He was older and we just used to have a banter over the counter. He used to come in and buy chips . . . and we used to joke with each other. And he knew that I'd got a daughter. That is it. Period. He just knew that I'd got a daughter. And then one morning, I was walking somewhere with my daughter and I saw him in a van. He was driving up the road and nearly crashed. He was looking—staring at me. And I knew immediately what he was staring at. He was staring at my daughter because she's black. But he didn't know whether that was my daughter or not. . . . My daughter was little. The next week I went in to work and he came into the chip shop. And he went, "I saw you the other morning." And I said, "Yeah, I saw you." He says, "Who was that little girl you were with then?" I said, "My daughter." And it was never ever the same since. When I came he never wanted to joke with me no more because she was black.

As this story demonstrates, Allesandra's whiteness is qualified by the presence or absence of her daughter. Her acceptance by her white male customer is contingent upon her not having transgressed racial codes that require white women to distance themselves from black men and to form monoracial families with white men.

In a study conducted in the early 1980s Anne Wilson, a British sociologist, concluded that the white mothers of what she called "mixed race" children often experience the marginality attributed to their children: "In discussions of racial incidents and the attitudes of other people, the mother made a distinction between situations in which her husband or children were present and those in which they were not" (1981, 208). Wilson described the centrality of intraracial boundaries among whites:

> Within the white group, the sense of "us" maintains fairly rigid boundaries excluding "them," boundaries which are affirmed and reaffirmed between whites in ordinary conversation and behavior. For the white mother of mixed race children this can mean a curious, unintentional dual role, for she may be the recipient of entirely different kinds of behaviour and communications, depending upon others' knowledge of her intimate connections outside the white group. These bonds "qualify" her white membership—she cannot belong completely with "us" if her family belongs with "them." (208)

In chapter 2 I argued that the criteria for inclusion and exclusion in white communities is class-inflected and mediated by capital, heterosexual gender regimes, marital status, migration status, and the political climate. In Allesandra's case, her rejection by a white working-class man exemplified the secondhand racism that she has learned to negotiate. Her racial literacy enables her to analyze her social networks and to secure the support that she needs to shield herself and her daughter from this type of rejection. The operation of racial literacy is evident in her decision to organize her social and domestic life around friendships with black women. She has chosen to exclude herself from white social spaces and social networks she perceives as overtly racist. She no longer socializes in predominantly white spaces that she frequented in her youth, such as working-class white pubs, yet she regularly attends black social events and spaces. Allesandra has also developed strategies to negotiate the forms of everyday racism she anticipates encountering and has organized a comothering alliance to support herself and her daughter. In addition to the ongoing support of her white parents and siblings, she now has a caretaking alliance with two black mothers who share resources and knowledge with her and provide her with forms of ethnic capital (see chapter 6) as well as forms of social support.

Reflecting on her life before and after her daughter's birth, Allesandra notes, "You make friends, different friends, new friends when you got children. . . . You tend to pick people that have got a common interest as you. So you make new support systems that are based on different things from your old ones." Allesandra understands that, although she has retained some of her friends (all black Caribbean) from her childhood network, she has less in common with the white people with whom she grew up because she is responsible for raising a black daughter. This responsibility required her to cultivate a new support network that includes more black women and white women raising children of multiracial heritage.

Another example of Allesandra's racial literacy is her negotiation of her relationship with her white boyfriend, who recently moved into her home. One dimension of racial literacy is the ability to identify and analyze the racial ideologies and racial logics that circulate among family members, friends, neighbors, teachers, and service providers to determine whether one's child is being routinely exposed to racist ideologies and practices in the private and public spheres. To do this one must continually monitor the discourses, practices, and culture in one's local community. In the past Allesandra was reluctant to date white men because of her fear that they would be racist toward her daughter or express racist beliefs. However, she is now in a serious relationship with a white man who has passed a series of tests. She staged conversations she had with him about racism and the specific economic situation of black people in Britain to evaluate whether he held racist views.

Chelsea Carrington: Political Experiences and the Value of Whiteness

Chelsea Carrington, who was introduced in chapter 2, is a forty-six-year-old white English welfare rights consultant who grew up in a small village in a rural farming community. She is the daughter of a postal worker and a full-time homemaker who had worked as a waitress prior to her marriage. She is five feet, six inches tall and wears her black hair short. She has intense dark brown eyes and a delicate face. Shortly before her thirty-ninth birthday she gave birth to her only child, a daughter whom she is raising as a single parent. When Chelsea first invited me into her home her daughter was seven years old. Living in a community that is centrally located, and without a car, Chelsea and her daughter spend much of their social life within a short walk of their home.

Chelsea and her daughter live in Highfields, an inner-city neighborhood that is the heart of the African Caribbean and Bangladeshi Muslim communities. In this neighborhood it is very common to see children of visible multiracial heritage. Chelsea owns her Victorian terraced home on a street whose affordable housing has been a magnet for successive waves of immigrants, first from Europe, then from the Caribbean, and

FIGURE 22 A row of terraced homes in Highfields built during the Victorian period to house workers at the shoe and hosiery factories. Chelsea lives on this street.

now from East Africa and South Asia. Chelsea has established a strong support network of black male and female friends and colleagues whom she describes as part of her "extended family." Her best friend, an African Caribbean woman who has no children, is her daughter's godmother; they regularly vacation together. Although Chelsea would be classified as a "lone mother" by social services, she is more integrated into a caring network of black women and men than many of the interracially married women who participated in this study.

In 1969 Chelsea attended Reading University, west of London, where she first met African students who went there to study agricultural science. She then went to Durham University before moving to Manchester for five years. Her time living in Manchester was difficult because she was a stranger, but it changed her vision of the world and her social networks, thereby transforming her life.

During the late 1970s Chelsea learned Urdu and began working among the Punjabi Muslim community (from Pakistan) in Manchester. While working at a law center on deportation cases, she visited people's homes to learn about the conditions they were enduring. During this five-year period she expanded and redefined her community to include South Asians and black Caribbeans. Her work and political alliance with these communities led her to develop friendships with black men and women, which is how she met her daughter's father. She has remained immersed in these communities and in community work and political activism for two decades now.

Shortly after the race riots in 1981 Chelsea moved to Leicester and became involved in what is called the "black voluntary sector." At one point in the late 1980s she was the sole white member of a black women's organization that provided cultural services to black and South Asian inner-city residents. Despite her tertiary education, Chelsea, like other university-educated English women, had learned little about the experiences of black people in England; she began to actively search for and read books about black experiences in Britain (see chapter 2), engaging in what could be called an antiracist campaign to educate herself about the experiences of ethnic minorities. This self-education occurred before she became intimately involved with a black man and gave birth to her daughter. Chelsea's awareness of everyday racism is acute, as these remarks illustrate:

I think racism in this country is very insidious . . . compared with some European countries where it's very overt. . . . I think here there is a traditional English hypocrisy that you don't actually say things openly. It's always behind the scenes, and I realized how closely [this hypocrisy] is woven into the English psyche, both gender phobia and racism. . . . I've learned about racism—that it's an insidious thing. That it's so much a part of all our traditions and our ways of thinking. That it's something that you have to be aware of all the time. It's almost made [me] much more critical, I think, of white liberal thinking because that can be, in a sense, more dangerous racism. You know, the so-called color-blind approach to things.

Chelsea has worked very hard to understand racism as a complex structure in which she is always embedded and implicated. Ongoing discussions with her black and South Asian colleagues and friends have helped her learn to separate her whiteness from this larger structure of racism. When asked to describe her perspective as the white parent of a child of African Caribbean ancestry, she talked about how her "vision" had changed. She now sees the world from the perspective of her daughter, whom she describes both as black and mixed-race. Chelsea brought up the issue of racism as she described her decision to remain in her current neighborhood, even though it is economically impoverished. She exhibits a form of dual consciousness that enables her to move between perceiving her whiteness or her position as a white university-educated woman with certain structural advantages over black mothers in specific institutional settings, and sharing struggles with black mothers. As the primary caretaker and parent of a daughter whose body will be socially classified as "not white," and thus subjected to some forms of racism, she has learned that she needs to protect her daughter. Her daughter's skin color, hair texture, and facial features do not conceal her African heritage, despite how she may self-identify.

When asked how British whites view her daughter, Chelsea responded without hesitation: "They'll see her as black. . . . If they look at her and think of her in terms of her origins, they will probably think of her as mixed race, but the way they will treat her, and the way that [a person of salient African ancestry] will be treated in the society where the cultural norms are white—you will be treated as a black person—in the sense that you're likely to suffer the same kind of discrimination and stereotyping."

Like Allesandra, Chelsea has labored to acquire a form of double vision, and her racial literacy sometimes enables her to "see the world through black eyes." She has concluded that having a birth daughter of black Jamaican parentage confers some advantages on her, while also simultaneously excluding her from respectability and social acceptance by some segments of the local white community. That is why she maintains at a critical distance from whites as a transracial mother:

> I'm very suspicious of white people. I notice how easy it is for me to be part of that community. And yet, I feel like I'm not a part of it and can't be part of it because it's always going to, in some sense, reject [my daughter]. . . . It's a culture that doesn't readily accept black people. . . . So I feel that if I have a friendship or a relationship with white people . . . I always think that there's a barrier that's *always* there with white people.

Chelsea's nuanced analysis of everyday racism has motivated her to strategically employ her whiteness as a resource in institutional settings in order to guarantee that her daughter has access to specific educational resources and social services, while also distancing herself from white people whom she fears will harm her child. She is acutely aware that her whiteness and middle-class professional status confer advantages on her that black women of the same class position who are parenting multiracial children do not have. In contrast to three-fourths of the white parents in this study, who do not possess racial literacy, Chelsea employs her racial and class privilege (as a professional) to mediate and minimize the effects of institutional and individual racism on her daughter:

> I've tried hard to kind of create good relationships with the school and her teacher. . . . I realize that I also want to pave the way for her. I'm very conscious of the fact that if there is an issue [the school personnel] will deal with me as a white person. . . . I may have access into sort of institutional society as a white person that a black parent wouldn't have. Do you follow me? And obviously, I will use that to her advantage. A black mother of a black child or a mixed-race child would have a very different experience in that respect because if there's an issue at school or something she wasn't happy with then she will immediately encounter some sort of racial stereotyping or, you know, a list of cultural expectations which won't be directed at me.

Like Allesandra, Chelsea understands that her whiteness is mediated by her accent, class location, and educational capital. As a university-educated professional Chelsea has learned to strategically utilize her whiteness as a valuable resource to counter and minimize the racial discrimination that her daughter might encounter. One could argue that purposefully deploying her white privilege in such a manner does not disrupt the broader system that rewards whiteness. However, Chelsea interprets these small acts as part of a larger process of subversion in which she attempts to use her white skin to reallocate resources to her child of African descent. Chelsea's acts are a form of racial literacy because they reflect her awareness that her whiteness, like her class and her university education, is a source of capital that can be employed to mitigate the blows of antiblack racism.

Barbara McBride: Negotiating Local Geographies of Race and Racism

When I was introduced to Barbara McBride in 1997 she was forty-nine, an adult educator, the mother of a white twenty-six-year-old daughter and a teenage son of Caribbean ancestry, and the wife of a native of Barbados, whom she met in leftist political circles in London in the late 1960s. At that time they had been married for twenty-four years. Born in London at the end of the Second World War, Barbara grew up in a family that belonged to what she described as the "servant class." Her father was from a working-class family in Lancashire and had been a professional soldier based in India and Kenya during the war. Afterward, due to injuries he sustained during the war he found it difficult to secure and retain employment. He held "very racist ideas" about black Africans, Asian Indians, and other people of color formerly colonized by the British.

Barbara described what she learned at home about race, and specifically black and South Asian people, as "kind-hearted racism." The only black people she saw were the four black babies fostered by one of her white neighbors, who was given an award by the queen for doing so. Barbara recalled statements made about blacks: "'They're really sweet and nice, and why are they all here? It's cold. Wouldn't they be better off in their own place where it's nice and warm?' . . . So it's a sort of kind-hearted racism."

When she was twelve her father died and her mother accepted a position as a live-in housekeeper with an upper-middle-class woman. As a teenager Barbara lived in a spacious, upper-middle-class home in a posh neighborhood while attending a secondary modern school with other working-class girls. There was "a real schism" between which she learned to move and negotiate two very different social worlds: the working-class world of her friends and peers at school and the upper-middle-class world of her mother's employer.

In 1964, when she was sixteen, Barbara went to a further education college (similar to a community college in the United States) to study for her advanced General Certificate of Education, which would give her academic qualifications that she couldn't acquire at her secondary modern school.[5] This experience served as a catalyst for the development of her political consciousness: "I became sort of politicized because there was the students' union in the college and some of the lecturers were involved in this sort of political activity." At school she was exposed for the first time to an alternative political community and to ideologies that challenged those of her parents. She became involved in the antiapartheid movement and the Campaign for Nuclear Disarmament and, like Chelsea, began to develop friendships with British-born black people and those who had migrated from the Caribbean and West Africa.

In 1968 she married her first husband, a white university student who was involved in the antiapartheid movement. Two years later, at the age of twenty, she gave birth to her daughter. When her marriage fell apart she returned to London with a suitcase and a two-year-old. In London she got involved with a left-wing political group and moved into a political household, where she raised her daughter. She returned to school and completed a three-year certificate course that qualified her to be a teacher. She then began teaching in inner-city, multicultural schools in poor communities. As a single mother and political activist living in a socialist household, she started dating men she met in her leftist political circles.

During this period Barbara also studied events that had occurred during her childhood, including the race riots in Notting Hill in 1958: "I learned that sort of history. I went to meetings and rallies and heard black speakers for the first time and I went to the Angela Davis rally. . . . I had a lot of arguments with white people." Her political education and experience in antifascist groups provided her with forms of knowledge that she converted into racial literacy. In other words, her political experiences and knowledge constitute a form of capital on which she continues to draw even though she is no longer living in London and involved directly in that work.

Barbara, like Chelsea, also possessed what C. Wright Mills called the "sociological imagination" (1959, 5–6). Both women were able to locate themselves and their problems in a broader historical and national context. For example, Barbara was able to describe the habitus in which she was raised, including the unquestioned assumptions that structure social relationships, along with how racial power is activated in working-class white communities. She identified the racial logics and racial ideologies that circulated among her family members and neighbors and how they attempted to regulate both blacks and white women through racial rules. She was conscious of the opinions white people in her circle held about interracial relationships during her youth in the 1960s, and what they revealed about racial logics that opposed interracial intimacy: "There was a real fear . . . if anyone got involved with a black man. It was all around. It was kind of accepted that [having an interracial relationship] was something that you didn't do. . . . If somebody's wife left them, people would say things like 'Oh, she's gone off with a black man.' It was used as an insult: this woman was [considered] a slut."

In London Barbara acquired an understanding of how her social position as a divorced, single mother of a young child was interpreted by her white comrades and the general white public. Serving as a liaison between her political group and black workers who were striking, she became more conscious of how black workers saw racism operating. While dating a black man from St. Lucia, they were subjected to a barrage of public racial abuse. They were routinely spit on, and she was called a whore and verbally abused by whites. As a white heterosexual woman in a dating relationship with a black man, Barbara learned which areas of London to avoid because they were unsafe for interracial black-white couples. She displayed a crucial dimension of racial literacy: how to evaluate local racialized zones so that she could protect herself and her partner from verbal and physical abuse. She also learned that her whiteness, in conjunction with her femininity, could be interpreted either as an asset or as a liability, depending upon the racial logics of her partner and the racialized zones they entered. Moreover, as an unmarried, sexually active woman, she slowly became aware of how she was perceived by her black boyfriend. She discovered that he viewed her as a source of status, an asset, and as evidence of a potent masculinity. And she came to realize that both her white political comrades in the socialist house in which she lived and her black partner strategically employed her whiteness as a resource in ways that she began to find problematic. She eventually ended this relationship and began dating another man, to whom she has been married for twenty-four years.

Barbara acquired a high degree of racial literacy as a consequence of her work in antiracist and antifascist political circles in London in the 1960s when she was raising her daughter from her first marriage. Yet speaking about this period three decades later, she is aware of the limitations of her knowledge because she had not yet experienced the refusal or inability of white people to perceive her as the biological mother of her son. Despite the forms of racial literacy she possessed as a young mother, she was not prepared for all of the racism that she would later encounter:

> I knew about institutional racism. I knew about racial harassment, so I knew that when I stepped out on the street with my black child, the chances were that I would get harassed in some way or another. And I was ready for that. I was ready for someone to call me a name. I was ready for somebody to throw something at me. . . . I had that in my head—that that could happen. I wasn't ready for somebody to doubt that he was mine. It just hadn't occurred to me at all. So it was a real shock for the first time. After that I was ready for it. Whenever a stranger questioned me about [my son's biological origins] my answer would just be straight: "No, he's mine. I bore him. He was in my womb. I carried him for nine months, just like any other child."

As this quote illustrates, Barbara learned that her whiteness was interpreted as separate from her son's race. Like Danielle Johnson, she came to understand that the anonymous white public might interpret her whiteness as a sign that she was a foster mother or an adoptive mother, because, as a white, educated, middle-class teacher, she did not fit the stereotype of the working-class women or prostitutes who acquired such children through casual, coercive, or commercial sexual relations.

Barbara is aware that her social position as a white woman provided her with varying degrees of social currency in specific geographic and demographic contexts. She is also very conscious of how she is racially marked and admits that if she had not become involved with radical politics and then developed friendships with black men and women, she may never have developed her racial consciousness.

In his ethnographic study among poor and working-class white residents in three neighborhoods of Detroit, John Hartigan Jr. (1997, 1999) argues that white racial identities are heterogeneous, contingent, and mediated by local racial geographies of social space. Elaborating on the work of Omi and Winant (1986), he found that a multiplicity of racial formations exist, each deriving from social, economic, and political forces that are distinctly localized. In Detroit, where whites have lost their majority status, Hartigan asserts that "the contours of whiteness have rapidly mutated and reformulated" (1997, 183). These cities provide a local context in which the meanings of whiteness and blackness diverge from what are commonly assumed to be the dynamics of racial politics in the United States. According to Hartigan, the most important difference is that "whiteness, here, is rarely an unmarked or normative condition. In fact, whiteness is often read as being out of place in this 'black metropolis'" (185).

As Hartigan asserts, white people's social and class status mediates how their race is read in neighborhoods where their whiteness is visibly marked. Like other respondents who have cultivated racial literacy, Chelsea and Barbara understand that interpretations of their whiteness vary across social spaces and demographic zones. Unlike Hartigan's subjects, who were poor and marginalized whites, Chelsea and Barbara's class position magnifies the *privileges* signified by their whiteness.

Lifting the White Veil: Learning to See beyond Whiteness

During the past decade sociologists and social psychologists have paid more attention to the conditions under which a white antiracist identity may develop. Beverly Daniel Tatum (1997) described the stages through which white people pass as they learn to understand the meaning of whiteness in the context of racism and racial hierarchies and to acquire a critical analysis of the ways racism structures their lives. Drawing on social psychology, she explained how whites rearticulate the meaning of race in their lives: "For whites, there are two major developmental tasks in this process, the abandonment of individual racism and the recognition of and opposition to institutional and cultural racism. These tasks occur in six stages" (94). Tatum's analysis of the early stages of this process mirrors themes addressed in the memoirs of white women who become romantically involved with black men (Lazarre 1996; Reddy 1996).

Tatum described the second stage of this process, which she called "disintegration," as "marked by a growing awareness of racism and white privilege as a result of personal encounters in which the social significance of race is made visible. For some white people, disintegration occurs when they develop a close friendship or romantic relationship with a person of color. The white person then sees firsthand how racism can operate" (1997, 96). Jane Lazarre and Maureen Reddy have described this situation in their memoirs in eloquent and moving language.

While Tatum's analysis is instructive, it fails to consider the significance of space and locality as well as gender. Unlike Tatum, I did not find evidence of this process of disintegration occurring neatly in six separate stages. Rather, I discovered a dynamic and dialectical process that involved ongoing negotiations and strategies. This occurred because the meanings and values attached to whiteness and blackness varied as individuals moved across ideological zones, residential neighborhoods, racialized spaces, and racial boundaries. Furthermore Tatum does not adequately theorize the ways class inequality, gender subordination, locality, nationality, and political experiences shape how whites perceive and revise the meanings of race and racism.

In this chapter I have argued that white people, as insider-others, the intimates of blacks, can reconstitute a sense of self that enables them to acquire sophisticated analyses of race and racism. Rather than occurring in neat and ordered sequential stages, this process is messy and ongoing and involves daily negotiations and revisions of the meaning and value of whiteness. In her early writings on black feminist thought, Patricia Hill Collins (1986) also spoke of a feeling of "two-ness" when she described the "outsider within" status that has historically provided black women with unique insights into white society. Because many black women have been positioned inside white families as domestic servants, "these women have seen white elites, both actual and aspiring, from perspectives largely obscured from their black spouses and from these groups themselves" (14). This feeling of two-ness can be applied to white people who share their world with blacks as domestic partners, mothers, wives, and daughters-in-law.

An analysis of how racism shapes the experiences of white parents of children socially classified as black is central to understanding racism and antiracism in postcolonial Europe. Ninety percent of the white women and men who participated in this study reported that they had encountered or witnessed racism as members of transracial families (regardless of whether they had acquired racial literacy). Twenty-five percent of the white mothers in this study articulated an understanding of the forms of racism encountered by their children or husbands. Although these women constitute a minority among whites, what is striking is that they identified the *same* areas as black women when questioned about where they experience racism: in education, employment, police harassment and surveillance, routine racial abuse, and anonymous interactions with the white public. They developed various strategies for securing networks of support that they anticipated their children would need to combat this racism in the public sphere.

Conclusion

Racial literacy is learned through an ongoing analysis of how bodies are racialized and resources are distributed across various familial, occupational, local, and institutional sites. Interracial intimacy provides one possible route for transforming one's sociopolitical vision, but it is neither an automatic nor a natural consequence of interracial intimacy. There are two reasons to focus on those white women who display racial literacy. First, whites have been neglected as sources of antiracism in sociological analyses of British multiracial families. While there is no doubt that white women, whether they are members of transracial or monoracial families, may engage in racist practices, recycle racist ideologies, and benefit from racial privilege, this is only part of the story of race. Sociologists interested in understanding the contemporary racial life of England must also provide theoretical maps of the conditions that can lead to more reflexive and sustained commitments to antiracism among members of the racially dominant groups.

Second, transracial families provide strategic opportunities for theoretical and empirical excavations of racial consciousness in action. This fits in with my intellectual investment in identifying invisible zones of racial labor that remain undertheorized by feminist race scholars interested in race, racism, and antiracism. My aim is to clarify how parental labor can, for *some* white interracial family members, become a catalyst for engaging in racial literacy projects.

Among white parents I classified as racially literate I found several similar turning points in their racial consciousness. One turning point was the decision to work for an antiracist or social justice community, which launched them on a trajectory toward a transracial friendship, an antiracist mission, and a multicultural life. For women like Chelsea, attending a university and becoming involved in legal work on behalf of recent immigrants from South Asia and the Caribbean forever changed her social networks and her priorities. She also met the father of her child through these networks. For others, such as Barbara and Allesandra, immersion in a residential community or attendance at state schools with a large ethnic population enabled them to develop close friendships and political alliances with blacks and South Asians. Barbara's work as a political activist in London led to close friendships with black Caribbean workers, to marriage, and to transracial maternity. As children or adolescents, women such as Allesandra were eyewitnesses to the antiblack racism of their parents, peer group, siblings, teachers, and service providers.

For white members of interracial families who actively engaged in racial literacy projects, there was a pattern across classes in which all learned to closely monitor themselves as they related to other whites and to members of racial and ethnic minorities. They carefully evaluated their everyday practices and the social processes that sustained or reproduced the racial and ethnic hierarchies that denigrated blacks and distributed various forms of privilege to whites. They possessed C. Wright Mills's "sociological imagination," were aware that they belonged to a particular historical moment, and operated in a larger racial (and regional) structure. Thus they were always implicated in the material and social residues of a postcolonial and post–civil rights world in which the forms that racism assumes are adaptable and in flux.

Du Bois's concept of double consciousness is instructive in understanding "dual vision" and the resistance to "constricted eyes" (Pratt 1984). Although Du Bois developed the concept to theorize the complexities and unique position of American blacks at the turn of the nineteenth century and early twentieth, his insights can be applied to interracial partners or other individuals who transgress or "cross over," thereby becoming witnesses to the antiblack racism that continues to characterize the experiences of the vast majority of blacks in the United States and Britain.

Examining the contexts that motivate white people to analyze the racial logics and larger racial projects that structure their intimate lives can also lead to theoretical insights. White members of interracial families become candidates for racial literacy projects during those moments when they are able to observe the ruptures or gaps between the realities of their lives and the assumptions others make about their lives. They learn to see the dynamic ways in which their whiteness is interpreted, negotiated, and implicated in larger racist projects and to perceive structures that had previously been invisible to them. It is as if until then they had been living behind multiple veils. Like the American blacks about whom Du Bois wrote, nonblacks can also find themselves in familial networks that require them to move between worlds, to lift their veils, and to adopt the perspectives of others.

Interracial intimacy is a dynamic, micropolitical site where white members of interracial families can learn to develop a critical analysis of how race and racism operate in their lives. Through interracial intimacy they may learn to distinguish between their whiteness and white supremacy as a racial project, an ideology, a line of vision, and a position of structural advantage that is affected by the interrelated variables of class, gender, generation, sexuality, and locality.

4

RACIAL LITERACY IN PRACTICE

In a racist society there is a hierarchical racial order, with much for young children to learn. There are complex racial rules to be comprehended and lived.—DEBRA VAN AUSDALE AND JOE FEAGIN, *THE FIRST R: HOW CHILDREN LEARN RACE AND RACISM*

Black people only see the white side of you and white people only see the black side of you.—RHEA DAWKINS, EIGHTEEN

I've always said to [my daughter], "Look, you're black. Society sees you as black, and it's best you know that because at the end of the day . . . it would be black people who would accept you. The white people don't see you as mixed."—JUSTINE MOONEN

On 16 September 2000, *The Guardian* published a story titled "Women Win Payout for Soldier's Racial Abuse":

Two black women who were subjected to a barrage of racial abuse at an army base have been awarded thousands of pounds in compensation by a judge. Sue Hunter and her sister Angie DeMeyer suffered racial chants of "nigger" and say that they had guns pointed at them when they attended a dance at Oakington Barracks, Cambridgeshire, in August of 1995. The women say their ordeal came at the hands of soldiers of the first battalion of the Cheshire regiments, based at the barracks, whose commander in chief is the Prince of Wales.[1]

Kenneth Bragg, the soldier who racially abused the two women, was dismissed from the army after a court martial in August 1997. He was ordered by the Nottingham Crown Court to pay £7,000 compensation to Angie DeMeyer and £5,000 to Sue Hunter. According to *The Guardian* this incident began when Hunter intervened on behalf of a black soldier who was being abused by Bragg. Hunter, described as black in the newspaper article, is the daughter of a white working-class English woman and a black American serviceman from Detroit. She was raised by her Irish-born mother on a housing estate in the East Midlands of England. Her mother, born in Belfast, met her father in the 1960s, when he was stationed at an air force base located about forty miles outside of Leicester. She reported that her mother and father had an amicable separation after her mother declined her father's invitation to relocate to the United States when he was discharged from the air force.

Sue Hunter's antiracist training, which she attributed to her mother, disappears behind the headlines of this story. Yet if we carefully examine the social process by which women like Sue are trained (or not) by their white parents to identify politically with the black British community, we gain theoretical insights into how racial hierarchies are managed at the micro level of the family. Her experiences are also instructive in illuminating how blackness is socially produced in multiracial families. Critical race scholars concerned with racism and antiracism in black Britain have not systematically examined the social practices of women like Hunter's mother.

In demographic terms Hunter is not an anomaly. While she may represent only a fraction of the larger British population, she is part of a growing segment of the black British population. In 1991 half of British-born black men and a third of British-born black women had selected a white partner. Thirty-nine percent of children born to black Caribbean mothers or fathers had one white parent, and in the majority of these cases the mother was the white parent (Modood et al., 1997).[2] The number of interracial marriages between blacks of Caribbean origin and whites continues to increase in Britain, posing significant theoretical and political questions about how racial formation operates in these families. Multiethnic families deserve more sustained attention when considering black community formation in Western Europe.

In this chapter I analyze how white transracial parents raising children of African Caribbean heritage negotiate racial hierarchies and manage their children's racialization in ways that privilege the black community. While a number of studies of people of mixed-race heritage have provided insights into how they manage their identity and struggle with their racialization and racial hierarchies, none has offered a conceptual frame for understanding how white parents respond to racial hierarchies. The sociology of race literature has not carefully examined the practices of white parents who embrace an antiracist position and are training their children to strongly identify with the black community.[3] My research departs from mixed-race identity studies by placing the experiences and practices of *white* parents who are members of multiracial families at the center of analysis.

I discovered three discursive and material practices among those parents who reported actively training their children to strongly identify with the political struggles of blacks. Combined, these practices constitute the racial literacy that I examined in chapter 3. These practices facilitate the acquisition and transmission of racial logics and black-oriented social networks and provide children of African Caribbean ancestry with the resources to assist them in countering what Philomena Essed (1991) conceptualizes as "everyday racism."

I further develop the concept racial literacy by focusing on the discursive and material practices that provide children of multiracial heritage with the resources they can employ to subvert or invert racial hierarchies that privilege whiteness. These practices and projects are not formalized and do not register in conventional sociological accounts of racial formation or antiracism. My analytical focus on the labor of white parents offers a partial and restricted view of the dynamics in these families. I analyze the racial vocabularies, conceptual tools, and forms of education that white parents provide as they train their children to identify culturally and politically with the black community as one strategy to resist antiblack racism. I focus on these practices because they constitute a particular type of antiracist project that studies of interracial families have neglected. Furthermore they illuminate the role of white members of transracial families in the social reproduction of black subjectivities.

Racism in the Local Schools: The Demographic and Cultural Context

On 13 January 1998 the Leicester *Mercury* published an article titled "Racism Is a Problem in City Schools":

> [A] survey published by the Leicester Young People's Council . . . shows that [of] 1,628 youngsters who responded, 52.5 percent had experienced racist behaviour towards them and 73.7 percent had suf-

First Prize Winner; YPC Racism Poster Competition.
David Watts From Beaumont Leys School.

"Racism, Racism, What does that word mean?
Inequality and name calling, a difference in the way I am seen"
By Anna Nathwani, Beaumont Leys School.

If you are one of the 52.5% young persons experiencing racism then:

★ Tell your teacher.
★ Tell your parent/s, people you trust.
★ Tell your youth tutor.

Telling someone about your experience of racism can help make things better.

Other sources of help:

Racial Harassment Project   Leicester Mediation Services   Leicester Racial Equality Council
(0116) 252 6755   (0116) 253 2900   (0116) 254 5918

RACIAL HARASSMENT PROJECT

FIGURE 23 The poster that won first prize in a design contest sponsored by the Youth Project on Racism.

fered racism at school. Among those who reported that they had been racially abused in the school playground, in the classroom or in the street near the school more than half reported that they had not told anyone about the attack. The questionnaire was sent out to 17 city schools after the council's first meeting last April.[4]

The local community was shocked by the results of this survey. In response, the Leicester City Council initiated a campaign and launched a poster design competition "with the view of raising awareness about racism and how to combat it, as well as designing a new poster for the Racial Harassment Project." More than 250 entries were received from fourteen secondary schools in the city and county. The winning posters advertised the services available to students who encounter racism. Samantha Black, the chair of the Young People's Council, evaluated the competition:

> The competition gave young people the chance to express how they felt on the subject of racism which was sometimes based on self experience. It has also opened up opportunities for discussions, increasing understanding. If people realize that they are racist, it may help them to think about what they are doing to others and stop it. And for those experiencing racism, information on the poster will direct them to find help and also ways to stop it.[5]

What remains unclear in the aftermath of the survey and the poster contest is how effective these initiatives were in promoting racial literacy among students.

Among the 50,000 students in Leicestershire (in 1995), there were 1,964 black students of African descent (Modood et al. 1997, 30).[6] Among these 1,071 were classified as being of "dual heritage"; presumably the majority were of black Caribbean and white heritage,[7] while another 702 students were of exclusively African Caribbean heritage. There were 191 students of exclusively black African heritage. Thus children of black Caribbean heritage with one white parent constituted the majority of black students of African descent enrolled in the Leicester state school system around the time of the poster campaign.[8]

Although at the time Leicester had an ethnically diverse population, black students constituted a numerical minority within the ethnic minority population, and a black student of Caribbean heritage was typically the only one of his or her ethnic background in any given class. Furthermore I was told by both black and white parents as well as black educational consultants that mixed-race students of black Caribbean heritage had recently been defined and pathologized as a "problem" group in several of Leicester's inner-city schools. The erasure of differences between the experiences and treatment of black and Asian Indian students was identified in a report issued in 1996 by the Office for Standards in Education and written by David Gillborn and Caroline Gipps. According to the report, observations, interviews with students of all ethnic backgrounds, and an analysis of school punishment records each suggested that, as a group, black students (of both sexes) were disproportionately criticized and disciplined by white teachers (Gillborn and Gipps 1996, table 2.6).

Racial Literacy: Antiracist Vocabularies

In *Black, White or Mixed Race? Race and Racism in the Lives of Young People of Mixed Parentage*, a study based on fifty-eight students of mixed-race heritage between the ages of fifteen and seventeen, Barbara Tizard and Ann Phoenix (1993) assigned scores to young people based on their answers to a series of questions about their experiences of racism. Although the authors did not find gender or class to be a significant variable,

> [the scores] *were* significantly related to the extent of family communication about racism, and the extent to which they believed their parents had advised and influenced their attitudes to racism. They were also significantly related to the centrality of their own colour in their lives, and the extent to which they held politicized views and saw black and white people as having different lives and different tastes. (105)

What is significant about these findings is that the student who scored the highest had a black parent who talked to her frequently about the racism she encountered. Tizard and Phoenix provide only two cases to support their argument, so we do not learn whether there were any white parents who discussed racism with their children. I extend and build upon the earlier research of Tizard and Phoenix by providing an empirical case that is parent-centered and draws upon a diverse group of parents who describe their parental practices.

The provision of conceptual tools is the first practice that I uncovered as I mapped the socialization practices of white parents who described themselves as antiracist. White parents who reported that they were training their children of African Caribbean heritage to be prepared to deal with racism reported that they discussed racism with their children regularly and shared their own experiences. In an analysis of the intergenerational transfer of race-related resistance strategies among American blacks, Janie Victoria Ward (1996) analyzed black parents' descriptions of their efforts to train their children to resist racism. Ward identifies the "homespace" as an important site for teaching black children to resist racism. She argues, "In the safety of homespace of care, nurturance, refuge, and truth, Black mothers have learned to skillfully weave lessons of critical consciousness into moments of intimacy between a parent and child" (87). In my study white parents and a number of their adult children described daily practices that prepared them to resist racism in ways not unlike those reported by American black parents.

Natasha Murray is the twenty-year-old daughter of Sonya Smyth, an unmarried mother who was introduced in chapter 1. The youngest of four children, Natasha is pursuing a degree at one of the local universities. She said that her mother routinely discussed race and racism with her when she was a child and thus provided her with a vocabulary for thinking about the political meaning of having black Anglo and Irish heritage. When she was younger Natasha self-identified as mixed-race but now identifies herself as a black woman. Explaining the change, she cited the alternative history lessons that her mother provided at home.

Natasha punctuated our first discussion with tears, crying intermittently while we sat in the kitchen discussing her childhood experiences. She described how her mother helped her cope with the racism and racial abuse that she encountered at school. She never mentioned her father, a native of Jamaica who lives in the same community, but consistently identified her mother's efforts to promote her political and cultural identification with black Caribbean people. She described practices that sociological analyses have not registered precisely because they are improvised, informal, and in response to children's particular daily experiences. These practices are not always part of a formal strategy, but over a career of child rearing they may cohere into strategies that are adopted. Natasha's mother learned from her experiences as a parent responding to her children's racialization. Sonya's experiences as a transracial mother led to a change in her racial consciousness and to her self-identification as an antiracist. Sonya also named racism as a recurrent and serious problem that required continual attention. She did not interpret incidents at school as isolated but as part of a larger pattern. This is what distinguishes Sonya from those parents who are not teaching their children how to resist racism and are not engaged in racial literacy projects.

In Natasha's analysis of how she learned to resist racism at school and maintain her self-esteem as a person of multiracial heritage, she said of her mother, "I guess she was always there for me . . . when I used to come home from school and tell her what I'd been through, and she used to talk to me about [racism]." When Natasha shifted her analysis to the con-

FIGURE 24 The Islamic Academy on Melbourne Street in Highfields.

tent of her school curriculum, she identified alternative history lessons and discursive space that her mother offered her at home that enabled her to detect which discussions of racism and colonialism were avoided, and when blacks were absent, in the school curriculum:

> When you're doing history, all [of] it is on the First and Second World Wars. They never tell you that black soldiers fought in the war, or that they were put to the front line to be killed first. They never tell you about colonialism. They tell you about the British Empire, but they never tell you . . . how they achieved it. And I was always lucky in the sense that I knew that history [from my mother]. I knew all of the things like slavery . . . and not just the negative but the positive things that black people had contributed to world history. There's nothing there for you to relate to [in the British curriculum].

Natasha believed that the informal and supplementary education that her mother provided was crucial. In her analysis of the British curriculum she argued, "Basically I think black kids are made by the educational system to feel ashamed of who they are and their heritage because there's never anything positive. It's always negative."

This supplementary education is a central feature of racial literacy training. As a form of socialization it facilitated Natasha's ability to analyze how racism operated in her life as a student and how racial ideologies circulate in the postcolonial British educational system. It is Natasha's belief that her mother provided her with conceptual tools, particularly a vocabulary and the concepts necessary to identify and analyze the absence in the curriculum of the contributions of Caribbeans to British culture. If we accept her analysis, we can argue that the conceptual training that she received from her mother constitutes a dimension of racial literacy, one that enables her to identify symbolic and systematic forms of racism in the texts and visual images that she encountered at school.[9]

It is important to note that Sonya has four children, and not all of them share Natasha's analysis or had her experiences. I met three of Sonya's children at several family gatherings. I learned that two of her children held contradictory views of Sonya's racial literacy. Several months prior to my conversation with Natasha, Sonya introduced me to Jessica, her eldest daughter, and explained my research interests to her. Jessica said, "I hope that you told her the truth." After an awkward silence Sonya replied that she had described her experiences accurately. Later, in a private conversation, Jessica told me that her mother doesn't really understand racism but had merely learned the right words and discourses to use when she was a mature student at the local university.

How do we explain these different and contradictory views of Sonya by two of her adult children? Jessica and Natasha were born eleven years apart: Jessica in 1976, and Natasha in 1987. By the time Natasha was born Sonya had been a parent for fifteen years and had accumulated a number of experiences which had changed her awareness and increased her understanding of racism. It is also possible that Sonya had only recently acquired her understanding of race and racism. In the late 1980s she returned to school as a mature student. I met her years after she had earned her bachelor's degree in sociology.

Jessica and Natasha had very different experiences growing up. In Jessica's view, her mother was not exempt from racism and had not acquired an understanding of her own racism. The differential experiences of Jessica and Natasha highlight the fact that white transracial parents can begin with little or no understanding of how racism operates and then accumulate experiences which alter their vision and enable them to develop racial literacy. On several occasions Jessica described a transformation in her racial consciousness that may have paralleled her mother's transformation. She told me that as a child she identified herself as a half-caste and now considers herself to be African Caribbean or simply African. Yet she was also aware that not everyone viewed her as African Caribbean because of her light skin, long hair, and facial features.

Home Interiors: Aesthetics and Antiracist Symbolic Culture

The second practice that I identified as an important dimension of racial literacy is the designing of black-centered home interiors. White parents who had been actively involved in antiracist and antifascist political work and race-awareness training prior to forming interracial families reported that the visual and material culture of their homes was one way they tried to create a black world at home and to respond to the social isolation and impoverished visual representations of blacks. Their homes also countered racist depictions of blacks in the public sphere. Parents training their children to identify with the black British community described material practices that included the selection and consumption of black-produced cultural objects to promote black aesthetics. They collected, purchased, and displayed visual art, toys, books, music, and decor that

FIGURE 25 A table made by Stephen Hawkes, decorated with African symbols and cultural icons and stacked with books on black history, philosophy, and literature and antiracist materials.

idealize black Africans, black Caribbeans, and North American blacks. The interiors of their homes provided their children with a symbolic and visual culture that facilitated their identification with blacks on both sides of the Atlantic.

One-fourth of the white parents interviewed argued that the selection of black-produced art, material objects, music, toys, and symbols was important for their children's self-esteem and would facilitate their positive identification with the black diasporic community. In particular, the search for visual images and literature that depict African-descent people as the social and cultural equals of the Anglo-British is a repeated theme in the narratives of racial consciousness among those parents who anticipated that their children would have to be prepared to resist racism and would need a heightened sense of self-esteem as black children.

Claire Tierney, a statuesque blonde with brown eyes, is the thirty-five-year-old parent of a teenage son whose father is African Caribbean. She and her son reside in a middle-class, white professional neighborhood located within walking distance of Leicester University. She is the vice principal of a school located in an inner-city neighborhood that now services a predominantly Muslim and immigrant student population. This same school historically served the African Caribbean community concentrated in this neighborhood. Claire belongs to a subset of university-educated white parents who have worked within communities of color and have struggled to educate themselves about racism and antiracism. She describes her efforts as a single mother to provide her son with black-centered images and books at home:

> I've always attempted to make sure that there are different images on the walls, that there are different books on the shelves. That, you know, there are these representations [of blackness]. . . . It was very, very difficult to do this at the time [1960s]—it's not so difficult now. I would sort of purposely hunt out books that had black children or Asian children or people of color in them, lots of different situations, and read those things. They were very difficult to find [when he was a child]. There were lots of books about Black Sambo, I think, but nothing positive. And it got easier. But I did feel at one point that home was the only place that [the display of antiracist images] was happening.

When asked to describe how they decorated their home interiors, white fathers who were involved in parenting described similar antiracist aesthetic projects. Brian Piper, a sixty-one-year-old trainer and consultant in Equal Opportunities and a church antiracism consultant, is the father of two black sons. He has been married for more than twenty-five years to Annette, a nurse who immigrated to England from Trinidad in the 1960s. Brian is part of a cohort of white antiracists who became active in race relations and antiracism prior to establishing families with black women. He is a member of the first generation of postwar university students and witnessed the rapid decline of the British overseas empire as it lost its colonies in Africa, the Caribbean, and South Asia and the emergence of an antiracist movement in Britain.

Brian's son was born in 1976, the year the National Front received 18 percent of the vote in the outlying suburbs of Leicester. Describing the formation of the National Front, John Solomos notes, "As a union of the right wing British National Party, and the League of Empire Loyalists, the National Front inherited the ideological baggage of anti-semitism and resistance to Britain's post-war decolonization, two prominent themes among the far right groups in the 1960s . . . and there is evidence that both its leadership and its membership were committed to a nationalist ideology based on a notion of racial purity" ([1993] 2003, 188–89). Solomos describes the political aims of the National Front as "provid[ing] a new arena for the far right activism, outside the Conservative Party and as an independent organization" (190).[10] In the mid-1970s Leicester was a site of intensive organized antiracism. When the National Front marched through Leicester, Brian took his infant son with him on antifascist political countermarches. He served as an elected member of the city council during the period when the National Front narrowly lost its bid for a seat on the council. He describes how he and his wife decorated their home to counter the rampant racism in the public sphere:

> We saw it as important for [our son] to grow up in a world where he saw successful black men. And also that the books and the images and the toys that he had reflected the cultural diversity. There were not many on the market, but they were becoming increasingly available twenty-one years ago. We had to look for it in those days. . . . We've made sure that there were images around the house which reflected black success and achievement, which were not stereotypes. It would be very easy to get figures which reflected stereotypical views of black people . . . and white views of their beauty and aesthetics and so on,

but we wanted [our son] to grow up in that kind of ethos, how black people portray themselves.

Brian believes that in the past two decades there has been increased access to antiracist and nonracist children's books depicting brown-skinned children (as well as black and multiethnic families, including African Caribbeans). Younger white fathers reported that their children have more access to multicultural books (many published in the United States) at the local library that do not recycle racist ideologies and that provide "imaginary possibilities" for black characters. In this case, racial literacy involves teaching their children to identify with black characters in fictional worlds and to critically evaluate the absence of black characters in their school books and formal school curriculum.

Supplementary Schools: Gender, Class Fractures, and Social Worlds

Debra Van Ausdale and Joe Feagin observed play groups of children between three and six years old to determine when very young children acquire and use racial distinctions and concepts:

> Early friendships are often precursors of relationships formed later in children's lives. How and with whom children form relationships at this stage can influence how and with whom they will choose to affiliate as they grow up. Early friendships inform children on what social groups are suitable for them and what groups they can expect to be included in over time. Some recent research suggests that these early relationships are the foundation for social understanding, intelligence, self-evaluations, social comparisons and social competence. (2001, 90)

In my conversations with white and black members of interracial families, parents expressed their fear that their children's social isolation from black children and possible rejection by black adults could become a potential source of injury to their children's self-esteem and well-being. This was of particular concern for middle-class families who live in predominantly or exclusively white neighborhoods. Their financial ability to live in historically all-white areas and to avoid areas that are poor and working class carries a social and emotional cost. Their children rarely, if ever, see other children of color and have virtually no opportunities to form friendships and social relationships with other blacks.

In an analysis of the U.K. census data of 1991, Tariq Modood and his

FIGURE 26 Nelista Cuffy, a founding member of the African Caribbean Education Group.

associates found, "Ethnic minorities are concentrated into the South-East region, and, in particular Greater London. Fewer than one out of ten whites lived in Greater London, but more than half of Caribbeans, African Asians and Bangladeshis lived in this area" (1997, 185) Anne Wilson (1987) identified spatial isolation from blacks and other ethnic groups, rather than isolation from whites, as a problem for the interracial families she interviewed in the late 1980s. This was also identified as a serious problem in my conversations with white parents of multiracial children. While blacks are concentrated in the major urban centers in Britain and are not evenly distributed across geographic regions, they nevertheless live in closer proximity to nonblacks and are more exposed to white people than their counterparts in the United States.[11] Susan Smith argues, "It is undoubtedly true that, at some spatial scales, indices of dissimilarity between black and white urban residents in Britain are less—by as much as 20 points—than in the USA" (1989, 38).

Unlike Van Ausdale and Feagin, the parents I interviewed were not able to observe their children at their schools or day care centers, so they had to rely on teachers' reports or their children's descriptions in evaluating the racial climate at their school. White parents who were training their children to self-identify as black and align themselves politically with the black community said that they trained their children to describe to them in detail their social interactions at school. This enabled parents to evaluate the racial and cultural climate at the school. This practice was central to cultivating a black identity in a context in which their children understood the meaning of having a black and a nonblack parent.

The "black voluntary" school movement emerged in Britain in the late 1970s. It has been described as "part of a broader political and education ideal that has directly risen from an assessment by Afro-Caribbeans of their social position in Britain and of the part that the existing white dominated education plays in its perpetuation" (Chevannes and Reeves, 1987, 147). In their analysis of how voluntary or supplementary schools differ from other educational projects, Chevannes and Reeves note:

> The schools have been set up for the benefit of children of Afro-Caribbean descent: they are indeed black schools in aim and composition. . . . The schools have been set up to provide a predominantly black environment for the needs of black children. Black children

attend because they are deliberately recruited from families where the parents believe in the need for their children to undertake extra study with children from the same racial group and to obtain support from teachers who understand what it is to be black in white society. (1987, 148)

The voluntary organization African Caribbean Education Group (ACE), founded and staffed almost entirely by African Caribbean women, operates the Saturday school in Leicester.[12] The primary goal of the school is to foster black children's self-esteem and racial and cultural pride rather than to pursue a specific curriculum. The supplementary school, known as Saturday school because it is held for two hours on Saturday morning during the official school term, has been operating since 1981. Children between the ages of five and sixteen are welcome to attend.[13] Until three years ago the school was free, but a nominal fee has since been charged to cover the cost of the workbooks. Because it receives no permanent funding, the Saturday school depends upon annual grants and volunteers.

Sending their preteen children to supplementary schools is a practice that differs from the other forms of antiracist education discussed earlier because, in addition to providing access to privileged racial and cultural knowledge, it encourages children to form social relationships with black adults and other black children. Parents informed me that they were concerned not only with the curriculum, but with the cultural experiences and black social networks that their children would access. This is of particular importance for multiracial families residing in predominantly white or middle-class residential communities, where their children do not routinely meet blacks in school or as neighbors. These families argued that it is important for their children to have regular social contact and form social relationships with less economically privileged black children who reside in working-class communities.

The desire that their children identify with the black community often masks the disagreements and struggles that some white parents have if their children strongly identify with them as positive role models. For example, a daughter's identification with her white mother may result in the daughter's embracing her European heritage rather than her African Caribbean heritage. Some white parents fear that such choices may lead their children to identify with white supremacy, British colonialism, and racism.

Justine Moonen, born in Brisbane, Australia, is the daughter of a white English mother and a white Dutch father. When her parents split up, her father took her to Ghana, where he was a teacher and where Justine attended her first school and established her first close friendships. Justine is one of the white women whom blacks described as "living in the black scene"; she has dated black men most of her life. She works as a youth and community coordinator at the African-Caribbean Centre with youths and young adults ages nine to twenty-five. She said that her job responsibilities were "to develop their educational and social skills." As a single mother of a teenage daughter whose beautiful cinnamon-colored skin conceals her white Dutch and English ancestry, she expressed her concern that her daughter does not strongly identify as black.

Justine left school at the age of fourteen without any academic qualifications. Describing her academic experiences, she said, "I was bored. I was too clever for them. The lessons were going too slowly." When I asked her to describe her expectations for her daughter, she explained why she was motivated to send her to the local African Caribbean supplementary school for black children:

> I sent her to [Saturday school] to educate her. I mean she gets her European culture here [at home] so I would send her to Saturday school, which provides classes which tell her the conditions around being black and black culture and being about Africa and the West Indies and all that. But if I ask her how she identifies, she doesn't see herself as black. . . . And I'm quite upset because I've always said to her, "Look, you're black." She goes, "Well, I'm not black, because if I say I'm black I'm disrespecting you." And I thought, "You have a good point there." But what I said to her was, "Okay, put it this way. Society sees you as black. And it's best that you know that because at the end of the day if it came to one or the other it would be black people that would accept you. The white people don't see you as 'mixed with white.' . . . At the end of the day it's the black people who will look after you. If push comes to shove, it's the black people. I'm not going to tell you any different. I'd rather you be safe than be in a position where you're not comfortable."

Justine is trying to socialize her daughter and to train her to locate herself among blacks rather than positioning herself as mixed. As a white woman who works in both predominantly white areas and racially mixed areas,

FIGURE 27 Justine Moonen and her daughter, Sasqua.

Justine has concluded that white people will not distinguish between her daughter, who is of mixed parentage, and a black person who has no European parentage. She argues that in the eyes of the white people with whom she is familiar, her biracial daughter will be perceived as "just a nonwhite person." In contrast to her mother's perception, Justine's daughter rejects this version of the one-drop rule and argues that her mother's racial and cultural relationship to her must be recognized and acknowledged. This is an example of the troubled terrain and competing conceptual maps that white mothers and fathers reported encountering as they attempted to cultivate cultural and political allegiances to the black community among their children of multiracial heritage, while not denying their biological ties to their children.

Justine belongs to a cohort of white mothers who argued that the black community will be a social and political resource for their children if and when they are in need of support. Mothers such as Justine who send their children to Saturday school identified exposure to the black community as their primary motivation. Their hope is that if their children are integrated into black social networks they will be better able to defend themselves against racism.

In *Streetwise* Elijah Anderson (1990) analyzes the acquisition of "street wisdom" and "street etiquette." He argues that "pedestrians" acquire more skills as veterans of public spaces and that "they understand how to negotiate the streets. They know whom to trust, what to say through body language or words. They have learned how to behave effectively in public" (232). Anderson's insights can also be applied to the motivations of white mothers and black fathers to send their kids back to the inner city on Saturday mornings. Several of these parents expressed their fears that their children would not be "comfortable" interacting with blacks from different class backgrounds and that they would not be able to function on the street if they did not have opportunities to interact with blacks regularly. They participated in the black voluntary sector and took their children to events organized by members of the black community so that their children would have social experiences that could provide them with the cultural knowledge and competence that would facilitate their acceptance by working-class blacks. Justine sent her daughter to Saturday school in part because she wanted her daughter to affiliate with black children and adults.

In her research on white women engaged in interracial parenting,

Ruth Frankenberg found that for some interracial couples "the desire to provide contexts in which their children could identify with their father's Chicano and Black heritages clashed with issues of class" (1993, 128). I found a similar pattern when talking to white mothers and their black partners of working-class origin, who were concerned that their children, growing up in middle-class households, would not strongly identify with blacks. For parents such as these, the struggle was to find social organizations, cultural events, and other contexts in which to maximize their children's exposure to blacks of working- and middle-class backgrounds. If they wanted their child to learn to conceptualize race in the ways that they thought "black people think," then they needed to maximize their social contact with black people in the local community. A number of them turned to the black voluntary organizations, supplementary schools, and other black-organized events to achieve this goal.

Insider-Other Dilemmas for White Parents in Black Organizations

Nelista Cuffy, a Saturday school teacher and founding member of ACE for more than ten years, introduced me to her colleague, Vanessa Robinson, a university student, a volunteer teacher at the local Saturday school, and a qualified teacher in a local primary school. Actively involved in ACE for eight years and previously the secretary of the organization, Vanessa is the thirty-four-year-old mother of two daughters of Jamaican heritage. Her daughters share their black Caribbean father with two half-sisters, who have a white birth mother. Asked about the primary purpose of Saturday school, Vanessa, like the other black women voluntary teachers I interviewed, identified "confidence building as being of central importance."

When I asked Vanessa whether white parents actively participated in the Saturday school, she described a recent political controversy that developed after she invited the white wife of a black Jamaican, who was also the mother of a child of black Jamaican heritage, to participate in the Saturday school. The woman was an experienced teacher and had taught in the Caribbean.

> I invited her to Saturday school. . . . That's the first *white* person we've had who came [into the organization] in that role—as a voluntary teacher. And there was unspoken problems about her [inclusion]. Saturday school itself has said that the children already get the white role models in the [state] schools. They say that the children must

see and identify with black adults—black teachers. Personally, I feel there is a problem [with that idea] because their mothers are white. And . . . we've had the mothers who come and stay, rather than the fathers, so then if it's the case that we have a mixed child whose mum wants to play an active part in Saturday school—what are we supposed to do? . . . At what level does this [white] parent get involved? . . . But it wasn't until after she left that the question started going around [among the black volunteers]. At the end of the day we have got mixed children anyway. What are we saying to these *white* parents? Surely, we should be encouraging all parents to be involved even if they are white.

This white parent eventually left and Vanessa never had any more contact with her, but her presence generated a controversy over the appropriate role of whites in the organization. The situation in which white mothers constitute a majority of the involved parents whose children are attending Saturday school exemplifies a paradox in this black community and demonstrates the complicated feelings generated by the participation of white parents of African-descent children in black voluntary organizations. It also illustrates the organizational context and discursive terrain that white parents of African-descent children must negotiate when they attempt to access services established for black children who have two black parents.

Returning to Patricia Hill Collins's concept of "outsiders within" (see chapter 2), we see that white mothers of children of multiracial heritage may be treated as insiders yet remain outsiders on the basis of their race. Lorraine Delia Kenny employs the term *insider-others* in her analysis of white middle-class teenage girls who occupy an ambivalent and contradictory position in their suburban communities: "At times, [insider-others] can appear fully ensconced on the inside, but upon closer examination there is something not quite normative enough about their identity or how they carry themselves in a normative world" (2000, 3). Although Kenny is writing about white girls in suburban New York, her analysis can be applied to the situation of the white transracial mothers I met. Their children were perceived as a normative segment of the black community and as "potential" blacks or possibly future blacks; they had the option of self-identifying as black or with the black community.

White mothers parenting children fathered by black men generated anxieties and occupied an ambivalent position in Saturday school. I was told by two of the ACE teachers that a majority of the children who regularly attend Saturday school were children from transracial families in which the mother was white. Their mothers were utilizing the Saturday school as a resource, yet in private conversations there was a lot of anxiety and ambivalence about both the mothers and their children. In focus groups and private conversations black women, both mothers and nonmothers, repeatedly told me that they feared that children of mixed heritage would be privileged over children with two black parents. They feared that having a white mother would translate into an advantage even in *black*-run organizations. At the same time, some of the same women criticized white mothers for not cultivating a black identity in their children or exposing them to their black heritage.

If the only goal of the Saturday school were to provide adult black role models, then excluding white parents from volunteering might be defensible. However, in the context of a labor shortage of qualified teachers, black out-migration to London, and a growing population of parents of multiracial children seeking access to black cultural spaces, this is a problematic strategy. If one goal is to keep the Saturday school operating and to expand its student enrollment, then all parents who volunteer, particularly qualified teachers, should be considered in the volunteer pool. White parents represent a relatively invisible yet potentially powerful reservoir of support to the local black community.

In a community in which a growing number of white mothers are responsible for nurturing and culturally training children who may be socially classified as black or mixed-race, black leaders cannot afford to exclude the parents of children they hope will identify with the political struggles of black people. If a politically viable antiracist coalition is to be built in the local community, an antiracist alliance that can accommodate white parents is needed. The inclusion of white parents in antiracist initiatives in the public sphere could benefit the black community, since having a white mother has become a normative experience for the majority of children of black Caribbean heritage in Leicester. Some of these children will be classified or will learn to self-identify as black or mixed-race. The parents of African-descent children need support and access to antiracist initiatives in order to counter the racism that their children encounter in the public sphere. White parents who are actively pursuing social relationships with blacks in support of their children need to have opportunities to forge alliances with black parents, black teachers, and black organizers. This may require that the black community give white parents the same access to black organizations that have been established for their children (both monoracial and multiracial).

The One-Drop Rule Revisited: The Limits of Racial Privilege

When enumerating the number of blacks in the nation, the U.S. Census Bureau has not used a scientific definition but a cultural one; this is known as "the one-drop rule." The one-drop rule refers to the practice of classifying a person as black on the basis of "one drop of black blood." Some courts have called it the "traceable amount rule." No other ethnic population in the United States is defined or counted according to a one-drop rule. Floyd James Davis writes, "Not only does the one-drop rule apply to no other group than American blacks, but apparently the rule is unique in that it is found only in the United States and not in any other nation in the world" (1991, 13).

In *Black, White or Mixed Race?*, a study of fifty-eight adolescents of mixed race, the developmental psychologists Tizard and Phoenix briefly sketch differences in the legal constructions of blackness in the United States and Britain:

> In Britain there [were] no legal definitions of a black person, or legal restrictions on mixed marriages. This may have been in part because until the mid-1950s the number of black people in Britain was very small—never more than 15,000, often less. The few "half-castes" were generally recognized by both black and white people as different from black. But they were stigmatized in Britain as elsewhere, perhaps more so, since they were usually born into the poorest sector of society, whilst in other countries they tended to be part of an intermediate class. (1993, 3)

Thus, while the census, state, and federal courts in the United States have generally upheld the one-drop rule, blackness has not been legally defined in Britain. Consequently, the social and legal classification of children of mixed ancestry in Britain has been characterized by more fluidity and more ambivalence (see Davis 1991). The absence of the one-drop rule does not diminish the complex forms of racism that British children of multiracial heritage face; however it may generate forms of ambivalence and dilemmas that are "peculiarly English." This absence of a state-sanctioned legal definition of blackness is an important consideration when analyzing the racial and cultural logics that motivate nonblack parents in Britain to counter racial hierarchies by training their children of mixed heritage to privilege the black community as its community of reference.

The transracial parents I interviewed were neither motivated by nor invested in a version of the one-drop rule. Their efforts to promote their children's cultural and political identification with blacks were a direct response to racism and to their awareness that their children would not be positioned as white. These parents did not perceive their children as only black or embrace a belief in a biological notion of blackness; rather they believed that their children would encounter racism and that they needed the resources to defend themselves against it.

During my eight years of field research, half of the parents I interviewed changed the terms that they used to describe their children's racial and ethnic ancestry. Other relatives and some adult children interviewed confirmed that both they and their parents had changed the language used to refer to race as their conceptualizations about race shifted. Some parents and grandparents continued to refer to their children as *half-castes*, while others switched to *mixed-race* and then later *black British* or *African Caribbean*. In most families I observed generational and educational differences in the terms used; for example, university-educated parents used the terms taught to them or suggested by ethnic monitoring forms. The language used to describe members of multiracial families was an area of contestation and struggle. Nevertheless only a minority of the white and black parents perceived children of multiracial heritage to be *black*, even when they expressed concern that they could be excluded or discriminated against on the basis of their African or African Caribbean ancestry.

Chelsea Carrington, who was introduced in chapter 3, is raising her daughter alone in a poor, inner-city district associated with drug trafficking, prostitution, and other forms of crime. This area has a high concentration of single-parent families that include white mothers raising children of multiracial heritage, although the population is largely African, Caribbean, Bangladeshi, Indian, Somali, Polish, and other East African

FIGURE 28 Naomi, the daughter of Glenda Terry, a white antiracist activist.

Asian. Chelsea has been the sole nonblack member of a number of committees and community organizations that service the black and South Asian communities. Her motivation for not moving out of this neighborhood is that her brown-skinned daughter is not an anomaly here; this minimizes the stigma she experiences elsewhere as the daughter of an unmarried white woman.

During my first conversation with her, when her daughter was eleven, Chelsea expressed concern that her daughter would internalize the racist ideologies and representations of whiteness idealized in the popular press, films, and the media:

> You know, subconsciously [children] very quickly take in the view that in [British] society . . . to be white is to be desirable. And occasionally [my daughter] has said to me that she wants to be white. . . . I think my main fear at the moment is that she will grow up sort of feeling that she's white. And I wouldn't want that. I would want her to embrace her African heritage, to put it rather grandiosely. I suppose I feel that I'm not perhaps up to the task of enabling her to do that.

In order to counter the influence of popular culture, Chelsea has cultivated a support network that consists of black Caribbean women as well as black male friends who have white partners. She told me that her closest friend is a black woman of Caribbean origin, whom Chelsea has designated to be her daughter's guardian in the event of her death. Chelsea organizes her daughter's social activities to maximize her contact with black children, paying ten dollars per week to send her to an after-school club run by one of her black male colleagues.

Chelsea also belongs to the Letterbox Library, a mail-order book club based in London that provides resources for children of color. She describes some of the difficulties of trying to provide pro-black messages for her prepubescent daughter in a national context in which there continues to be aesthetic hierarchies that privilege blonde blue-eyed girls in popular culture. She relies on a range of material and social resources:

> I order books from [Letter Box Library] which show black children and stories about black children. . . . I mean, that's just an example of trying to look at books, and things like that give a positive image and actually show black people. . . . Now she's getting older. I'd like to do more sort of structured things . . . perhaps look at things like the

history of the Caribbean. . . . She goes to an afterschool club, which a [black] colleague of mine at work has sort of been instrumental in setting up, where they've done quite a bit with the children on things like African history and so on.

Parents such as Chelsea are motivated to socialize their children to be proud of their African Caribbean heritage because they recognize that they are not able to transfer their white status and the privileges that accompany it to their children. The risk of racial discrimination motivates these white parents to cultivate in their children a strong sense of pride in their African Caribbean ancestry. Racial and ethnic affiliation is not taken for granted but actively negotiated. These parents are not motivated by a belief in the one-drop rule, but a recognition that racism and racial hierarchies continue to structure British life and that they need to prepare their daughters and sons for this reality.

Conclusion

One dilemma that white transracial parents encounter is how to provide their children with the resources they need to cope with the varied forms of racism that they may encounter in public institutions such as schools. The educational work that occurs at home can best be characterized as one way that transracial parents translate racial hierarchies and negotiate the racism that their children encounter.

Some parents decide to privilege their children's African Caribbean heritage as a sociopolitical resource and thus promote their children's alliances with other black adults and children as a method of strengthening their children's emotional and cultural defenses when they encounter racist practices or ideologies. The boundaries between "black" and "mixed-race" are permeable. The transfer of racial positions (particularly white racial privilege) is unpredictable, incomplete, and contingent not only on a child's ability to physically "qualify" for whiteness, but on the decisions that white parents make about how to socialize their children as members of multiracial families. My empirical data point to the complex negotiations that occur within multiracial families as they manage racial hierarchies and racial fractions in their genealogies. The experiences of transracial parents who self-identify as antiracist prompt us to consider the conditions under which some parents who are classified as belonging to racially privileged groups may socialize their children to position themselves alongside members of the less-privileged racial and ethnic groups as an antiracist strategy.

The growth of multiracial families requires a reconceptualization of the ways that racial identities are translated, transferred, and transformed. Rather than transmitting their racial identity and status to their children, white transracial parents may actively attempt to transfer dimensions of their black partner's identity and status to their children as one way to manage racial hierarchies and to protect their children from the damaging effects of racism.

Returning to the case of Sue Hunter and her sister, Angie DeMeyer, who won a historic suit against a British soldier for racial abuse, we see that their genealogy, in particular their mother's whiteness, is unremarkable to *The Guardian*. In a national and demographic context in which nearly 40 percent of children of black heritage have a white parent, the readers of *The Guardian* are not informed that a working-class Irish woman stands in the shadow of this historic legal victory for the black British community. This raises provocative questions about racial boundaries and antiracism in a context in which so many children of black Caribbean heritage are being raised by a white parent. The labor and experiences of Hunter's mother disappears behind the headlines of this story, yet we can gain much by paying careful attention to the process by which women like Hunter have been trained (or not) by their white parents to identify politically with the black community. Her experiences illuminate the ways that racial hierarchies are translated and countered under particular familial, cultural, and demographic conditions.

Although white parents of African-descent children constitute neither an ideologically nor culturally homogeneous group, an analysis of how they informally train their children to negotiate or challenge racial boundaries provides critical race theorists and sociologists of race with insights into how white people conceptualize blackness, whiteness, and antiracism as the intimates of blacks. Their labor as the parents of children who may join the ranks of the black community is not often visible or recognized as "racial" labor or as constituting an antiracist project.

In chapter 5 I turn to a different form of racialized and gendered labor, that of socially reproducing "ethnic belonging" on the body via grooming practices and the consumption of specific foods. I examine the work that mothers, daughters, and daughters-in-law perform as they inscribe ethnic differences onto themselves and thus culturally reproduce racial-ized boundaries, mapping these distinctions onto and through their bodies. Hairstyles and heritage cooking are two arenas that are crucial when examining the social meanings of race, blackness, and whiteness, as well as the ways that racial logics are naturalized through intensive labor.

5

WRITTEN ON THE BODY

Ethnic Capital and Black Cultural Production

> Visible minorities are not recognizable merely through racialisation as an epidermal schema constituted through skin colour, texture of hair or other physiognomic markers, but also embodied a second time over through hair styles, clothing, comportment, movement of the body, hijabs, beards and salwaar-kameez.—DENISE NOBLE, "REMEMBERING BODIES, HEALING HISTORIES: THE EMOTIONAL POLITICS OF EVERYDAY FREEDOM," IN CLAIRE ALEXANDER AND CAROLINE KNOWLES, *MAKING RACE MATTER: BODIES, SPACE AND IDENTITY*

The body is a place, a construction site, upon which individuals cultivate, display, and perform ethnic, gender, and class identities. Bodies are also utilized by young girls and women as forms of embodied cultural capital to assert aesthetic agency, affirm social relationships, establish feminine identities, and secure respectability (Brumberg 1997; I. Banks 1998; Ali 2003). Anoop Nayak (2003) has described the body as a "corporeal canvas" upon which identities can be written, negotiated, and contested. Feminist and critical race scholars have argued that in addition to discourses and state practices, race and femininity are performed via the body (Bordo 1993; Alexander and Knowles 2005; Adkins and Skeggs 2004).

British sociologists studying the cultural politics of representation in black British communities have provided instructive analyses of the ways that aesthetic and cultural practices can emphasize cultural or biological sameness. Denise Noble (2005) points out that a second phase in black cultural politics in Britain differs from an earlier one, which responded to the "invisibility that comes with Britishness." This second moment is "exemplified by struggles over representation, which emerge when internal differences around gender, sexuality, and class begin to weaken or unsettle 'Black' as a composite racial category. . . . These 'new' liberation struggles take place largely outside of the old forms and arenas of politics, increasingly emerging at the level of the individual and acted out in the contours of the everyday, the personal, and on the body, producing a poetics and aesthetics of the self" (135). Informed by the work of black British feminist scholars such as Noble, this chapter focuses on the pivotal role of the body in the cultivation of black ethnic identities. I show how white transracial mothers assist their daughters in responding to racism, in part, by using their bodies to display and stylistically represent the African or African Caribbean side of their heritage. This occurs in a local context in which blackness is also commercialized and homogenized by white and black parents in their efforts to construct an "aesthetics of self."

The consumption and caretaking regimes of transracial mothers are critically linked to the social reproduction of versions of black ethnicity, black femininity, and black ethnic capital. White mothers and white fathers (as well as black family members) can transfer black ethnic capital to the children of multiracial heritage through relatively mundane caretaking practices.

Body care services and food preparation, or heritage cooking, are *gendered* cultural practices in which white mothers and their daughters negotiate black ethnicity. Both white transracial mothers and their black sisters-in-law identify these sites as central to the cultivation and maintenance of a black ethnic identity. These cultural practices are forms of ethnic capital used by white and black members of transracial families in my study. An analysis of this form of reproductive labor and the grooming and cooking practices of *white* members of transracial families offers theoretical insights into the way blackness, in its local, transnational, idealized, and commercial forms, is negotiated within British interracial families.

Bourdieu and Ethnic Capital

Extending the theoretical arsenal of Pierre Bourdieu, what I call *ethnic capital* refers to a variant of cultural capital that is valued by members of ethnic minority communities but is deemed by members of the racially or ethnically dominant group to be irrelevant, evidence of a refusal to as-

FIGURE 29 Close-up of Eshe Mitchell's braids. Photograph taken in 2004 at the Lerris Hair Salon.

similate, or even a liability or barrier to achievement. This form of capital can include cultural knowledge of a group's history, fluency in one's native language (e.g., the ability to speak patois), music, and cooking skills.

Although Bourdieu was not specifically interested in race, racism, or the ways that racial hierarchies structure fields, his discussion of the four forms of capital—economic, social (relations with significant others), cultural (legitimate knowledge), and symbolic (prestige and social honor)—is instructive in understanding how white members of transracial families negotiate the meanings of blackness and black ethnicity. My analysis of the role of white mothers in the transfer of ethnic capital and the reproduction of ethnic distinctions is not intended to cover all of the sites at which ethnic distinctions are routinely produced in these families. Rather, it is limited to those practices that I directly observed during my participant observation and that were identified by white transracial mothers and their black sisters-in-law as central to black ethnic identity in their lives.

Global Hair Care Market: Black Consumer Circuits

The value of the global ethnic personal care market is estimated at $5.1 billion, of which $1.6 billion is in retail and the rest is in professional products and body care services. In the 1990s the competition for black hair care dollars became more intensive. Revlon and other historically white firms began to expand to new markets by turning their attention to blacks and other ethnics for the first time, and black family-owned businesses, which had developed innovative products and established the foundations for the global ethnic hair care and beauty market, began to see their sales decline.[1]

The global ethnic hair care market was born in Chicago (Silverman, 1998; M. Wilson 2004). After the Second World War Chicago, then the second largest city in the United States, became home to the world's first and largest black beauty and hair care companies, which include Johnson Products and Soft Sheen. These companies were founded by black families on Chicago's South Side who identified a need among working-class blacks for commercial products that could clean, condition, straighten, and style their hair. Black family-owned firms established a parallel industry in a context in which blacks constituted a segregated and neglected market. American blacks, along with those white ethnics who did not have straight, silky, or oily hair, demanded specially designed hair care products.[2]

Soft Sheen was the worlds' second largest producer of hair care products targeting black communities, exporting its products to Canada, the United Kingdom, West Africa, and the Caribbean; by the time it was purchased by the French firm L'Oreal its gross sales were close to $80 million. In 2000 L'Oreal opened the L'Oreal Center for Research and Development, the world's only state-of-the-art research center devoted to ethnic hair care, on Chicago's South Side and hired Laila Ali, the daughter of Muhammad Ali, to launch a new promotional campaign.

L'Oreal's corporate officers appear to view ethnic minorities in Europe, including black Africans and South Asians, as an important segment of their international market. The company devotes one-third of its $360 million annual budget to research on black hair and skin care. Market research has consistently shown that blacks and other ethnic groups spend significantly more dollars, and a higher percentage of their income, on hair care.

Hair Care as Ethnic Capital: A Black Aunt Speaks

Black women invest great energy to socialize their white sisters-in-law and friends to purchase services and products that will position children of multiracial heritage as members of respectable and upwardly mobile black families and communities. The cleaning, conditioning, cutting, styling, and daily management of hair was described by black members of interracial families as a definitive arena in which respectability, femininity, and authority were asserted. White women parenting children of African or African Caribbean heritage were evaluated and ranked based on their cultural knowledge of hair grooming. In those transracial families in which white mothers had regular contact with black extended family members, I observed such family members continually evaluating and monitoring them to ensure that they replicated a particular grooming regimen that was deemed best for the self-esteem and appearance of the children involved. Black sisters-in-law outlined clear expectations about how their nieces' hair was to be shampooed, styled, conditioned, and managed. Describing their relationships with their white sisters-in-law and their nieces of multiracial heritage, black women invariably pointed to their hair as evidence of cultural competence or maternal failure.

FIGURE 30 Maureen Dover, the highest ranking black woman employed by Leicester City Council and the aunt of six nieces and nephews of multiracial heritage.

Maureen Dover, a forty-five-year-old black woman who was born in the Caribbean, migrated to England at the age of twelve with her family. She is the social services manager for Home Care in Leicester. Her three brothers have all established families with white English women; she described six of her ten nieces and nephews as being of "dual heritage," though she believes that they would be classified as black by those outside of the family. When asked to describe her relationships with her white sisters-in-law, she ranked the women based on how they groomed their daughters' hair, the books and toys they bought their children, and the degree to which they prepared their children to function as members of a black ethnic community.

At a Sunday gathering at the home of her mother, who lives next door, Maureen introduced me to Marie Cunningham, one of her white sisters-in-law, and two of her black sisters. Marie's daughter was having self-esteem issues because her hair was not long and straight like her mother's. Maureen explained to me why she admires and respects Marie: "I feel she very much wants the child to have a black identity. So every Sunday she would bring [my niece] up to my mum's house so that she knows her black family. And she's asked for advice about her hair. And you'd see her plaiting it. And her hair is always so pretty."

Maureen and her other black Caribbean family members considered this niece to be ethnically black. In their view she will be so classified despite her white mother because her physical appearance does not qualify her for inclusion in the white socioracial category. For this reason it was imperative that she be culturally trained to embrace a black ethnic identity. This involved femininity training, whereby she was taught by her black aunts and other black relatives to clean and style her hair in ways that enhanced her self-esteem and affiliated her with black cultural tastes.

Braids as an Ethnic Body Project

On 19 December 1991 Helena Mitchell, a white native of Leicester, gave birth to her first child, a daughter fathered by a Nigerian. Helena named her Eshe, the Swahili word for *life*. Helena has raised Eshe with the active involvement and support of her mother, Anita O'Riley, her maternal grandmother, and her two maternal uncles. Eshe has African kin in England, France, and Austria as well as Nigeria.

Although Eshe's father is Nigerian, her experiences do not differ from

FIGURE 31 Anita O'Riley (left), her granddaughter Eshe Mitchell (center), and her daughter Helena Mitchell.

the pattern I found among the teenage girls whose mothers and fathers are of Caribbean origin. All of Eshe's closest girlfriends are the daughters of women who are first-generation African Caribbean or black British. She lives in a residential community in which her multiracial heritage does not distinguish her from many of her neighbors. Eshe's mother and her maternal grandmother have made a commitment to teach her about her Nigerian father's heritage. Her mother regularly took her on holidays as a very young child with other children who share her background and enrolled her in Caribbean dance groups and other afterschool programs that support her ethnic identification with her black family. Eshe's experiences illustrate a pattern of integration into black friendship networks and black groups that I found among teenage girls being raised by single white mothers.

British sociologists have identified the stylistic repertoires of young children of multiracial heritage as central to the way they manage their racial and ethnic identities (Ali 2003). In an ethnographic study of young children in London of mixed-race heritage between the ages of eight and eleven, Suki Ali found, "For girls the reading of attractiveness and whether it was 'raced' or not was often articulated through hairstyles" (78–79).

Specific demands are placed upon the bodies of the light-skinned daughters of white English mothers who are actively cultivating their African English identities. Eshe's West African heritage was inscribed on her body via her braids. Her hairstyle declared to the black and nonblack community that she was living an "authentic" black life, despite having a white English mother. For a young woman whose facial features may have positioned her slightly outside of narrow definitions of blackness, her hairstyle was a crucial ethnic marker. Braids enabled her to establish her racial authenticity through a stylistic convention that is strongly associated with blackness. She secured her sense of belonging by conforming to popular and commercialized versions of blackness.

The labor of black women was essential to Eshe's ethnic identity and to the cultivation of her place in a black female network. Having her hair professionally braided by a black woman repositioned Eshe as the symbolic daughter of a black woman while strengthening her cultural bonds with black peers. In other words, this style de-emphasizes her biological and cultural links to her white English birthmother. Braids encoded onto

FIGURE 32 Eshe Mitchell's hair is being braided by Lerris at the Lerris Hair Salon, a local salon owned and run by a black woman, located in Highfields, the heart of the African Caribbean community.

her body her public identification with black people of transnational origin. Furthermore, by adopting an "African look" she legitimated herself as a black woman with a white mother.

Braids and dreadlocks have been authorized and identified as an idealized version of blackness by a segment of vocal and powerful members of the local black community. Weekly and bimonthly trips to black-owned hair salons enabled Helena to establish and sustain her reputation as an ethnic equivalent of a black mother who knows how to properly care for her daughter's hair. Whether Eshe chose to wear her hair braided in elaborate patterns or to have her hair chemically straightened (as she did recently), the work was done at a black salon by black women, who styled her hair for daily wear as well as for holidays and special occasions.

Kobena Mercer, a black British cultural theorist, conceptualized black hairstyling as a "popular *art form* articulating a variety of aesthetic 'solutions' to a range of 'problems' crated by ideologies of race and racism":

> As organic matter produced by physiological processes, human hair seems to be a natural aspect of the body. Yet hair is never a straightforward, biological fact, because it is almost always groomed, prepared, cut, concealed and generally worked upon by human hands. Such practices socialize hair, making it the medium of significant statements about self, society and the codes of value that bind them, or do not. In this way hair is merely raw material, constantly processed by cultural practices which thus invest it with meanings and value. (1994, 100–101)

In an analysis of black American women's conceptualization of hair and hairstyling practices, Ingrid Banks argues that "black hair, in general, has not escaped political readings about how blacks construct identities, as well as how whites construct identities about blacks by reading the biological (hair) through a sociopolitical lens. . . . Beaded braids . . . display a black aesthetic that is linked to an authentic or radical blackness in the imagination of many whites" (1998, 13–14). In focus groups with black American women of diverse ages, Banks found that women distinguished between "good" and "bad" hair and argued that hairstyles signaled specific lifestyle choices and social networks. According to one black woman interviewed by Banks, a crucial social aspect of hairstyles was their significance in attracting and sustaining friendships with particular types of people: "Depending on who you want to socialize with dictates pretty much what kind of hair, what kind of style you have to wear" (39).

Like the women interviewed by Banks, the participants in my study stressed that hairstyles and grooming practices were crucial in securing membership in specific friendship networks. Women of black African and white English heritage often employed their hairstyles to affirm their relationships with their darker-skinned family members and peers of African or Caribbean ancestry.

In her analysis of the culture of intimacy and femininity in beauty salons in Cairo, Casablanca, and Paris, Susan Ossman describes the job of the hairstylist as "allow[ing] women to move gracefully through the webs not of meaning but of engagements with others who are known and whose judgments count" (2002, 106). In the case of Helena and Eshe, the judgments that mattered were those of Eshe's black girlfriends, their black mothers, and black members of the local community who could evaluate Eshe's hair as a marker of both her ethnic identity and of her mother's cultural competence.

By signaling an investment in and public commitment to black cultural styles, Helena aligned herself with the black mothers of her daughter's friends. Through the act of taking her daughter to black hair salons, she provided Eshe with access to a black public space in which she could learn how to perform acts of black femininity and engage in rituals that structure the lives of black women. The adult black women validated Eshe's membership in the black community by mapping a style onto her body that displayed and communicated to others her African heritage. For Helena and her daughter, salons owned and operated by local black women provided a space for Eshe to form and *perform* a racialized black feminine identity in which the ethnic differences between West Africans, West Indians, and British-born black people were erased. This bimonthly hair grooming ritual reinforced both Eshe's status in this black community and the boundaries between Eshe and white English girls. For teenage girls from multiracial families in which the white parent is the most visible and the most involved in daily care, hairstyles are a crucial "body project" that can serve as a powerful statement of allegiance to their blackness. White mothers, often with the support of their black female friends or black sisters-in-law, thus employ hairstyling practices as a "flexible social resource" to mobilize a black ethnic identity among their children (see T. Reynolds 2006).

Heritage Cooking: Culinary Skills as Ethnic Capital

Between 1963 and 1968 Bourdieu and his research associates surveyed 1,217 individuals living in Paris, Lille, and another French town about their cultural activities. There were twenty-five questions on cultural tastes in cooking, clothing, interior decoration, reading, cinema, painting, music, photography, radio, and other leisure activities. This survey of lifestyles was designed "to determine how a cultivated disposition and cultural competence are demonstrated in the types and quality of cultural goods consumed" (Bourdieu 1984, 13).

As part of his comparative analysis of working-class and bourgeois lifestyles Bourdieu systematically examined differences in the patterns and structure of consumption of various food items. He identified "three structures of the consumption as distributed under three items: food, culture, and presentation (clothing, beauty care, toiletries, domestic servants)" (Bourdieu 1984, 185). Following Bourdieu's model, I selected five families who allowed me to shadow them as they did their weekly grocery and household shopping. By observing and comparing different family members' choices, I uncovered distinctive patterns of consumption associated with particular racialized lifestyles. The subset of white transracial mothers who expressed a strong identification with blacks, particularly African Caribbean culture, and who described themselves as living a black lifestyle invested more time and spent more of their weekly income purchasing ethnic foods. They cooked labor-intensive dishes that required overnight seasoning and adherence to a specific set of rules regarding hygiene, spicing, and cooking. These meals involved the transfer of ethnic and cultural capital: tastes which were valued by upwardly mobile black Caribbean families attempting to maintain cultural ties to their communities of origin. The consumption and preparation of ethnic food was a cultural practice that also enabled white transracial mothers to achieve respectability and acceptance among their black family members and to position themselves as the cultural equivalents or "clones" of black women in their extended families.

The Caribbean Supermarket is located on the corner of St. Stephens Road and Guilford Road in the heart of Highfields. It was established in the late 1960s by an East African Asian, who sold it in 1999 to a Bangladeshi. It remains central to the black Caribbean and African diasporic communities because it provides easy access to fresh, canned, and pack-

FIGURE 33 A view of the Caribbean Supermarket from the halal meat market across the street.

FIGURE 34 The Caribbean Supermarket in Highfields was founded in 1969 by a Ugandan Asian. Half of the families that participated in this study shop regularly at this market.

aged ingredients required to prepare West Indian, West African, and East African cuisine. The white women and black men who cook black food reported that they shop regularly at this market.

In this store one can buy hair care products, spices, beans, rice, and corn meal, shipped from a London-based Asian distributor. A series of advertisements posted on the front of the store reflect the clientele's desire for one-stop shopping. Eight of the nine glossy posters are advertisements for American-made black hair care products, "relaxers" that chemically straighten hair. To the left of the entrance are three large Soft Sheen posters of black American women whose silky, straight hair shows the benefits of using Dark and Lovely, a brand of chemical straighteners. An orange handwritten sign in black letters contrasts with the glossy American ads and reads, "English Pony Hair from Zimbabwe/Kenya Is Available Now."

Kassim Haque, the son of the current owner, has a degree in chemistry from University College London and comes up from London on the weekends to help run the store. He described his clientele as 50 percent "real Africans" (i.e., those born in Africa, as opposed to British-born people of Caribbean heritage who self-identify as African Caribbeans) and 30 percent members of multiracial families that include a white partner.

During a tour of the store Kassim describes the national origins of all of the various dry goods and other products. Pointing to a bag of maize meal, he says, "This is for the Zimbabweans and Kenyans. This is why the Kenyans can run so fast." He explains that this is "energy food." There are rows of forty-five-kilo bags containing a colorful range of beans in the corner next to the refrigerated case of water and soda. He shows me Gungo peas (West Indian), white beans, kidney beans, crab-eye beans, and Great Northern beans (United States). There is long-grain rice and "easy cook" white rice. There is also an array of canned and partially cooked beans. He emphasizes the diverse national origins of his African customers. The shelves are packed with canned goods, dry goods, and prepackaged meals from the black transatlantic world. There is hot pepper sauce from Barbados, corn meal from the United States, maize, flour, black-eyed peas, kidney beans, white rice, and Jamaican ginger beer soda. This is a global market where transnational identities and tastes are satisfied. Rows of human hair in all colors, textures, and lengths hang on the wall behind the checkout counter and can be bought with other hair care products. He explains that "pony hair" is hair that is sold to wear as a pony tail. The quality of the hair sold is quite spectacular.[3]

The Caribbean Supermarket, which is within walking distance of about one-fourth of the families in my study, is a sociocultural resource that provides white transracial mothers with the ingredients required to prepare meals similar to those prepared by their black Caribbean relatives. By adopting the culinary tastes and learning the spice regimes of the mothers and sisters of their black partners, white women hope to secure approval from black family members and to feel that they culturally belong in their transracial families. White women who have convinced themselves that they are "running a black household" evaluate themselves on the basis of how closely their cooking approximates that of their Caribbean-born family members.

In a study of the cultural identities of young children in London who are from mixed-race families, Suki Ali describes the material culture at home, which includes cooking, cleaning, and shopping:

> The majority of the mothers were responsible for the everyday cooking, whereas fathers were linked to cooking for a chance to "help out," and perhaps washing up after a meal. In the cases where the fathers are from minority ethnic groups and the mothers are white British, the fathers were responsible for cooking food that has strong cultural and national connections. In a few cases the mothers learned to cook these dishes, and the fathers reverted to occasional helping out. . . . There was a special role for the fathers of minority ethnic status in families of inter-ethnic backgrounds, as "authentic" cooks of "authentic" cultural foods. This circumvented the more usual gendered divisions of food production. The role of the father in these cases was also to provide the special and "traditional" link to the "other" culture and it was this specialness that facilitated cooking. (2003, 107)

Ali's observations are similar to what I observed in the families that participated in my research. The vast majority of the fathers did not regularly prepare any meals, either ethnic or English; instead, white English and Irish mothers were expected to do all of the daily cooking. During periods of advanced pregnancy and following the birth of a child, their mothers-in-law, sisters-in-law, or girlfriends might cook for them. In a few cases the white wife was taught how to prepare specific dishes by her black in-laws. The four second-generation black Caribbean husbands whose mothers lived nearby returned to their mother's home every week to eat a "traditional West Indian" dinner.

The cooking skills of white partners were regularly denigrated by some black extended family members. In interviews and casual conversations with black husbands and their black mothers, the mothers considered it their duty to cook an "extra pot" for their sons if they were married to "English wives who were not [able] to cook like a black woman," as one black mother with three white daughters-in-law explained. One wife, after fifteen years of marriage, enrolled in a West Indian cooking class at the local community college. Although she learned to cook a few dishes very well and even prepared one for me, one of her black sisters-in-law dismissed her newly acquired skills as disrespectful to the black women in the family, saying, "She should have asked my mother to teach her."

Ethnic Equivalents or English Wives

Justine Moonen, a vivacious blonde in her late thirties and the mother of a teenage daughter, whom we met in chapter 4, was described to me by several black Caribbean women as "a white woman who lives black." Justine is employed as a youth and community coordinator for the African Caribbean Centre and lives with her daughter on a housing estate in a neighborhood that has more children of dual heritage than black children. Justine met the father of her daughter when she was fourteen, and although they never married, they remain close friends. She strongly identifies with the political and cultural battles of the African Caribbean community and views black women as her reference group. This motivates her to provide her daughter with black cultural experiences such as food, dance lessons, music, and social events. She is invested not only in cultivating particular tastes but in integrating her daughter into black social and friendship networks.

In 2000, when I visited Justine, her infant son, and his Jamaican British father, I was surrounded by the smells of acke sautéed in onions and spices. A large pot of peas and rice was cooking on the stove. Their home had the same aromas, sounds, and colors as those of many first-generation Jamaican British families. Proud of her culinary skills and her ability to "cook like a black woman," Justine did her weekly grocery shopping at the Caribbean Supermarket. Food was a cultural tool she used to establish her strong identification with blackness and her membership in the

FIGURE 35 A Caribbean vegetable stall located at the Leicester Outdoor Market is operated by an interracial couple. This stall is in the heart of the city center and provides customers with root vegetables, meats, and dry goods that are essential ingredients in West African and West Indian cooking.

Anglo-African diaspora in England. By preparing West Indian and Caribbean food regularly and teaching her daughter to like this food, she was transferring a form of ethnic capital.

Sharon Dawkins, the mother of four daughters, has been married for more than twenty years to a black British man of Jamaican parentage. Describing her life as a member of a black extended family, Sharon expressed pride in her cultural achievements, which include fluency in patois, cooking West Indian foods, and running a household that meets the approval of her Jamaican British husband and his family. Commenting on her struggles during the early years of her marriage, she identified cooking as a significant site: "I've had to prove myself worthy of being in their family because I do cook black food, and I do cook it very well. And like, [now], my [black in-laws] will even eat at my house, whereas before they wouldn't . . . because as far as they're concerned 'What do white people know about black people's food?' My [mother-in-law] never thought I'd be able to cook for [my husband] like a black woman could." Over the years Sharon worked hard to earn the respect of her black mother-in-law and the honor of preparing food for important family events such as funerals, memorials, weddings, and other annual get-togethers. She has distinguished herself from the other white women who have married into this family and has become the only white daughter-in-law to be treated as the cultural equivalent of a black woman in the family.

In her analysis of the ideals of love among American white, middle-class couples, Ann Swidler called for new metaphors to understand how culture works:

> Perhaps we do best to think of culture as a repertoire, like that of an actor, a musician, or a dancer. This image suggests that culture cultivates skills and habits in its users, so that one can be more or less good at the cultural repertoire one performs, and that such cultured capacities may exist both as discrete skills, habits and orientations, and, in larger assemblages, like the pieces a musician has mastered or the plays an actor has performed. It is in this sense that people have an array of cultural resources upon which they can draw. (2001, 24–25)

The concept of cultural repertoires is also useful when considering the new skills and habits that white English women acquired as members of black extended families. Among the cultural skills common to Jamaican

FIGURE 36 Lisa Hackett's mother-in-law teaches her how to prepare seasoned Caribbean chicken for a Sunday meal.

families that Sharon learned were seasoning meats, washing and preparing foods, properly washing dishes, and training her children to display formal respect and obey their elders without questioning them.

Over the past ten years Sharon has repeatedly said to me that she runs a "black household" and that one of her primary achievements as a wife and mother was to become the cultural equivalent of a black Jamaican woman. This required her to adopt specific gender regimes and consumption patterns that convinced her black Jamaican in-laws that she was the functional equivalent of a black woman and thus a competent mother to her four daughters. By learning how to properly prepare jerked chicken, peas and rice, and other Caribbean dishes that are highly valued by her black family members, Sharon has achieved respectability. Since eating specific foods regularly, and particularly on holidays, demarcates the boundary between a white English and a black household, Sharon also learned to negotiate her whiteness by performing authorized versions of black culture and training her daughters to behave in a manner that is socially acceptable to their Jamaican grandmother and their Jamaican British relatives.

Conclusion

Cultural practices such as hairstyling and heritage cooking mobilize a black ethnic identity while also homogenizing blackness by erasing crucial distinctions between children of black parents and children whose parents have different national origins, different migration histories, and varied cultural practices. For women of multiracial heritage who may also be ambiguous in their ethnic appearance, these practices entail contradictions; according to Noble, they "[threaten] to reduce you to an essence or caricature of your own or someone else's making" (2005, 134). Noble argues for the need to contextualize the situations in which "a Black identity as a racialised embodiment is deployed strategically and non-strategically. . . . [In national contexts such as Britain where] being a 'visible minority' produces specific environmental and social risk that must be managed and overcome, critiques of essentialism must be historicized and contextualized, for there are no identities devoid of essentialist elements and moments" (135).

White transracial mothers play a pivotal role in the cultivation of their children's ethnicity. Through their heritage cooking and hair grooming practices, they can transfer ethnic capital and other forms of cultural

FIGURE 37 Sharon Dawkins and her youngest daughter, Imani, preparing jerked chicken for the Sunday meal.

capital to their children. This includes teaching them distinct sets of cultural skills and specific tastes so that they can demonstrate their right to be included in black ethnic communities. In black Caribbean diasporic communities in Leicester, segments of the community calculated ethnic belonging and determined criteria for inclusion and exclusion based on symbolic capital such as tastes in food, clothing, hairstyle, language, and music.

In their study of the relationship between the state, women, and ethnic processes, Anthias and Yuval-Davis identified five ways in which women have participated in ethnic and national processes, one of which is "as reproducers of the boundaries of ethnic or national groups" (1993, 114). The white women discussed in this chapter trained their children to strongly identify with the cultural tastes privileged by members of the African Caribbean diasporic community and culturally reproduced ethnic distinctions and thus ethnic boundaries between their multiethnic families and monocultural families.

One-fourth of the white transracial mothers who participated in this longitudinal ethnography identified black mothers as their reference group and worked very hard to function as an ethnic equivalent of their black sisters-in-law. These same white mothers exhibited a strong identification with their black female relatives and black friends as they labored to serve as an ethnic resource for their children. They engaged in care-taking and consumption projects that positioned them as race-conscious mothers who had adopted the cultural style and culinary practices of their black in-laws. By adopting the consumption regimes of their black relatives, they reified certain aesthetic styles and ideas of what constitutes blackness within multiracial households. This cultural signature distinguishes them from white transracial mothers who neither embrace a black aesthetic nor believe that they need to adopt African Caribbean or black-centered cultural practices.

The labor of transracial mothers who are socially immersed in black diasporic communities provides important theoretical insights into the myriad ways that ethnic capital can be mobilized and black ethnic identities cultivated by nonblack members of transracial and black extended families. Among members of transracial families, the cultivation of ethnic identities and the transfer of ethnic tastes depend heavily upon the gendered labor of women, who spend a great deal of time learning how to select, purchase, prepare, and consume ethnic foods, hair care products, and beauty salon services. Their labor sustains and cultivates an identification with a transnational or global black community among their children of multiracial heritage. Because this gendered labor is part of routine caretaking it is often taken for granted both by the women themselves and by their family members.

6

~~~

ARCHIVES OF INTERRACIAL INTIMACIES

Race, Respectability, and Family Photographs

> With the invention of the paper roll film and the handheld Kodak
> camera in 1888, photography pervaded the family as one of its self-
> identifying mechanisms.—SHAWN MICHELLE SMITH, AMERICAN ARCHIVES:
> GENDER, RACE, AND CLASS IN VISUAL CULTURE

How do members of transracial families employ photographs, particularly family albums, to manage the social stigma that may attach to these
unions? How do white working-class women utilize material culture to
demonstrate and display their respectability? In this chapter I examine
the family photographs of a couple who have been married for more
than twenty years. I treat their private photograph collection as a crucial
site where respectability is managed and racism countered. My analysis
of the family photographic archives of the Dawkins family, an upwardly
mobile middle-class family of working-class origins, provides theoretical insights into how racism and respectability are negotiated by members of transracial heterosexual families. Family photographs constitute
a form of material culture that can be found in homes of all class origins
and thus provide insights into the role of material culture in the management of respectability.

Shawn Michelle Smith (1999) has provided a historical analysis of
how baby photographs came "to emblematize a racial fantasy as eu-
genicists claimed [them] for scientific evidence" in the United States.
Smith's analysis of how family photographs became central to middle-
class visual culture in North America inspires and animates my analysis

FIGURE 38 Sharon Dawkins at age ten in a family studio portrait taken in 1970 after the birth of her younger sister. Six years after this photograph was taken, Sharon's parents expelled her from their home for dating a black man. Reprinted with permission of Sharon Dawkins.

of how photographs may be deployed by upwardly mobile, transracial families to negotiate racism and opposition to interracial intimacy as they project middle-class respectability:

> [The] family photo album remains the most enduring colloquial register developed during the period of photographic expansion. Over the course of the nineteenth century, the album came to function as a visual family archive, a record of ancestral legacies—the site where individuals were positioned within a family history. . . . George Eastman aggressively targeted middle-class consumers with his popular advertising campaigns, and by the turn of the century the camera had become an accessible source of home entertainment. The photographic portrait, once the sole domain of professional photographers . . . became a product of family life itself. By the 1890s, the family became a social unit increasingly imagined through the process of photographic representation. (118)

Following Marcus Banks (2001), I treat photographs as "tiny mirror fragments" that are not an accurate "visual record" of what really happens, but provide a partial view of the social fabric of people's lives. Banks has argued, "All visual forms are socially embedded, and many visual forms that sociologists and anthropologists deal with are multiply embedded. Using archival photographs to prompt memories or comments from informants in the course of an interview, for example, involves an appreciation of at least three forms of embeddings or frames" (79–80). He goes on to identify three contexts in which photographs are read: the original production of the photograph, subsequent histories of the photograph, and the context in which the social researcher deploys the photograph in the course of an interview.

Anthropologists and sociologists have used photographs from a wide range of sources in photo-elicitation interviews. They have used archival photographs (Modell and Brodsky 1994), photographs taken by the researcher (Bunster 1977; Harper 1984; Gold 1986), photographs taken by professional photographers working with researchers (Dublin 1998; Duneier and Carter 1999) and by participants in the research (Sprague 1978; Harrington and Lindy 1998), and snapshots taken by family members (Twine 1997b). Douglas Harper employed photo-elicitation interviews in his analysis of the social impact of mechanization on dairy farmers in rural New York, and Steven Gold has used photo-elicitation in interviews with two subpopulations of Vietnamese refugees.

I used photographs as primary source data, a visual record to study the material and social settings in which my research subjects live, and as evidence for theory. This popular method of documentation also helped me to clarify how the white birth mothers of African-descent children strategically employ family photographs to stage "presentations" of their domestic lives for private intrafamilial as well as public consumption (Goffman 1959).

Visual Sociology in a Discipline of Words

In 1901, while conducting research for an article that he was writing for *The World's Work*, W. E. B. Du Bois collaborated with Major A. Radclyffe Dugmore, a German photographer who accompanied him to Albany, Georgia. Dugmore shot photographs of black men and women to document their lives as agricultural workers in what was known as the Black Belt. Eighteen of these black-and-white photographs illustrated an article that Du Bois published in June 1901, "The Negro as He Really Is." Little has been written about Du Bois's collaboration with this German photographer. How did Du Bois view these photographic records of black life at this particular historical moment? They were not reprinted or included in the 1903 edition of *The Souls of Black Folks* and have only recently been reunited with the text in a centenary edition of that book. Why did Du Bois exclude photographs from the original edition? Did he fear that their inclusion would risk positioning his scholarship as photojournalism (S. M. Smith 1999)?[1]

When Albion Small became the editor of the *American Journal of Sociology* in 1914 he banished photographs from the pages of the journal. Describing the status of visual evidence within mainstream sociology journals during the early twentieth century and the motivation behind Small's decision, Elizabeth Chaplin has written, "Small believed the presence of photographs in a sociological text threatened the theoretical status and purpose of sociology itself. He claimed that although photographs might be an invaluable tool in the hands of those who argued for social change, the relationship of such a project to pure sociology was analogous to the relationship between public hygiene and biology" (1994, 198).[2] For nearly a century sociologists have debated the contribution of visual methods to sociological theory and to their use as "evidence of theory"; on one

FIGURE 39 Imani Dawkins, the youngest of four daughters of Sharon and Everal Dawkins. This family portrait behind her was taken in 1997, when Imani was two years old.

side are social scientists who employ visual methods, and on the other are those who eschew them in favor of less messy and more generalizable methods (206). Ninety years have passed since photographs were banished from the *American Journal of Sociology*, and they remain marginalized in the pages of mainstream sociology journals that are not devoted specifically to qualitative sociology or visual sociology.[3]

Howard Becker (1995) distinguishes between visual sociology, documentary photography, and photojournalism. Clarence Stasz explains why visual materials have been marginalized in the discipline of sociology since its inception:

> Since visual imagery has not been conventional in sociology since its beginnings, when it was more tied to social reform, most sociologists not only do not accept that obligation, they see few legitimate uses for visual materials other than as "teaching aids." It is as though using photographs and films in a research report constituted pandering to the low tastes of the public or trying to persuade readers to accept shaky conclusions by using illegitimate "rhetorical" means. In short, visual materials seem "unscientific," probably because "science" in sociology came to be defined as being objective and neutral, just the opposite of the crusading spirit which animated the early muckraking work, itself intimately tied up with photography. (Stasz 1979, 9)

Why do certain forms of data collection become defined as inherently political, while other forms are defined as neutral and scientific? Historically photographs were discredited as a legitimate form of evidence in part because in the early twentieth century sociology was engaged in a campaign to establish itself as a science. Visual images were associated with photojournalism and political activism rather than apolitical academic inquiry.

In his analysis of the marginalization of image-based research in visual anthropology and visual sociology, Jon Prosser argues that the orthodox qualitative research community undervalues images: "Contemporary orthodox qualitative researchers are very limited in what they count as acceptable use of images. For them an image is useful: as a way of breaking the boredom of the written text; as illustration of an object, place, person or event that [is] fully (and 'more properly') explained by language or via traditional visuals, namely tables, graphs and diagrams; and as a 'record'" (1998, 102).

Family photographs are not a straightforward representation of social reality; rather they are to some extent staged, selected, and assembled images that can convey contested aspects of a family's interior life. Photo albums are edited versions of family life since they rarely represent the total number of photographs that were taken or could have been taken. How do families decide which photos are taken, collected, arranged, and chosen for display, while others are discarded, destroyed, and left buried in boxes in basements or attics? I view photograph albums as socioracial maps that provide insights into how families archive their intimate lives and project particular racial and ethnic identities.

A Case Study in Photo-Elicitation Interviewing: Sharon Dawkins

Sharon Dawkins is the daughter of Julia Moult and Raymond Charles Moult. She was born on 15 July 1959 in Leicester. She met her husband, Everal, in 1979, and they were married on 30 July 1983, after living together for three years. When I recruited Sharon into my research study in 1995 she had been married for twelve years and was the mother of four daughters between the ages of nine months and thirteen years.

I was introduced to Sharon and Everal in September 1995. Mandy Burke, the wife of a childhood friend of Everal's gave me their number. I conducted my first racial consciousness interview with Sharon that year. My participant observation and home visits began in 1997, when I moved to Leicester and established a residence for eight months.[4] Between 1997 and 2003 I conducted seven semistructured interviews with her. In addition to participant observation, I observed her in her home and spent four overnights.

I conducted my first photo-interview with Sharon in her home in 8 March 2004; this involved her showing me and discussing her family photos.[5] Michael Smyth, a professional photographer based in Dublin, accompanied me to shoot additional photographs of Sharon's home.[6] Sharon directed me to specific aspects of the photographs that were meaningful to her, and thus she provided a frame that brought into relief her racial logics. These photo-interviews allowed Sharon to revisit selected moments in her life and to discuss the meaning of race in the photographs.

The smell of the smoke of Mayfair cigarettes floated in the air and encircled me. The sound of Sharon's contagious and throaty laughter filled the room. She has always given what my black relatives call a "perfor-

FIGURE 40 The author in Sharon Dawkins's kitchen examining photographs in Imani's baby book. Imani and Tanika look on. Everal Dawkins's mother, sister-in-law, and brother-in-law are in the photograph we are discussing.

mance." On the previous evening her husband put on blue work overalls and went up into the attic to retrieve close to five hundred photographs that are uncatalogued, unframed, and unremarkable to the family. As we opened the first box of photographs, I felt like a detective in a BBC drama about to make a discovery. I viewed these photographs as partial maps that I hoped would direct me through the racial territories of Sharon's life.

PHOTO-INTERVIEWS: MAPPING THE SOCIORACIAL CONTOURS OF INTERRACIAL FAMILY LIFE

There is a photograph of Sharon and me sitting side by side on a couch in her living room. We are sorting and reviewing the first set of a hundred photographs lying in shoe boxes scattered on the floor. I tape-record her describing her emotional state and the political issues that the photographs document. She clarifies the identities of everyone in the photographs and gives me her analysis as we systematically count every photograph and discuss them. She provides the historical context and her analysis of the meaning of her whiteness, while I listen and ask questions. I was particularly interested in the unidentified white women who occasionally appeared in these photos. We revisit recurring themes that we have discussed over the past eight years, including her place on the "white spectrum" in her black family.

We examine a series of photos that show Sharon in an advanced stage of pregnancy with her fourth daughter. The first photograph we discuss in detail was taken in July 1995, only one day after Sharon and I were first introduced and had our first formal interview. This photograph documents an annual family holiday. Sharon and her close friend Roxie (also a participant in my research study) are pushing baby carriages, accompanied by several of their other children. Roxie is a white woman of working-class origin who is also married to a British-born black man of Jamaican parentage. Roxie's daughter and Sharon's daughter are best friends. The next photograph, taken by Sharon's husband, shows various configurations of their children, playing, laughing, and dancing at what appears to be a leisure club.

In a photograph taken in July 1994, only three months before Imani, her fourth daughter, was born, Sharon is standing in a group shot with twelve black members of her husband's family. Her three daughters are

FIGURE 41 Sharon Dawkins.

also in this photograph. Smiling as she examines the photograph, she says, "I am the only white spot in the family." Positioned in the exact center of the photograph in the first row, Sharon is smiling; her red hair against her pale skin exaggerates her whiteness.

I listen carefully for changes and continuities in her narrative of her life. I listen to how she racializes herself. I am particularly interested in the ways that race figures as a character in the family dramas depicted in the snapshots. Sharon shows me a snapshot she took from her hospital bed of her husband and her youngest daughter, just moments after her birth. In the photo Everal is holding Imani in his arms. The next photograph, taken by her sister-in-law, is of Sharon talking on a cell phone after the birth of Imani. We then encounter several photographs of family gatherings in hospital rooms, celebrating the birth of her two youngest daughters, Tanika and Imani. This is followed by a photo of the postpartum party at her home, with Sharon's father sitting on the couch next to her sister. I listen carefully as Sharon analyzes this period in her life, comparing my own analysis to her translation and interpretation of this photograph. I had already developed a theory after years of recording conversations in which she discussed this same period.

A WEDDING ALBUM: OFFICIAL REGISTERS THAT CONCEAL AND REVEAL

The wedding album is bound in white leather and consists of fifty pages. It is a treasured family archive of Sharon and Everal's marriage, stored within easy reach of family members in a cabinet in the dining room that faces the garden. This album bears testimony to the official formation of a multiracial family and displays a "white wedding," distinguished from "civil registry" weddings because the bride wears white and there is typically a church ceremony followed by a reception with family members and close friends. Sharon and Everal were married five months after Sharon gave birth to their first daughter, Rhea.

Sharon takes me on a visual tour of her wedding day in 1983. The album depicts a handsome couple that has achieved respectability and appears to have the acceptance and support of their family. There is a photograph of Sharon and Everal smiling with his white parents-in-law. However, this photograph conceals the dramatic conflicts and struggles that took place the year prior to the wedding. Sharon describes being coerced by her mother, father, and future mother-in-law into aborting her first child one year before giving birth to her eldest daughter. Describing

FIGURE 42 Sharon Dawkins and the author during a photo-elicitation interview.

that period to me in 1995, she explains what led her to terminate her first pregnancy:

> My mum and dad weren't very happy either. And it was, well, they all came down [to Leicester] for a family discussion. Everal's dad didn't come because Everal's dad isn't at all—he wasn't racist. He loved anybody and everybody. . . . The family discussion consisted of Everal's mother, me, Everal, and my mum and dad. . . . Everybody thought I should get rid of this baby. And they were like discussing me like I wasn't there, you know. . . . Then Everal went and had a good talk with his mum and decided that he was going to finish with me [end the relationship].

These wedding photos conceal the trajectory of social suffering that preceded Sharon and Everal's marriage. The abortion and subsequent breakup are not captured in any of the photos that appear in the wedding album or boxes of photos. The photos that Sharon shows me provide documentary evidence of a successful and happy marriage.

Sharon and Everal were married after a three-year struggle and a three-month separation following the termination of her first pregnancy. According to Sharon, when Everal recommitted to their relationship, they agreed to what Sharon terms "new ground rules" in which she renegotiated her role in his extended family. Within the first year after their reunion, Sharon became pregnant with Rhea. She described her pregnancy as unplanned. In my private discussions with Everal he never mentioned the abortion or their separation, although he did acknowledge that his mother made it clear that she wanted him to establish a relationship with a black woman, preferably of Jamaican parentage. One of my favorite wedding photos, taken by a professional photographer, shows Sharon looking up directly into the camera as she signs the wedding registrar. The remaining photographs in the wedding album include Rhea, their infant daughter.

Family photo albums are a conventional form of storing, recording, and negotiating the memories of individuals and families. Photographs tell particular versions of events in familial lives. In the case of Sharon and Everal Dawkins, a journey through their album tells the story of two upwardly mobile people of working-class origins, both born in England, who fall in love and establish a family. It is a love story. It is the story of a white woman and her London-born Jamaican husband, who are par-

FIGURE 43 Sharon Dawkins signs the wedding registry at the city hall. Reprinted with the permission of Sharon and Everal Dawkins.

FIGURE 44 Clockwise, Raymond Charles Moult (Sharon's father), Sharon Dawkins, Everal Dawkins, and Julia Moult (Sharon's mother) standing in front of the Leicester courthouse on Sharon and Everal's wedding day. Reprinted with permission of Sharon and Everal Dawkins.

enting four daughters and now live in a spacious five-bedroom, three-bathroom home in a posh section of Leicester. Their boxes of photos chronicle twenty years of their relationship.

Yet another story remains outside the frame of these family snapshots. A set of photographs that were not taken would provide a different set of images and tell another story: of abortion, abuse, alcoholism, alienation, and redemption. As a young woman Sharon watched her mother physically battered each weekend by her father in routine rituals of domestic violence.

As we look at the post-wedding photographs I recall the previous day, when Sharon gave me a tour of her childhood home and the street where she grew up. After visiting the hair salon that Sharon co-owns, she drove me to the house where she lived between the ages of two and twelve. A council house consisting of three bedrooms, a living room, and an outdoor toilet, lacking indoor plumbing and hot water, and with rats in the backyard, this was a "purpose-built" home for poor families. Sharon lit a cigarette and began telling her story as we sat in her red BMW: "That's the place where my dad would beat my mother to a pulp. I was never allowed to have friends come to the house. I was never allowed to invite anyone to tea after school." Neither Sharon nor her mother was allowed to have friends visit. No one else entered this house except the police, who were occasionally called by the neighbors when her mother was beaten unconscious.

Sharon told me stories of younger versions of herself, the story of a thirteen-year-old girl who worked as a "Saturday girl" giving shampoos at the local hair salon; the story of a fifteen-year-old girl who dated black men, and whose parents kicked her out of the house one year later. At sixteen this girl was exiled for violating her parents' race rules, a delinquent daughter who took a position by dating the person she desired. At eighteen she learned to drive and purchased her own car. At twenty she was supporting herself and living in her own apartment. This is when she met Everal.

These are the stories that remain outside the frame of the photographs that Sharon is showing me. The photographs I see are the Kodak moments of joy, belonging, reunion, and redemption. The pictures that document a happy and successful marriage, that have been preserved and are available for display, do not reveal the strong opposition and disapproval that Sharon and Everal encountered during the first years of

FIGURE 45 Sharon and Everal Dawkins, leaving for their honeymoon. Reprinted with permission of Sharon and Everal Dawkins.

their relationship and their marriage. The story that is concealed by the photographs is that of a couple in love who encountered strong opposition from both families. It is the story of a coerced abortion, followed by depression, followed by reunion. It is the story of redemption, of a second pregnancy, and a wedding twelve months later. The snapshots of smiling and happy family moments conceal this story. Sharon's struggles for agency and control over her sexual and reproductive life remain outside the frame of the five hundred photographs that we examine and discuss.

I read these snapshots of Sharon and Everal's intimate life as their refusal to be constructed as deviant—as anything other than a respectable and loving family. These photographs insist on their respectability. Sharon has repeatedly said that she did not want her mother's life and states that she married "the opposite of [her] father." She married a man who is neither white nor an alcoholic nor an abuser. None of the family photographs that Sharon pulls out of the boxes depicts the conflicts and tensions of the first seven years of her marriage. Rather, they depict social cohesion and interracial harmony, the joyful years and events, the mundane and the momentous, the birth of children, the weddings, the annual holidays, the diaper changes, the laughter on couches, the children playing, and the Christmas holidays.

The Presentation of Self in Photo-elicitation Interviews

Sarah Pink cautions that photographs are ambiguous and unpredictable in their meaning: "Visual images have their own biographies. When they move from one context to another they are, in a sense 'transformed.' . . . Photographs and video images are interpreted in different ways and by different individuals at different points in ethnographic research, analysis and representation" (2001, 95). A comparative analysis of the content of the photographs that Sharon collected and displayed in her family albums and the content of our semistructured interviews and conversations over eight years (1995–2003) reveal tensions between the two. These family photographs of intimate moments present idealized representations of Sharon's family life and her position in her extended family as an "insider-other."

Hours of taped conversations over her kitchen table, at restaurants, in bars, in store checkout lines, and at "girls-only" nights with her friends provide the context for my theoretical analysis of the photos as Sharon

FIGURE 46 The entrance hallway in the Dawkins home is lined with photographs. In the top row is a formal studio portrait of Sharon and Everal, followed by individual photographs of each. In the bottom row is a group portrait of their daughters, followed by four studio photographs of the children as infants.

reads these same photos to me. Photo-elicitation interviews provided a reflexive space for Sharon and I to discuss the meanings that she attaches to these visual representations of her family life. This research method enabled me to compare how Sharon narrated her life over time, with and without the photographs. In the context of eight years of conversations, her analysis of her family photographs sheds light on the racial struggles and drama occurring outside the camera frame. The photographs trigger memories, but they also provide an opportunity for me to examine shifts and changes in the frames Sharon employs in her analysis of her marital career. She explains the changing dynamics of her relationships with her husband, mother-in-law, sister-in-law, friends, and daughters. Her life is not frozen in one moment, nor is her racial identity fixed; rather we can visit her at different moments in her life through the photographs.

Sharon's analysis of her situation has changed over the years. During the ten years that I conducted research for this book, I saw Sharon as she revisited, reframed, and analyzed her familial relationships and developed new repertoires and strategies for managing race and racism and her whiteness. Her readings of her family photographs occasionally challenged or contradicted my analysis of her transracial social life. The photographic archive that she selected and discussed provided me with a reflexive method of evaluation and enabled us to revisit themes that we had discussed over the previous eight years. It also enabled us to critique and challenge the socioracial maps that I had produced of her familial and friendship networks.

The photographs also show Sharon belonging to a cohort of white women who have formed long-term domestic partnerships with black men. These other women appear regularly in the family snapshots; she is not the lone white woman in her black extended family. These are women we have not discussed before. We came across a photograph of a white woman with blonde hair holding a baby, standing next to Everal's older brother, a handsome dark-skinned black man. This is Tracey, Sharon's white sister-in-law, the second wife of Everal's brother. When Sharon fails to comment on or identify this woman, I ask her to explain who she is. I thought that she might be Sharon's biological sister. Another photograph taken from the perspective of Sharon's hospital bed in 1995 shows a woman with a blonde ponytail holding Imani shortly after her birth and smiling directly into the camera. This is Nicole, the best friend of Sherrill, Sharon's black sister-in-law. Nicole is married to a black man and regularly appears in photographs of family dinners and at hospital births. It appears that she is invited to most of the major family holiday dinners and private events. Sharon had never mentioned her. I was surprised by the images of these white women because in our previous conversations, in the absence of photographs, Sharon had emphasized her racial isolation. Her white sisters-in-law have not been central in Sharon's narration of her life. Nevertheless they regularly appear in the photographs of intimate family moments, of births, weddings, and annual family holiday dinners—events that display social cohesion. During the photo-elicitation interview it became apparent that several other white women have been incorporated into her black extended family.

What distinguishes Sharon is not her whiteness, but her class origins. She appears to be the only white woman in her family who is marked as being of working-class origins. Her commentary on these photographs suggests that it is not her *whiteness* or racialization that has contributed to her feeling marginalized, but rather her working-class origins and her cultural style. In other words, her discussion of her whiteness may sometimes be a code for her *class* disadvantage and her working-class tastes that threaten to disrupt the upward mobility of her husband's Jamaican family (Bourdieu 1984).

The family snapshots and staged photos of interracial harmony that depict family members smiling, kissing, hugging, eating, and vacationing together also conceal the opposition to interracial formation from both sides of their family that Everal and Sharon have discussed with me. Sharon's mother-in-law, Mrs. Eileen Dawkins, and her sister-in-law, Sherrill, agree that there have been conflicts. Mrs. Dawkins argued that it was not Sharon's whiteness, but the cultural values that she inherited from her working-class parents that posed a threat to her family's respectability. Sharon was perceived as not being capable of running a household that was morally and culturally appropriate for Jamaican British children. The conflicts and tensions between Sharon and her Jamaican mother-in-law are concealed by photographs that show them laughing and engaged in playful banter on Christmas Day. The conflicts that they each described were performed beyond the frame of the camera lens. Should we dismiss the scenes of harmony and laughter depicted in these family photos? Do these scenes represent partial truths, or do they reflect what this family aspires to and desires, the ideals of intimacy that they share?

Ten years ago, when I first met Sharon, she appeared to still be struggling with her grief and anger over the termination of her first pregnancy. In our earlier interviews (1995–97) she focused primarily on conflicts and tensions with her mother-in-law. Sharon may have emphasized certain aspects of her family life while de-emphasizing others because of what she was enduring at that particular moment in her marriage. At that time the questions that I posed may have directed her to focus more on issues that concealed the degree of social cohesion and affection that exists in this family. Another interpretation is that Sharon may have viewed my research study as an opportunity for her to voice her concerns and frustrations about her experiences of marginalization in her extended black family.

During the photo-interview Sharon viewed her life from the perspective of a twenty-year marriage that had produced four daughters, marital stability, financial security, and immersion in a black extended family. Our photo-interview called my attention to how much she appeared to enjoy her social life with her black in-laws. I could almost hear the laughter in the photographs. This interview combined with my analysis of the photographs brought into sharp relief the emphasis that I had placed on conflicts, tensions, and racial troubles while not considering the degree of social cohesion that existed.

The tensions between these staged and harmonious images of Sharon smiling, laughing, and playing with her family members and the private suffering she reported to me over the years, including over the termination of her first pregnancy, demonstrate how photographs can be used in photo-elicitation interviews to revisit themes and introduce reflexivity by creating the discursive space for family members to re-vision and re-frame past struggles in the context of the changes that have occurred in their lives.

In the context of a longitudinal ethnographic study of race, feminist race theorists can employ photo-elicitation interviews to evaluate how individuals reframe, redefine, and rework the meaning and significance of race and racism over the course of a marriage. They provide a rich source of empirical data that can advance theories of how race and racism are negotiated in the context of aging, class mobility, heterosexual marriage, racial hierarchies, and gender inequality in longitudinal studies of interracial intimacy. Race recedes and comes back into relief as individuals respond to crises in their life. They develop repertoires for negotiating race and racism. Deaths, divorces, births, weddings, illnesses, and

FIGURE 47 Sharon and Everal Dawkins in 2003.

career changes can alter the ways that individuals interpret, narrate, and present their intimate lives. Members of interracial families, like members of monoracial families, continually edit their previous narratives as their story lines are disrupted by personal and family events.

Sharon presented varied analyses of the significance of race and racism in her life, in part due to the dynamic nature of her relationship with her husband and her in-laws. The photo-elicitation interview generated data that complemented and challenged my field notes, participant observations, and racial consciousness interviews. During the photo-elicitation interview, Sharon emphasized what she had achieved during her marriage and her inclusion in the family as "an honorary black." In contrast to earlier interviews, the themes of social cohesion and respectability were more prominent than the themes of isolation and alienation. She projected a racial self and a family profile that was more racially unified than the one that she had presented in previous years.

7

~~~

WHITE LIKE WHO?

Status, Stigma, and the Social Meanings of Whiteness

> What is this whiteness that threatens to separate me from my own child? Why haven't I seen it lurking, hunkering down, encircling me in some irresistible fog? . . . The obsessive denial that race mattered was obviously a white creation.—JANE LAZARRE, *BEYOND THE WHITENESS OF WHITENESS: MEMOIR OF A WHITE MOTHER OF BLACK SONS*

> Socialized to believe the fantasy, that whiteness represents goodness and all that is benign and non-threatening, many white people assume this is the way black people conceptualize whiteness.—BELL HOOKS, "WHITENESS IN THE BLACK IMAGINATION"

How are white women raising children of multiracial heritage perceived by their black partners and sisters-in-law? How is their whiteness interpreted and managed by black British family members? Within transracial families the value and meaning of whiteness is contested, and varied interpretations compete. Ruth Frankenberg has argued that whiteness is a "set of practices." Black family members may perceive whiteness as an asset, a liability, a cultural disadvantage, or a harbinger of ethnic erasure. In this chapter I explore these questions by analyzing the discourses of black men and women as they present their views of the social, cultural, and symbolic meanings and value of the whiteness of their wives and sisters-in-law.

Competing racial narratives and representations of whiteness circulated among the transracial families I studied. Overall I found gender fault lines among black family members. Regardless of their racial or

FIGURE 48 Marie, the sister-in-law of Maureen Dover, and two of her sisters-in-law at a Sunday gathering.

ethnic identity, they adhered to a strict code of respectability and certain gender regimes that place accountability for race training on the shoulders of white and black mothers. This contradicts the assumption held by some of these same family members that white people are culturally unqualified to prepare children of African Caribbean ancestry to cope with racism.

An analysis of the discursive and ideological terrain within these families illuminates how white people get symbolically positioned in a hierarchical system of class inequality, heterosexual gender regimes, and cultural norms that privilege specific performances of femininity. When black members of transracial families analyze the cultural impact and value of whiteness, they employ one of four discourses: (1) white family members are an asset—a source of economic and social capital; (2) white family members are a source of injury because they increase black family members' exposure to racism; (3) whites are a cultural liability because they don't understand racism; and (4) white family members, accelerate assimilation into white English society, and thus dissolve the ethnic boundaries and threaten social reproduction of the black community.

Jeffrey Smith: White Family Members as an Asset

A probation officer at the local jail, Jeffrey Smith is the only child of a middle-class black Jamaican preacher. Born in 1942 in the parish of Manchester, Jamaica, he went to fee-paying schools and the top boarding school in Jamaica. After completing the senior standard Cambridge exam,[1] he immigrated to England in 1961 intending to pursue a degree in engineering. Arriving in London at the age of nineteen with his childhood friend Herdle White, he was shocked by the racism he encountered. Describing his and Herdle's perceptions of whiteness at that time, Jeffrey stated:

> As far as we were concerned, England was the mother country. And although we weren't expecting any red carpets, we still weren't expecting to be treated badly. . . . We had this stupid, silly idea, which I think is to do with how you've been socialized [in the Caribbean], that because a person was white, they were sort of educated, intelligent, and well off. You have all those sort of things attached to them because . . . the assumption was that anybody who was white was better off educationally, financially—and it's a real stupid daft idea.

Jeffrey grew up with servants, a cook, and other privileges shared by middle-class families in rural Jamaica. When he arrived in metropolitan London, he was not perceived as middle class and lacked the social and economic currency he possessed in Jamaica. The white English simply failed to recognize the color hierarchies and social distinctions that West Indian immigrants brought with them:[2] "In the 'Mother Country' no regard was paid to the complex hierarchy of shades by the 'host' society: the patterns of racism which the Caribbean migrants experienced here did not correspond to the pigmentocracy which they left behind in the Caribbean. They were regarded monolithically as 'coloured,' 'West Indians,' 'blacks,' 'immigrants,' and even 'wogs' with no reference to differential shades" (James 1993, 239).

Shortly after his arrival in London, Jeffrey met Chloe, a fourth-generation artist and white native of London, whom he would marry. He described how her class background immediately gave him access to social experiences, elite social events, and forms of protection from racial abuse. In contrast to Chloe, he was conflict-avoidant and never challenged white people who stared at them or treated them in a racist manner in public, due to their hypervisibility as an interracial couple in London in the 1960s:

> From the moment she opened her mouth, they would know that they're not in her class. And if I'm with her then it means that I'm from her class because in London they're a very class-conscious society. And [my wife] is . . . from an upper-class white family, socially. They might not have the money and the wealth and all that goes with it, but socially they're from an upper-class background, a much higher class that I was from. . . . . I've been to silver wedding celebrations, which were with ex-Rugby school people who I know through [my wife], through her connections with the school. So all I'm saying is that if I wasn't her husband I would not have gone to all those sorts of events.

Having a white wife from an upper-class background provided Jeffrey with a racial shield that protected him from some forms of racial discrimination. For example, after several unsuccessful attempts to buy a home, he asked his white father-in-law to intervene:

> So I said to my father in law, "If you find a house that you think we would like, you should sort of hold it for us." So that's what he did. He

put the bid and he put the deposit down to hold the house. So when we came, we went around to look at it. But I didn't go in. We just walked up the street and looked at it. . . . [My wife] went with her dad and looked around and decided that it was something that we would like. So everything went ahead. And because we also paid cash for it, there was no long-drawn-out rigmarole. . . . So after the contract and everything was signed, we came down for the weekend and [my wife] rang the [white] lady and said, "Look, my husband is with me, can we come around and look at the house?" And we went around with Alex, and the [owner] opened the door. She had a shock when she saw me and [our son]. But she wasn't insulting or anything like that. We didn't know that she had resented [us] to that extent until we moved there. The neighbor told us that she had told them that she was so sorry she left them with a "nigger" for a neighbor.

Thus Chloe's whiteness and that of her father enabled them to purchase a spacious three-bedroom house in an exclusive district of Leicester from a white woman who would have refused to sell her home to a black person. Utilizing his social relationship with his father-in-law gave Jeffrey access to capital that shielded him from vulgar racism.

Netifnet Arthur-Hawkes: Whiteness as a Source of Symbolic Capital

Netifnet Arthur-Hawkes, a thirty-eight-year-old attending Nottingham Trent University, is a striking woman with medium brown skin who wears her hair in dreadlocks that hang to her waist. Netifnet has been married to Stephen Hawkes, a white man, for seventeen years and is the mother of two multiracial sons.[3] She was born four months after the Nottingham race riots of 1958 to first-generation immigrants from Barbados. Her parents, who migrated during the mid-1950s, raised Netifnet as a member of the Seventh Day Adventist Church, where she met her husband. Stephen grew up in a white middle-class family and works as a residential social worker.

Netifnet and Stephen began dating in 1980 and married shortly thereafter in a religious ceremony. She explained her parents' response to her marriage to a white man:

They're fundamental Christians, right, Seventh Day Adventists. So they consider all people as equal in the sight of God, so you get filled

FIGURE 49 Netifnet Arthur-Hawkes.

with all of this nonsense for the whole of your life and "in God there is no black and white." . . . My mother thought it was wonderful, but that's because she's of the side that says having a white person in the family's quite prestigious. That was when we first started going out. Since then her opinion of him has changed quite drastically.

When I asked why her mother changed her opinion, Netifnet responded, "Well, he's got locks. He hasn't kept me out of the ghetto. He didn't give me a nice, middle-class life in a nice middle-class area. He didn't, you know, wave the magic wand of success and fame and fortune for her little girl."

In Netifnet's family there was initially a gender split between her parents. While her father disapproved of her marriage to a white man and wanted her to marry a black man from their church, her mother viewed his whiteness as an asset, given that he was also a Christian. She perceived his whiteness as a valuable resource that would provide economic, symbolic, and cultural capital to her daughter and, by extension, to the entire family. Her mother engaged in a double discursive move, both acknowledging the value of his whiteness and also claiming that "race doesn't matter." Her mother became frustrated, however, when her son-in-law did not move her daughter up the class and cultural ladder to middle-class respectability. After seventeen years of marriage her daughter and son-in-law lived in a small terraced home in a district referred to as "the ghetto" of Leicester. Rather than transfer class privilege or respectability to her daughter, her son-in-law, who grew up in a middle-class family, instead became a Rastafarian and a socially marginal member of the white community.

Like the other black women I interviewed, Netifnet maintained that there was a double standard in her local community. Black men tended to support and endorse their sons' relationships with white women while opposing their daughters' with white men. Describing her father as very patriarchal, Netifnet believed that he viewed her marriage in terms of his losing her or "giving [her] up to a white man."

Netifnet's experience represents a pattern I found in three-fourths of the families I interviewed. Black men, including those who were married to or had previous relationships with white women, strongly disapproved of interracial relationships involving their black sisters or daughters. Black men of all ages, however, consistently endorsed their own and their sons' interracial relationships. The only exceptions were among male Seventh Day Adventists.

Netifnet said that both her parents and her husband's parents disapproved of their relationship. Like the white women whose white parents opposed their interracial marriage (e.g., Andrea MacKenzie, Simone Carpenter, and Sue Farrell, chapter 2), she was disciplined by her parents and the black community for her transgression:

> I've been accused of being a traitor. I've been accused of watering down the race—by both black men and black women. But they'd never necessarily hold that against the black men because, at times, they feel, well, because white women have got more economic power—they feel there's a lot more for a white woman to be able to seduce away a black man with. There have been occasions where black men have their baby-mother—a black woman—but the woman they get money from is going to be a white woman.

Netifnet's statement identifies one of the dominant racial logics and controlling myths: that interracial relationships are motivated by economic incentives. These racial logics were invoked across race, class, and gender in my conversations. This discourse, which is used to argue against interracial family formations, shifts the analysis away from noneconomic dimensions of the relationship and minimizes issues of sexual desire, attraction, companionship, and shared cultural values. It also denies that relationships that begin as teenage love affairs (not generally based on rational calculations) are not emotionally or sexually driven. It thus recuperates black female sexuality by suggesting that black men do not reject black women because they don't desire them, but because black women don't possess or offer as much economic capital or economic security as white women. In other words, it turns raging hormones into a rational decision based upon the calculation of value.

While Netifnet may have witnessed this behavior, and there are merits to her analysis, this line of thinking softens any perceptions of rejection. Her theory enables her to argue that white women are being chosen not because they are perceived as more beautiful or rank higher than black women on the aesthetic ladder of desirability, but because white women treat black men like a commodity whose sexual and emotional services, not unlike those of sex workers, are being purchased. Even if some black men actually do benefit financially from their intimate relationships, does this distinguish interracial relationships from intraracial relationships, particularly among the upper class, where consolidating and retaining wealth has always been a primary consideration? What explains the tendency to interpret interracial relationships but not intraracial relationships in economic terms?

Although virtually all of the black women I interviewed argued that whiteness is a form of capital—a resource associated with material privileges—family members' opinions varied on the value that individual white women and men brought to their relationships. I discovered gender fault lines and class fractures in which black men tended to overvalue white femininity as a resource, while black women called attention to the gender gaps in their family's degree of acceptance and support of interracial relationships.

Black and white members of interracial families agreed that black men either appeared to or in fact did sexually exploit white women and that they utilized white women as a form of economic support. A related argument was that some white women were class-climbers and pursued only economically successfully black men from whom they could extract money. These arguments exaggerate the symbolic and material value of whiteness while minimizing the affective and emotional dimensions of interracial relationships.

Interestingly, however, the emphasis on economic capital associated with white men and women plays out across classes and stigmatizes whites who are of working-class origin or display a cultural style associated with working-class whites. Black family members invoke these class distinctions to describe the motivations of working-class or poor white women who pursue employed black men, as well as middle-class white women who pursue upwardly mobile black professional men.

Michael Lewis: Managing Intraracial Class Distinctions

The black men I interviewed who had married their childhood sweethearts or married women they met in their youth argued against the notion that these relationships were driven by economic motives and that they used their white wives to climb up the class ladder. In fact, unlike Jeffrey Smith, who was the exception, the majority of black men in this study married white women who *shared* their class position and whom they met in class-segregated and socially stratified spaces such as pubs, nightclubs, work, and school.

FIGURE 50 Michael Lewis holding his third son, three months old.

Michael Lewis is representative of three-fourths of the men in this study. He married his wife when they were in their twenties after a long courtship. Like Everal Dawkins, he was part of the same social circles of upwardly mobile, second-generation black men who had been raised in working-class families by Caribbean-born parents.

Born in 1961, Michael Lewis is the only black community librarian in Leicester. The son of a nursing assistant, he grew up in Highfields, an inner-city working-class community described by blacks of Caribbean origin as "the heart of the black community." His mother, a native of Barbados, raised him as a single parent; his father, the manager of a bakery line, lives in London. Like other second-generation black men of Caribbean origin, he expresses a strong identification with his mother's native Barbados. He described the intraracial island distinctions among black Caribbeans: "If you want to go into anything that's controlled by Afro-Caribbeans in Leicester, they're all controlled by Jamaicans. If you're not Jamaican, you're classed as an outsider, so I used to get this 'Oh, where are you from?' I said, 'Well, I'm from Barbados.' 'Oh, you're from the small island.' . . . The Jamaicans class us as inferior to them because we come from small islands."

Michael identified the class distinctions and social stratification within the black community as a major factor in his life. He believed that he was consistently rejected by black women he dated because of intraracial class hierarchies:

> A pattern emerged for me when I was older, when I started going out with girls really. And I would go out with black girls first, and you would go into the family. You'd sit down and you'd meet their parents. They never asked you about your parents. And me being honest, truthful because that's the way I was brought up, with telling what I want, I would say, "My mum's not married to my father and my father lives in London. She lives in Leicester." . . . You were usually lesser. About two more weeks with this girl and her family would say, "No, you don't want to go out with him. He's going nowhere. . . . He's not going anywhere." Because there was a stigma about Highfields.

As the son of a single mother, he was viewed by black families as possessing neither cultural, social, nor economic capital and as a high risk. Michael's wife, Anne, unlike black women from his community, accepted him when he was not financially secure and had no symbolic or cultural capital to offer. She was his childhood sweetheart and also grew up in Leicester. She did not evaluate him on the basis of his mother's marital status or his family's residence in a poor community.

Michael received criticism from his black female friends, who questioned his marrying Anne, a white woman. He recalls how he responded to their questioning:

> I've got a lot of black friends and black women friends. And they were sitting there and they were going, "But Michael, you're a strong, healthy, black man. What are you doing with a white woman?"
>
> And I went, "I fell in love with a white woman. I can't help, you can't help who you fall in love with."
>
> And they were going, "Yeah, but you should have married a black woman. You're upwardly mobile. You're going places. You should be with a black woman. That's the problem with you black men. As soon as you get anywhere, you have [to get] a white woman."
>
> I went, "Come back. Come back. When I had nothing, I had Anne, and if I have everything I have Anne. That's the difference." Most black women in Leicester want the good times. They forget when you used to be poor and walking the street and had no job.

Michael's experience of being rejected by a series of young black women from his class background illustrates the significance of the perception of social and economic capital within the black community and challenges the notion that black men select white women simply because they are trying to move up the class ladder. His experience also highlights the residue of Victorian attitudes toward single mothers, which stigmatize their children and position them as undesirable. In Michael's case, he simply fell in love with a white woman after being excluded from the pool of desirable young black men by the parents of the black girls he dated.

Joyce Chase Stephens: Whiteness as a Source of Injury

Joyce has a round face, flawless skin, and like Netifnet wears her hair in dreadlocks, although Joyce keeps them covered. Her dark brown eyes occasionally contain a glimmer of sadness that is countered by her electric smile. She is the thirty-eight-year-old mother of five children and she opposes interracial marriage. Like a number of other university-

FIGURE 51 Camille London-Mayo (on left) and her sister-in-law Lisa Hackett at a Sunday meal.

educated black women with whom I spoke, she was involuntarily incorporated into an interracial family.

Following her divorce in 1996 she left Brixton, a working-class multiethnic community in south London, where she had lived for twelve years, and moved her family to Leicester, where her mother lives. As a cancer survivor and divorced mother, Joyce needed her mother's emotional and financial support. According to her brother, their mother cooks, cleans, and takes care of Joyce's five children on a daily basis. Without this support, Joyce could not manage her job.

Joyce began our discussion about her white sister-in-law, with these words: "I had cancer in 1997. I was always the strong one and then I got cancer and [my ex-husband] couldn't cope with it." She continued:

> When I discovered that [my brother and sister-in-law] were going out together, I didn't want to meet her. He had had a few white girlfriends and this had always been a contentious issue between us. He let the relationship develop before he told me he was going to marry her. So it was a fait accompli. . . . He was quite a fairly successful black man. She hadn't established herself yet. . . . He had already bought his first house. I helped him buy his first house. It was a house I had owned and I sold it to him. I was vexed. . . . If he didn't have a job and didn't have status she wouldn't have paid attention to him.

Joyce's interpretation of the relationship echoes the popular perception that white women are likely to economically exploit black men. This presumes that romance is not the primary factor in these relationships and that black men constitute a resource for white women and are being exploited for their labor (sexual and emotional). This interpretation applies particularly to financially stable and employed middle-class black men.

Joyce also identified a type of white woman who is attracted to black men for a different reason: "Historically, the white women who went out with black men just wanted to party." These are primarily daughters of the industrial proletariat or semiskilled working class. These women have been coded as sexually loose by blacks and whites alike, and are assumed to be engaged in commercial or casual sex, particularly if they remain unmarried and give birth to children fathered by several black men. This also depletes the pool of available black men for black professional women. Joyce described her first meeting with Danielle before her marriage in Barbados: "When I finally met her, I had already been diagnosed with my illness. She was so nervous. I actually had a big thing [argument] with [my brother] over the phone. She realized she was going to have opposition from me. . . . I decided to just watch her. This was a decision that he had made. At the end of the day I wanted him to be happy. I was very cool towards her. I felt that she knew I disapproved of the relationship."

Joyce's justification for her initial rejection of Danielle was her whiteness and the fact that she wanted what was best for her "baby brother," Adam. Her concern was that her brother would be treated as inferior, that he would be exploited and then discarded. In her words, "[White women] . . . thought they were better than [black men]. They used them and moved on." This is not what happened, however; instead Danielle offered forms of emotional support that Joyce's former husband and her friends had failed to provide. By doing so, she directly challenged Joyce's perceptions of white women and caused her to reevaluate their relationship:

> I was going through my chemotherapy. . . . She was very supportive. She sent me little cards and little gifts, which I remember to this day. She didn't have to. I had friends who couldn't cope with my cancer. We don't see a lot of each other and that's about work. I get on better with her than with my brother. [My sister-in-law] is very proactive. She recognized that she is a white woman and she has a child of dual heritage. She wants him to own his blackness. She wants him to identify with his roots. [My nephew] doesn't need me to teach him about white culture. [My sister-in-law] is more radical than [my brother].

As a result of Danielle's behavior, Joyce was able to see her as a white person who understood racism. She realized that Danielle was more racially conscious than her brother, even though he had grown up in a black family: "She reads extensively. . . . She reads Terry McMillan, Zora Neale Hurston. Because she has taken the step of educating herself, there is less of a need for us to educate. She's really aware of appearances. She just wants [my nephew] to be whole . . . not fractured."

Two significant issues arise from this discussion. First, Joyce's sister-in-law is not representative of the type of white women to whom she referred earlier who become involved with black men, because she is a university-educated social worker and does not regularly frequent pubs or nightclubs. Second, Joyce views her brother as racially unaware, and

FIGURE 52 Owen London with his son Oshi in 2001.

thus as culturally distant from the black community. In Joyce's view, since her brother is not pro-black, he cannot be expected to transfer a black identity or consciousness to his children. This means that the responsibility for race training necessarily falls on the women in the family.[4] In contrast to his white wife, Joyce believes that Adam does not prioritize issues of race and racism in his children's lives and is not invested in his children's immersion in or ties to the black community. He resides in a predominantly white community with a white wife but doesn't compensate for this in any way.[5]

Although Joyce no longer views Danielle simply as either a white trophy wife or exploiting her brother, and though they have established a close and affectionate bond, Joyce remains opposed to interracial relationships, arguing, "We [the black community] cannot afford to allow our strength to be dissipated." Her overall philosophy about interracial relationships has not changed:

> I love [my sister-in-law]. I think she's a lovely person. But that doesn't mean that I think we should promote mixed relationships. Not everyone is coming from her background. . . . I do think there's diversity [among white women]. I have a friend. She's white. She doesn't go out with black men. I don't think I could handle that. . . . I don't want to upset [my sister-in-law or brother]. They know what my philosophy is. They know what my value system is. I have to respect their decision to be together.

Because Joyce's brother minimizes his contact with his mother, his children spend more time with their white English grandparents. Danielle's parents showed me photos documenting numerous birthday parties and weekend celebrations they had organized for their grandson and appeared very emotionally attached to him. Danielle and Adam also confirmed that they receive a lot of support from Danielle's family and that their son spends nearly every weekend at the home of his maternal grandparents. This was also one of Joyce's biggest complaints: "[My nephew] spends a lot of time with Danielle's family, more so than with our side of the family. So it doesn't matter how pro-black Danielle is, then, his socialization will be more white." Despite [my son's] strong identification with his black father, from the perspective of his black family members the fact that he spends more time with his white English grandparents accelerates his identification with his white English family and promotes the adoption of English cultural traits. What they fear is that, as he gets older, he will become more identified with whites and feel more comfortable socializing with them.

Unlike Joyce, who held her brother responsible for his children's race training, several of the other black women I interviewed were more likely to see this form of labor as the exclusive domain of the mother. Black women of all levels of education exempted their brothers from this responsibility, adhering to a fairly conservative gender division of household labor and child care. In families in which the mother is white, this resulted in a racialized and gendered division of labor that made the white parent responsible for socializing the children into some version of a black or "off-black" identity.[6]

Even though Joyce was critical of her brother's racial politics, she idealized him as highly desirable: "[My sister-in-law] has a man who has a degree, is upwardly mobile. He doesn't drink excessively. He doesn't smoke. At the end of the day many black women would love to have a man like [my brother]." Joyce's views were representative of two-thirds of the black women I interviewed. Virtually all of the black women I interviewed had a brother who was dating, had married, or had established a domestic partnership with one or more white women.

To my surprise, regardless of the type of relationship they had with their white sisters-in-law, none of the university-educated black women argued in support of interracial relationships. This was true even for black women who were married to white men (typically after a failed marriage or domestic partnership with a black man). Instead they argued that interracial relationships threaten the sociopolitical reproduction of a black collectivity. This was the norm in the local community, as was the different standard held for black women in these families. Black women were not encouraged by their fathers or brothers to establish relationships with white men, a fact that is a strong source of tension in the families and the community.

Vanessa Jamieson: Whiteness as a Position of Disadvantage

Vanessa Jamieson is a thirty-two-year-old African Caribbean achievement teacher. As a qualified teacher who speaks Creole and has an extensive knowledge of the Caribbean community, she is ideally positioned to explain how white mothers of children of African Caribbean heritage are perceived in the school system. She grew up in the Seventh Day Adventist Church and married a man who was also raised in the church. I interviewed Katrina Nash, her white sister-in-law, in 1995 (see chapter 2), as well as Katrina's former husband and her brother-in-law in 2001.

Vanessa is the mother of two children, ages one and three. She has a duel master's degree in criminology and education from Leicester University. In contrast to some of the other black women I interviewed, Vanessa has positive impressions of her white sisters-in-law and identified their efforts to learn about black culture. In our interview she assessed the white women who have married into her family. Seven of her nieces and nephews have white birth mothers.

From Vanessa's perspective, white women in her family and those she has met in her capacity as a teacher who have married into black families perceive black women as their reference group, which can generate feelings of cultural inferiority or inadequacy about being white. These white women view whiteness as not "hip," not culturally interesting. Describing one of her sisters-in-law, Vanessa noted:

> I find them as being quite keen and enthusiastic to take on board what might be regarded as the black culture. . . . "Tell me everything I need to know. Tell me how to cook the food. Tell me sometimes how to speak the lingo." So wanting to kind of grasp everything there is to know, which I think is about them being included in the family and also about something that gives them some kind of kudos because it's hip to be black or at least have that kind of *style* and cultural thing that is associate with being black. But generally there's an eagerness to taking on the black culture, whatever that is.

Vanessa's sisters-in-law and the other white women she described could be considered "ethnic converts" because they have essentially adopted the cultural style and lifestyle of their black Caribbean partners and changed their way of cooking and cleaning, their dress and discipline, and their social network in exchange for inclusion in the black family. White women who are perceived as multicultural navigators can earn the status of "honorary blacks." The black women who had established close relationships with their white sisters-in-law supported this type of ethnic conversion and viewed it as positive, while those black sisters-in-law who remained categorically opposed to their brothers' relationships with white women were critical of this conversion.

Vanessa views most white women parenting interracial children as "culturally disadvantaged" because she believes they often have less support than black mothers. According to Vanessa, this is because the white women don't have the support of a religious community or the black community; their children have been socially constructed as a bigger problem than black children in the local schools; and these women are often stigmatized and seen as morally compromised.

David: Whiteness as Lack of Racial Empathy

Like Vanessa, David, the black husband of his white childhood sweetheart, Simone, views white mothers of black children as culturally disadvantaged. David has been married to Simone (see chapter 2) for more than twenty years; they have two sons. When asked to describe his relationship with his wife, he expressed admiration for her and respect for her "character" and also remarked on her "strength." However, when asked to compare his wife's experiences as a white mother to those of black mothers of African-descent children in his family, he turned to an ideology of "racial empathy" to argue that as a white woman, his wife could not feel the pain of racism that her children would inevitably experience: "My wife is always going to see things differently [from] a black mother anyway. Black mothers traditionally are very strong and very protective of their children, but when the ugly head of racism starts rearing its head, black mothers deal with it a lot. For example, they know, they can *feel* racism. They'd [be] doing it from an empathic position. They [experience] the racism themselves, so they know how to challenge racism."

Like many of the black women and men I interviewed, David assumed that if one experiences racism firsthand, then one automatically knows how to challenge it. He did not consider that the social ostracism, racial exclusion, and other forms of rebound racism that his wife experienced (from her natal family and other whites) provided her with experiences she could draw on. Although he acknowledged how much privilege she had "lost," for example, he did not consider that experience a parallel one that could enable her to empathize with their children's experience of racism. In other words, he did not appear to recognize that her racial privilege was contingent upon her willingness to form familial relationships exclusively with white men, even as he recognized that his wife had been subjected to certain forms of racial abuse. For example, he noted, "She's classed as a second-class citizen. It's a deal [black men] can never pay back [to their white partners]. And the majority of them don't realize it. They don't realize how much their partners have lost—none of them. But I see what she's lost when I go to the family get-togethers and I look around the room and I'm the only black face and my children are the only black kids in that environment." Recall that Simone related that her brother had not spoken to her since she married David. Although her twin sister remains close to her, she has experienced considerable hostility from other white family members.

The view among black family members that white mothers are unable to "feel" racism or cannot "equip" their children to cope with it was also extended to white fathers. For example, one black woman who has been married to her white husband for five years and appears to be in a very satisfying and stable marriage expressed her fear, not uncommon among the black mothers married to white men, that she might die before her children reach adulthood. She was especially concerned that her white husband would be unable to respond adequately to racism on an emotional level:

> I don't think [their white father] could deal with [racism]. And I don't think he could equip them because, again, he doesn't have the understanding. I think he would deal with them in *sympathy*, but he couldn't deal with them as I would, in *empathy*. I some ways, that's perhaps not a bad thing. The first time [my daughter] came home from school and said she'd been subjected to racism, I just sat on the bottom of the step and cried because I just felt it so personally.

However, because fathers are not expected to parent to the same degree as mothers, most of the analysis is focused on the mothers. Black women and men tended to interpret whiteness, in and of itself, as an undifferentiated marker of inexperience with racism. They rarely acknowledged that age, education, class inequality, marital status, and political experiences mitigate the ways that white women and men experience race, racism, and racial privilege. White mothers in particular were typically described to me in terms that emphasized their whiteness without recognition of the ways their marital status and tenure in the local community might hyper-whiten or un-whiten them. Even when class was invoked to position them, their whiteness often trumped class in the final analysis. Their maternal and familial ties to blacks were sometimes de-emphasized in these discourses. In his research on whites in Detroit, Hartigan (1997) examined a similar phenomenon. He emphasizes "the uneven reproduction and experience of whiteness" and provides the example of a white woman, Esther, whose grandchildren are of African descent. Describing how ideologies of racism and racial difference impact her as a member of a multiracial family, he argues:

> Relating to her grandchildren racialized her because it brought her into zones where only her racialness would be read; attending to her "black" grandchildren made her even whiter even though she promoted no notion of racial superiority. It is notable that in such heterogeneous family sites, race retained an indelible content, no more diluted than if these members were in homogenous family groups. . . . For Esther, the complexity of their racialness (hers, her daughters,' their children's) had expanded exponentially. Whereas as an individual she could efface the significance of race with her friends ("we don't get into that stuff"), as a family member she had become racialized in a manner outside of her control or will, both by her nurturing role and by the positions in which it placed her. (202)

Like Hartigan, I found that white transracial mothers, were racialized by their family members in ways that they could neither anticipate nor control. This had particular consequences for white mothers who lacked an education and had not been involved in organized antiracist politics. Because in Leicester this group of women does not constitute an organized political constituency, their concerns as white parents of African-descent children rarely, if ever, register in public debates. Moreover they were not recognized as having struggles that parallel those of black parents of African-descent children, as demonstrated by David's interpretation of Simone's inability to empathize with racism.

Everal Dawkins: Whiteness as Assimilation and Sexual Adventure

Everal, a born-again Christian, is a tall, thin man with a broad smile and perfect posture. His eyes display that form of serenity not uncommon among Christians who have "made an agreement with God." Everal has a wife he adores and a successful marriage entering its twenty-third year. His Christianity serves as a firewall that offers protection and isolates him from danger. He repeatedly told me that all he needed was God, his wife, and his family.

Born in London in 1961 to Jamaican parents, Everal grew up in a two-parent, intact family. His parents were part of the first post–Second

FIGURE 53 Sherrill Dawkins (Everal's sister) and Eileen Dawkins (Everal's mother) in 2004.

World War wave of migration from Jamaica. The second eldest of five children, Everal has a very close relationship with his family. His sister and mother live close by and visit on a weekly basis. They also regularly attend church together. A trained engineer, Everal is responsible for setting up and repairing equipment all over Britain, including Wales, so he travels frequently. When I first met him his youngest daughter was six months old; she is now a teenager. Everal and Sharon have remodeled and renovated their three-bedroom home and turned it into a five-bedroom, three-bath mansion. Over the years I have watched them move up the class ladder and achieve their goals.

On a Friday afternoon we sat down at his dining-room table to discuss his childhood and events that led to his current life. I could hear the laughter of his youngest daughters playing outside with a white friend in a plastic swimming pool. Our conversation was punctuated by the constant ringing of the telephone, sometimes the landline, other times the cell phone. Rhea, his eldest daughter, called to tell her father that she loves him. Several minutes later Sharon phoned from work. Then we returned to our discussion of his values and his friendship network.

Everal distanced himself from his childhood friends. He criticized their failure to provide for their children and their constant pursuit of sexual adventure with multiple women. In his view, his wife and his "agreement with God" have kept him on track and distinguish him from those friends, who remain unmarried and have fathered multiple children by different white women. Everal shifts from an analysis of the behavior of his black male peers to make two arguments. First, he situates interracial sexual relations within a demographic context, before moving to an analysis of the sexual style and cultural differences between black and white women. In his view, black men are aggressively pursued and desired by white women because they are viewed as offering something culturally and sexually different from white men: "We were predominantly around English people. We had to make do with what [women] were available. . . . English girls were intrigued by the character of the black man. You could create an intimate relationship more easily with an English girl. Black girls weren't entertaining that. A sexual relationship with English girls—quite often they would be approaching us more than we needed it."

Everal drew racial and gender distinctions regarding what is sexually acceptable among black Christians in his family. He expects his four daughters to follow a strict code of premarital sexual abstinence that protects their reputation and ensures their virginity. The black women I spoke with confirmed this expectation. They also argued that they supported sexual abstinence before marriage (even though they themselves had not abstained), that they were not willing to engage in the same sexual practices as white women, and that, in contrast to white women, they would not sexually subordinate themselves to the desires of black men: there would have to be a negotiation. Black men and black women argued that white women had different expectations about intimacy and were willing to engage in sexual practices that the black women in their circle considered deviant, such as anal sex, oral sex, and group sex.

Everal continued to describe his former life, before he became a Christian, and the gender code that he and his male friends followed in his youth: "A girlfriend in every town . . . no serious relationships. We always used to have two or three girlfriends. That was classed as normal. It wouldn't have been common to use contraception." In Everal's view, the performance of urban masculinity still requires engaging in unprotected sex with numerous partners and no long-term obligations; thus the women often end up pregnant. It is for this reason that Everal fears his daughters will follow the practices of their white English peers, engaging in unprotected premarital sex and thus becoming pregnant prior to marriage. He is convinced that all of his daughters are virgins, including his eldest, who is twenty-one. His insistence on a Victorian code of chastity that places all of the responsibility on girls is clearly informed by his practices as a young man. He stated with complete confidence and no irony (and this was confirmed by his wife) that he expects his daughters to remain virgins until marriage, because in his view, "At the end of the day the boys can walk away and [my daughters] can't. That's my view. Take this into consideration: if I wasn't a married person with a house, I think I could have settled into that lifestyle. I've got to achieve something. I have no alternative." The paradox for Everal is that his daughters strongly identify with their white English mother, with whom they have a close and affectionate relationship. Although Everal was sexually active as a young man prior to his marriage to Sharon, he expects his daughters to reject sexual adventure and promiscuity, which he considers a central part of English culture.

Everal views Sharon's cultural style as inappropriate for girls being raised in a Christian household, and thus a potential source of injury to his four daughters. He fears that she will assimilate them into an English way of life. As a young unmarried woman, Sharon engaged in premarital sex, frequent partying, and drinking, which are associated with sexually loose working-class white women. Although she is monogamous and faithful to her husband, the weight of her past sexual promiscuity and the culture of her parents can always be invoked to blame her if her daughters violate this Victorian gender code. Despite all the cultural adaptations that she has made Sharon continues to be stigmatized by her class background, her cultural style, and her sociability.

During a dinner with Sharon and Everal in 2004, Sharon said that she and Everal have had to make compromises and adjustments, and that she doesn't tell him everything that goes on with their daughters. Everal acknowledged being aware that Sharon distributes information to him in an edited form and sometimes withholds details about his daughters' activities that would upset him. He did not challenge Sharon when she claimed, "Anything bad that they do is blamed on me and my whiteness," thereby demonstrating that they both agree that Sharon's whiteness is interpreted through a "class lens" and that her black relatives fear that she is not transferring their cultural values to her children.

Conclusion: Multicultural Navigators and the Whiteness Spectrum

The signs of whiteness were historically equated with economic and cultural supremacy, sexual purity, and respectability; however, the value and meaning of whiteness has shifted among certain segments of postcolonial English society. Black members of transracial families in Leicester conceptualize whiteness as an elastic position that can accommodate both status and stigma. Upwardly mobile black members of transracial families carefully consider economic and cultural distinctions among white mothers. They recognize the varieties of whiteness on a class-inflected spectrum. Class inequality, anti-black racism, pre-marital and pre-maternal sexual histories, and religious commitments shape how black family members evaluate their white wives, partners, and sisters-in-law as morally adequate, culturally competent, and racially conscious mothers. Whiteness, like blackness, is an achievement. In a field of shifting power relations, whiteness has multiple meanings and its value can vary depending on the family dynamics, the local community, and the resources available to the family.

The value of whiteness is diminished for white women of working-

FIGURE 54 Owen Brown, the husband of Sharon Dawkins's close friend, and the author.

class origins who possess little or no educational capital, symbolic capital, or cultural capital save for their femininity. Their whiteness, rather than being a source of status or a social resource, can become a stigma, and in some cases a liability, if it is a degraded version of whiteness associated with excessive drinking or alcoholism, sexual indiscretion, religious indifference, and other characteristics that are ascribed to white working-class English culture. White women who become the partners of black men may become positioned within their families and communities as both cultural and racial outsiders.

8

~~~

GENDER GAPS IN THE EXPERIENCE OF INTERRACIAL INTIMACY

> It's my view that women, be they white or black, who are in inter-
> racial relationships have a harder time. They're abused more by both
> black and white people. I think men don't have as difficult a time,
> as difficult an experience.—CAROL, THE BLACK FORMER WIFE OF A WHITE
> BRITISH MAN

Generally speaking, white men in committed relationships with black women have been absent from analyses of whiteness and interracial intimacy. To fill this empirical and theoretical gap I analyze four interracial married couples who formed relationships between 1972 and 1984 and were between the ages of thirty-three and sixty-one when I recruited them into my study. These couples varied in their analyses of the impact of race and racism on their lives. The two white fathers, who were involved in antifascist and antiracist political action, expressed the most sophisticated understanding and analysis of racism, although all the men were able to discuss how they came to understand the impact of their whiteness and gender. Of particular significance is the finding that white and black women, when compared to white and black men, are more likely to experience racial abuse in the public sphere. They typically express more intense fears of social rejection by friends and the isolation that accompanies this.

Stephen Hawkes: A Racially Literate Rastafarian

The father of two black sons who wear their hair locked in dreads, Stephen, a graphic artist and residential social worker, is married to

FIGURE 55 Stephen Hawkes with his eldest son, Zizwe.

Netifnet Arthur-Hawkes (see chapter 7). They met in 1982 at the pre-dominantly black Seventh Day Adventist church in Leicester, which her parents attended. Six months later they married in a religious cere-mony in a Baptist church (1983) — two years after the race riots that swept through urban areas of England. They are now Rastafarians, having since rejected the Christian network that brought them together.

With a soft-spoken voice and long dreadlocks reaching past his waist, Stephen is very different from middle-class white fathers in multiracial families who live relatively conventional lives in white middle-class neighborhoods, with their black wives and brown children the only dis-tinguishing features of their life. His dreadlocks increase his marginaliza-tion. He lives in a working-class black world and all of his closest male friends are working-class black men. The art he produces, the music he listens to, his friendships with black men, and his residential community reflect his deep roots in and ties to the African Caribbean community and its culture.

Stephen differs from the other white fathers I interviewed in that he and his wife shared the same scripts as they narrated their lives. They seemed to speak with one voice, even when interviewed separately in private discussions. He described himself as stigmatized and as having relinquished the value of whiteness. His beard, his spiritual beliefs, his dreadlocks, his black wife, and his two sons restrict his ability to convert his whiteness into capital.

Stephen has a nuanced analysis of the forms of racial abuse his wife has endured. When asked to describe how racism shapes his life, he described a routine form of abuse and social rejection that Netifnet has experi-enced: "I've actually seen it's not about me. [My wife] has been called a traitor, a Judas because of being with a white man. There are times where I think the silent or hidden way that racism manifests itself is tied with the need for survival within a black community under siege."

Stephen also differs from other men I interviewed by living a black rather than a multiethnic life. Describing his social network, he said, "My dominant group of friends are black men. . . . The acceptance by black men is greater than by the white men." He also described being perceived as a vagrant because of his dreadlocks and long beard. He and his wife lived in Barbados for two years, a period he described as a time when he "spoke to two white people in two years." Living in Barbados had a pro-found impact on him and also distinguishes him from whites who live and work in Africa as employees of Christian organizations but remain immersed in white networks. Stephen was not employed in Barbados and did not go there to work as part of a British corporate structure. He worked and saved money for their trip and they lived slightly above poverty during their time there.

As a young man Stephen took part in antifascist campaigns in the 1970s. He participated in solidarity marches against the local fascists, though he was not involved in electoral politics and did not belong to any organized network. In the late 1970s and early 1980s he was a member of what he described as a "nonaligned left-wing group." Looking back on this period seventeen years later, he said, "Now I feel better able, just on a daily basis, I think with other white people, to question racism and not feel that I'm likely to get in a fight from doing so. . . . Whereas in the past . . . all of my previous experience was such that I felt the world was so hostile."

Like working-class white women raising their children of multiracial heritage alone, Stephen is one of the rare white fathers who have to manage a stigmatized identity. It is not his status as the father of children of African descent and the husband of a black woman, but rather his dreadlocks, beard, and residence in a poor, inner-city district that reposition him outside of respectability. He described his efforts to manage this stigma: "I think there's a strong tradition of [Christian] men not having beards and . . . a man wearing a beard is almost akin to not [taking care of] yourself. . . . At times, I felt that I was treated [by white people] as though I was a *tramp*, as someone whom people would define as a homeless person, a vagrant, by appearance." Stephen's appearance stems from his decision to embrace Rastafarianism and to adopt a cultural style associated with blackness, which distances him from white people of middle-class origin. He is conscious of the choices he has made: "I try very hard to disassociate myself from many of the ways I associate with being stereotypically white, which is reliant upon racism." This includes rejecting conventional rules, such as being clean-shaven, wearing his hair short, and distancing himself socially and politically from black people. He also sees himself as a racial outsider: "There'd be a lot of white men who would choose not to be involved with black women on a long-term basis."

White men like Stephen occupy a paradoxical position. Although he is white, he lacks the resources and the cultural motivation to transfer his racial or class privilege to his sons. Raised in a white middle-class family, he has rejected all of the cultural norms and gender conventions that structured his parents' life. He is no longer affiliated with the white community and does not consider himself a member of the white community. He has moved from an "off-white" position to that of "honorary black." While he continues to be physically qualified for whiteness, he is no longer racially privileged.

Derek Inham: An Honorary Black in the Music Scene

A tall, thin, olive-skinned white man with dirty blond hair and tattoos on his arms, Derek Inham stands out among his black friends. Born in 1964, he is the son of a Dutch woman born in Ceylon (now Sri Lanka) and an English man. He left school when he was fifteen and has no academic qualifications. He is employed as a forklift driver for an American overseas firm. In 1997, when I met Derek and his wife, Alexis, the daughter of immigrants from Antigua and Montserrat, they had been married for more than four years and had one son. They live in a modest two-bedroom, terraced home in a white working-class neighborhood of Leicester. During the third year of my field research, Alexis gave birth to their second son; by the time I finished my research their older son was sixteen and their younger seven.

Derek belongs to a small cohort of white men in Leicester whose love of black music moved them into black male friendship networks and brought black women into their lives. In fact, one-third of the white men interviewed reported meeting their wives through music or dance. There are four avenues that lead to interracial marriage for white men: going to black nightclubs, having friendships with black men, attending a black church, and participating in antiracist political activism.

Explaining how he became socially integrated into a predominantly black network, Derek described being rejected by the white boys in his school because his mother was an immigrant and he was perceived as not being English, despite his father's English background. This motivated him to distance himself from English culture and drift toward his black schoolmates: "[This was] one way of like rejecting that side of the culture . . . the white side of the culture, because as far as I could see, there was no need for [whites] to [reject me]." Of greater significance than his feeling of alienation from whites was his love affair with music that inspired him to socialize with blacks: "The major force . . . I liked soul and disco and

FIGURE 56 Derek Inham and his sons, Jamal and Caleb (in his arms).

everything else. That was the main reason I started mixing with every-body, with people from *that side*. I generally went to black clubs, black nightclubs, dances, whatever else was going on."

At the same time that Derek was discovering black music as a teen-ager in the late 1970s, the gender and racial composition of the second-ary schools was changing from being gender-segregated and all-white to being multiethnic and coeducational. The numbers of Asian and black students increased dramatically. When he was fourteen Derek started fre-quenting black clubs, socializing with blacks, and establishing friendships with black males. He became accustomed to being the "only white guy in a group of thirty or forty." He established close friendships with black men and women and began dating black women at seventeen. Although he became accustomed to being a minority among his new acquaintances he never described a moment of epiphany in which he could suddenly see racism and his own racialization. Instead he continued to frame the narrative of his life in terms of music and being "in a gang."

His future wife was a member of a larger social network of people with whom he went clubbing. They met in 1984.

> I started taking interest [in her] while we were going out and things like that because we all used to dance together. . . . We all used to dance as a group kind of thing. . . . We all used to dance as a group instead of dancing by the woman. . . . We spent most of the time together anyway when we were going out because I spent most of my time [clubbing] anyways. It just seemed like . . . the next thing to do was probably move in together. Alexis would say that the reason I moved in with her is because my mum was selling her house and gen-erally I had nowhere to go. But I wasn't thinking that way.

It is evident that racism is not a central concern of Derek's. In our con-versations he never explicitly mentioned racism when he described his relationship with Alexis or discussed the birth of his children. His life continues to be organized primarily around his interest in music.

What is striking about Derek and his racial consciousness is that his understanding of the meaning of his whiteness and of racism does not ap-pear to have changed as a consequence of his marriage to a black woman. He told me (and his wife confirmed) that he had never discussed the issues of racism or race with her. There is no evidence that he experienced anything that might have motivated him to think more carefully about how race shaped his wife's life.

When I asked Derek about his parents, he carefully avoided any mention of his mother's racist treatment of Alexis or of her threat to socially distance herself from her grandchildren before their births because they might be "too dark." The only statement he made about race or color was that he had suffered discrimination because he was darker than his white male peers at school. He embraced a race-evasive discourse and emphasized that birth order, rather than race, was his mother's focus: "As far as my mum was concerned . . . he was their *first* grandson so that was the major factor for them. It didn't matter whether he was black or white or whatever. . . . I think it's brought them closer to Alexis as far as that's concerned. . . . I think they accepted her a lot more that way because . . . they've never had contact with blacks." Although Derek carefully avoided any mention of his mother's possible racism, he alluded to cultural distance between his parents and his wife prior to the birth of their first son. This was one of the only moments when "difference" was mentioned as significant.

When I asked Derek how he would describe the culture of his home environment, he replied, "I think we're more—it's probably more white, white things, more towards white culture than anything else. . . . The things we eat . . . fish and chips. Alexis's not too big on Caribbean cooking because generally her mum will do that kind of thing, so she'll eat at her mum's if she wants that. I don't mind. I'll eat anything." Derek's reference to food when asked about the ethnic culture of his home supports the argument that food is a central marker of ethnic boundaries and identity (see chapter 6). Given his attachment to his music, however, it is surprising that he used food, rather than music, to define the ethnic character of his home. Moreover, although Derek's family may eat "white food," the amount of time that his older son spent with his black Antiguan grandmother, who taught her grandson the folktales with which she grew up, fed him Antiguan food, and socialized him into Caribbean humor, speech, food, and friendship networks, must be considered when analyzing the cultural world of the Inham family.

Interestingly, Derek's analysis of the ethnic culture of their lives was very different from Alexis's. Where Derek minimized the significant role his black in-laws play in the lives of his sons, his wife maintains that her older son lives a black life because he goes to school in her old neighborhood and spends all of his leisure time and afterschool time with his black grandparents. The perceptual gap may be partially explained by their experiential gap, since Derek spends significantly less time than his wife caring for their sons. Thus he may not be conscious of the cultural impact his black in-laws have on his children.

Alexis Inham: Intrafamilial Racism

Like her husband, Alexis is a native of Leicester. Born in 1962, she is the third of four daughters of first-generation black Britons of Caribbean origin. Her mother, a native of Antigua, and her father, a native of Montserrat, immigrated to England in the 1960s. In 1992, when their son was three years old, she married Derek in a religious ceremony in the Church of England. All of their relatives attended. She described her parents' attitudes toward race and ethnic boundaries: "My mum and dad classed it that you're one race. You're human beings and it doesn't matter what your color you are. . . . We've all got to learn to live on the planet together, so if you get on with them, why make an enemy of somebody just because of their color? Why toss [a potential friendship] away just because of their coloring?"

Employed as a housing officer for the DeMontfort Housing Authority, a nonprofit organization that provides housing to poor people who cannot afford to pay rent or buy a home, Alexis's income puts her family in the lower-middle class.

Alexis described her closest friends growing up: "[There was] a set of four black girls who went to the same school as me, one Italian, and three white English girls." Until her twenty-first birthday, she had never experienced any racial abuse or racism because she attended a multiracial school in a poor inner-city area where whites were not culturally dominant, and like the Asian Indians they self-segregated. Her friendship network was ethnically mixed and included white girls who were accustomed to being ethnic minorities.

When Alexis was seventeen she followed her sister on the path to Rastafarianism and was a Rasta for several years: "I got fed up with it because they're hypocritical. They'd be saying 'We black sisters should wait for them [black men].' [Black men] can go off and do their thing—which is to date anybody they wanted: black, white, Chinese. We couldn't date anybody except for black men. You would be letting the black race down." Every black woman I interviewed agreed that they had been

FIGURE 57 Alexis, Caleb, Jamal, and Derek Inham in their living room.

strongly discouraged by their black male siblings and friends from dating white men, while black men readily endorsed romantic relationships with white women.

Despite this inconsistent male position, only a few black women admitted that black men had physically threatened them with violence for dating interracially. Alexis described an incident that occurred one year after she began dating Derek, which illustrates one form of policing that black women encountered in the mid-1980s: "I had been going out with [my husband] for a year. And two Rasta guys actually came up and told me exactly what I just described to you: 'You're letting the race down. You're a traitor. Think about slavery.' And if I didn't stop going out with Derek, they threatened to actually cut him up." It is significant that this threat was made to Alexis, not Derek, and that during our conversations Derek never mentioned experiencing any tensions or hostilities with black men or being policed by them in any way. In fact, he described nothing but very close and affectionate bonding with black men. This incident suggests that Alexis (and her white female friends) were targeted by black and white men opposed to interracial relationships, while Derek, her white boyfriend at the time, could continue to socialize and circulate in these same black clubs and interzones with little awareness of the problems Alexis was encountering. Despite the fact that the men threatened to harm Derek, they never did, and Derek was not aware that he was at risk.

Although the intraracial gender gap remains, and there are more black men romantically involved with white women than black women with white men, in Alexis's view this "gap is closing":

There are a lot more black girls going out with white guys now. . . . When I first started going out with Derek, [one woman] actually said to me . . . "I can't understand why you would ever go out with a white guy. I would never be able to go out with a white guy." She now will only date white men. . . . And when she told me this, I gently reminded her of what she actually said to me [in the past]. According to one of my other friends, they think that white guys treat them better than black guys. The examples they gave me was they are more considerate. They respected them and didn't mess around with other women when they were with them. And they treated them like they were the only thing that matters. . . . Basically they were generalizing [to all white men] because the ones that they've been out with are nice. And I said to them, "That's not the case. You will find that there are some [white men] that are just as bad, if not worse than a black man." So even though I go out with Derek and I married Derek, I still think that there's good and bad in both [races].

Alexis's description of how she and Derek met in the black club scene was the same as her husband's. Like Derek she described a good friendship that was organized around music, dancing, and clubbing. According to Alexis, Derek was a respected deejay and a standout musician. He asked her out after several years of friendship. Their analysis differed when his mother's response to their relationship was mentioned. Alexis recalled the first time she was brought home to meet his mother:

He brought me into the house. [His mother] said, "Oh, hell." She sat me down in the dining room and then she took Derek into the kitchen, forgetting that there was no door there. Or she did it deliberately. I never did know to this day. And she turned around and she actually said to Derek, "Oh, no Derek, how can you go out with one of *those* again."

I actually heard her and I sat there. And this was the first time I ever went to her house.

And Derek says, "Well, you know, you know what she's like."

I said, "Well, no. I don't actually know what she's like because that was the first time I ever met your mum."

He goes, "Well, you know, she's a bit of the old school."

And then the second time, I really found that she didn't like me because I was black. . . . Derek left me in the house with her and she ignored me. I said, "You've got a problem with me, haven't you?"

She looked at me and said, "I don't know what you're talking about."

I said, "You've got a problem with me. Is it because of my color?"

And her exact words—I remember them to this day—were "What mother wouldn't want her son to go out with a nice, respectable, white girl?"

"How do you know I'm not respectable? You're judging me based on my color and not on who I am," I said. "You don't even know me," I said. "You haven't even made an effort to get to know me, but you've already prejudiced that because I'm not white, I'm not respectable."

And she wouldn't look me in the eye.

"What have I done? Have I got two heads? No, I haven't. The only difference is the fact that my skin is darker than Derek's and it's darker than yours, so I can't understand it."

She just sat there and totally ignored me until Derek came home.

These experiences led Alexis to fear how her white mother-in-law would treat her children, the same fear described by close to half of the white transracial mothers I interviewed. When she gave birth to her first child she didn't know how much social contact, if any, she should allow him to have with his white grandparents. When Alexis discussed her fear with her parents, they cautioned her not to restrict her son's contact and suggested that he needed to be given the opportunity to negotiate his own relationship with his grandparents. Her parents believed that if his white grandmother made racist comments, he would eventually learn to evaluate them and challenge her, and that if Alexis restricted the contact he might later resent her for it. While Alexis struggled with this issue, Derek continued to avoid directly challenging his mother's racism and minimized its impact.

There were, however, shifts in her mother-in-law's behavior over time. For example, although there were tensions between Alexis and her mother-in-law for years and although Alexis perceived her as overtly racist and unwelcoming, she actively participated in their wedding by sewing Alexis's wedding dress and her bridesmaids' dresses. Alexis explained this change as follows: "I think she's learned to accept the fact that I'm still here. And because we're married, she's got to live with it. I still think she's racist, but she's learned. It's only over the last couple of years that me and her have actually started to have a conversation because when we were getting married, she did actually help with everything." Like some of the white mothers I interviewed, Alexis learned how to negotiate the racism of the white members of her family, while her white husband avoided the issue of racism altogether.

The nature of intrafamilial racism is often dynamic. In Alexis's family, the birth of a grandchild was a catalyst for changes in the behavior of her white mother-in-law, if not in her racial attitudes toward blacks as a group. Alexis's son has developed a close and affectionate relationship with his grandmother. Alexis acknowledged that her mother-in-law's racism had softened, at least toward her mixed-race grandson: "At the end of the day, she does, she does love Jamal. . . . She does love him one hundred percent. She'd do anything for him, even now. So that's why I continue to allow him to see her."

Kevin Hudson: From Color-Blindness to Racism Awareness

Kevin Hudson, the son of a central heating engineer, was born in 1960 in Birmingham, a city in the West Midlands of England. In 1992, one year after Kevin's first marriage ended, his closest male friend got a job in Leicester and moved out of Birmingham, and Kevin began visiting each weekend. During one visit he was invited to a party organized by a black music group. Describing how he met his wife, Dorothy Francis, he identified the significant role of black music as an interracial zone and a leisure space that provided him with social access to black women:

> This is a big story. This is the one I usually tell when I'm drunk because I'm ashamed to tell anybody how much I love [my wife]. I am absolutely in love with my wife. . . . One night—it was at a friend's house so I got to the party. Had a good dance. Ended up being taught to dance by Dot's sister and some of her friends. . . . I was really into reggae music, but you know, this particular white boy couldn't dance, so they're trying to teach me to dance, which was very good fun. . . . I'd been drinking quite a bit. . . . I must have seen Dorothy scooting around at some point. But gradually people were drifting away. . . . In the end, I think there were about four people left at this party. . . . And Dorothy's there and she's got [her daughter with her, who was eight months old at the time]. So Dorothy says, "Can you look after my daughter?" and plumped her on my lap. I said, "What do I do now?" She said, "Well, entertain her."

Over the next several months Kevin became a fixture at these black-organized events and a central member of this black music group. He helped serve drinks at the bar, collected money at the door, and cleaned up afterward, which brought him into regular contact with Dorothy, one of the group's organizers. She had a young daughter from a previous relationship with a black Jamaican. Eventually he developed a casual friendship with her, but he wanted more. One evening she invited him to accompany her to a gospel music concert. Although he disliked gospel music, he went on what was their first date. Within a few months he was spending every weekend and some weekday nights with her. Because

FIGURE 58 Dorothy Francis and Kevin Hudson.

Dorothy was enrolled in an intensive university course and needed child care so that she could focus on her studies, Kevin began taking care of her daughter on the weekends. He would pick the child up on Friday night, take her to his place in Birmingham, and bring her back to Leicester on Sunday evening.

Kevin and Dorothy now live in a four-bedroom terraced home in Clarendon Park, a middle-class neighborhood adjacent to the University of Leicester. Besides Dorothy's daughter, they are the birth parents of a second daughter who was born in 1994. When asked to describe how he changed after being married to a black woman, Kevin cited his increased awareness of "everyday racism" and his shift in consciousness:

> Now, having spent time with [my wife] I realize that I am a bit [racist] in terms of . . . preconceptions and ideas that you have [about black people]. . . . There were jokes about the length of a black man's penis. . . . My attitude then was, "Well, I'd quite like somebody to make a joke about . . . how big mine was." . . . And [my wife] sort of explained to me, and once it had been explained to me, I thought, "You're right." . . . I used to tell jokes like that, but I've avoided those now. . . . As soon as somebody starts to tell a joke that's got any mention of the race or whatever of the person, I tend to frown. And then afterwards I dissect the joke.

Kevin has learned to analyze and critique cultural practices that he previously took for granted, such as jokes about the genitalia of black men. After his wife taught him to deconstruct these jokes and to understand why they are dehumanizing and degrading to black people, he can no longer listen to them with "white ears." He has acquired a form of racial literacy that enables him to evaluate routine practices that he identifies as "everyday racism."

His discussions with his wife have not only altered his understandings of what race and racism mean; they have led him to radically change. Although his friendship network remains predominantly white, his current friends' social practices and racial ethics distinguish them from his previous circle of white friends: "Going back twenty years to when I was seventeen, there would certainly be an element within my social circle and people that I met regularly who were racially prejudiced. . . . I've moved out of those circles now, and those circles still exist, but they're somebody else's circle. . . . I don't have any people in my immediate con-

tact that [I] have any problem with [in] regards [to] their racial ethics."
As Kevin has made changes in his social network and his definitions of
racism have changed, he has left his predominantly white working-class
network for a middle-class and multiracial world that includes his black
in-laws and his wife's black Caribbean friends and colleagues. His assessment of his own behavior has also shifted because he now analyzes many
of his social interactions from the perspective of his dark-skinned Jamaican British wife. He now perceives forms of everyday racism and is able
to decipher racial codes that were not visible to him prior to his marriage.
He no longer thinks of racism as something outside of his social experiences.

What is striking about Kevin's description of his experiences is their
sharp contrast to those of the white women I interviewed. He reported
no opposition from his white friends or family members to his relationship with Dorothy. Instead his primary struggles involved Dorothy's ambivalence and anxiety about being involved with a white man, given
her political opposition to interracial relationships. Kevin struggled to
understand why Dorothy closeted their relationship for the first year, and
he felt hurt, frustrated, and helpless when she did not invite (or allow)
him to accompany her on a trip back to Jamaica to visit her relatives nine
months after they had begun dating.

When Kevin began dating Dorothy, he embraced a color-blind discourse, to which he sometimes clings, although he has learned to recognize some forms of everyday racism. When asked how the black community viewed interracial relationships, he replied that he didn't know
because he had been "shielded" from that issue by Dorothy:

> As far as I was concerned . . . people are people, and I didn't see black
> or white. I just saw friends or people that I didn't know. And yet
> Dorothy had apparently said at some point that . . . she'd never go out
> with a white man or she'd never marry a white man. . . . She did say
> that to somebody at some point. I felt really helpless. . . . There was
> clearly nothing I could do about [past racism, slavery, British colonial-
> ism]. . . . I just felt that I had to just keep doing what I was doing. . . .
> I would just keep loving her.

That Kevin embraced a color-blind discourse while white women
in interracial relationships became even more aware of their racialization and how they were treated suggests that both the white and black

communities are more punitive toward the *women* in these relationships. The women are more often the targets of verbal abuse and criticism, and white working-class women endure the most verbal abuse. Kevin's gender and racial privilege appeared to protect him from criticism and from the negative assaults that concerned Dorothy. On the other hand, Dorothy had a fear shared by many of the white women in this study: the fear of suffering rejection and disapproval from her close friends and associates. Although the fourteen white men I interviewed cannot be considered a representative group, it is nevertheless striking that none described being verbally abused or feeling that their respectability or morality was called into question. By contrast, virtually all of the white women I interviewed described being ridiculed, rejected, or disciplined for their relationships.

Dorothy Francis: From Rejection to Acceptance of Interracial Marriage

The daughter of immigrants from rural Jamaica, Dorothy Francis moved to Coventry at the age of five. She described being subjected to constant routine racism as a child at school. Married to Kevin Hudson in a church ceremony in 1994, she became pregnant with her second child during their honeymoon. Dorothy's analysis of the early years of her relationship with Kevin differed dramatically from her husband's experience: "Kevin always paints a bit of a fairy-tale romance. In some ways it was, but what he doesn't seem to remember is the bad times we had whilst I made up my mind as to whether or not we stayed together." In striking contrast to the black men I interviewed, she focused on the problems his whiteness generated for her as a politically conscious black woman. Dorothy had been strongly opposed to interracial marriage:

> I was very adamant that I wouldn't have relationships with white men because I didn't think they were politically correct. And also I wasn't prepared for that hostility [from the black community]. And there were lots of nice black men around, so I thought, "I will stick with my own because it makes life easier." The first thing my mother said when I said I was going to marry Kevin: "I would never ever have expected you to marry a white man. Any of my children—I didn't expect you to." Because I was always so adamant. I was always so political. I had many, many arguments with my mother about how wrong it is to marry white people. And how wrong it is to have, what I would have

then called "mixed-race" children because of the burden it puts on them of not knowing where they are. . . . I had many a debate with my mother because my mother doesn't actually feel that way. My mother is actually very liberal. . . . She's a church woman. She believes that there's good in everybody. And you can't damn a whole race just because of their skin color.

Eventually, however, Dorothy shifted her position on interracial marriage and agreed to marry Kevin:

Even with Kevin, it was very difficult because what he probably didn't say [when you interviewed him] . . . is that I finished with him time and time and time again when we first started going out together because I felt that our relationship was wrong, until he got really frustrated one day. "If I kept finishing with you and saying 'I cannot see you any more because you're black,' you would accuse me of being a racist."

And I said, "Yes, I would."

And he says, "So why is it okay for you to continue finishing with me all the time and telling me to go away because I'm white."

I said, "Because it's different. It's politically different. It's different for me as a black woman in a relationship with a white man. It's your coming from, not just different angles in terms . . . like gender, but in terms of the history."

But in the end, I looked at [the relationship] and I thought, "Well, this guy doesn't beat me. He doesn't abuse me. He treats me well. And I actually realized that he did love me." And I thought, "Well, why are you fighting this?" And I realized the reason why I was fighting it is because he was white. If he'd been what he was, but black, we'd have not been having any of those debates. We were only having these debates because he was white. And really what I wanted—if I could have waved a magic wand—I'd have wanted him, at least, a little bit brown, you know, just brown, just black so I could deal with it. I just wanted him in black skin, then I wouldn't have to worry about all these issues. And I thought, "Well, this is real life. You ain't got a magic wand, and he's not going to be brown, so you either finish with him or you continue with it and you deal with the issues." . . . I decided to continue with it . . . because I really knew that I loved him, so therefore

I thought, "I can deal with situations. I can deal with people rejecting me."

None of the black or white men I interviewed described going through this type of excruciating evaluation of the social costs of committing to an interracial relationship. It was only the women, and particularly the black women, who struggled like this.

It took Dorothy several years to resolve her feelings of ambivalence and anxiety about how she would manage Kevin's whiteness:

> From the moment we got serious, then I always knew that we would marry because I wanted the black community to see that I was not being abused by him, because a lot of the black community would look at it and think, "Oh, there's another white man with a black woman just taking advantage of her. . . . And I wanted the white community to see that it was legitimate. . . . I wanted them to see that it wasn't, you know, this master-slave relationships thing again, but it was a matter of choice, so it was important that we marry.

In contrast to her husband, Dorothy struggled with how the black community would perceive their relationship and whether she had the strength and courage to sustain a relationship her black friends and associates would not support. Like several of the white women I interviewed, Dorothy had to reconstitute her community once she made a decision to marry a white man.

The Racial Closet

More than half of the white women reported closeting their interracial relationships, concealing them from friends and members of their family, for periods ranging from a few months to several years. This is one strategy they employed to protect themselves from racial abuse, rejection from family, and exile. They negotiated their relationship in private or until family members discovered them or a pregnancy forced them to reveal it. None of the white men expressed concern about the reaction of their families, and none reported concealing their relationships.[1]

The black women involved in interracial relationships experienced forms of rejection and discipline similar to the white women I interviewed. Dorothy's experiences illustrate this point. During the first years of her relationship with Kevin, she was not certain about its future, which made her reluctant to invite him to Jamaica and introduce him to her Jamaican relatives.[2] When she went to Jamaica for several weeks in 1993, she did not invite him to accompany her. Kevin found this upsetting and challenging. Initially he was unable to recognize her concerns, but he slowly began to see the perceptual and experiential gaps that separated them. While he was not facing pressures from his social network to date intraracially, Dorothy had to negotiate the negative attitudes of her close friends and associates, who did not approve of interracial relationships but whose support she did not want to lose. In Kevin's words, "[Rejection and disapproval were] a problem that Dorothy felt she was going to have with some of her associates . . . where I was, to a degree, shielded from that." All of the black women I interviewed, whether or not they were married interracially, expressed either strong opposition to interracial marriage and had initially rejected white men as desirable partners.

In contrast to their white male partners and their black male siblings, black women admitted their discomfort with taking their white partners to black events. Carol, a divorced mother of a four-year-old daughter, presents a view that was representative of the university-educated black women I interviewed. Born in 1961 in London, she married a white man in 1983. They met when she was doing her student training as a nurse on a medical unit: "I know there are [places] where I would not have taken a white man." She expressed feeling more accepted socially at black events as a single mother than she did when she was married to a white man. Although it is known that she is raising a daughter fathered by a white man, she doesn't anticipate verbal abuse or criticism from black men or women at these events. In striking contrast, none of the white *men* reported experiencing verbal abuse from black men or black women at black social events. They rarely encountered any explicit criticism of their choice of partner. Adam Chase is an exception (see chapter 7), but he didn't report this to me or discuss it with me; I learned of his sister's (Joyce Chase Stephens's) opposition to his relationship directly from her. Although some black men knew that their mother did not initially approve of their interracial relationships, nevertheless they did not restrict their relationships in response to this disapproval, nor did they express (to me) any anxieties about their black female friends or the black public.

In contrast to the black husbands and black sisters-in-law of the white mothers whose voices we heard in chapter 7, Kevin knows that he can rely on Dorothy to manage the problems of racism if they emerge as an issue. As the father of two daughters, he is not expected to be responsible, either by himself or with his wife, for preparing his children to cope with racism. Thus despite the racial literacy that Kevin acquired as a consequence of the ongoing antiracist education that he received from his wife, like the black men married to white women he believes that his wife has the primary responsibility for their children's racism-awareness training and dealing with racist incidents. He expects her to perform this labor because, he argues, she has "more experience." For almost all the black and white women who married interracially, there is a similar gendered expectation that they will take the lead in dealing with race issues. As a general rule, this is considered maternal and thus *gendered* labor, regardless of the race of the mother.

Brian Piper: A Professional Antiracist

Born on a Royal Air Force base in 1936 in Hampshire, on the south coast of England, Brian Piper grew up in Braunstone, a white working-class area. After completing two years of compulsory military service for the British Army (1955–57), he went to the University of Birmingham, where, in 1960, he earned a social science degree with a double major in sociology and social psychology. He thus belongs to the first generation of university students to be trained in race relations during a period when Britain was losing most of its overseas possessions. He earned his Post Graduate Certificate in Education in 1961. He was "involved in antiracist activities" as a student and did research on social distance scales (also called "hostility" scales), which measure how much intimacy white people are willing to allow blacks and people of color. This was a radical and new form of research that began in the United States and was later adopted in Britain.

Brian became an antiracist in the early 1960s, when the Methodist International House in London hired him to seek funding for international students and to organize social events for them. In 1963 he was hired by the Methodist Church to "develop organizational structures to welcome foreign university students" at one of their international hostels in London. His job involved implementing strategies to counter the rampant racism that foreign-born university students encountered in London in the late 1960s. He developed strong relationships with some of these students. He met his first wife, a white university student, in London, and they married in 1966. Shortly after their marriage they went to

FIGURE 59 Brian and Annette Piper in their kitchen.

Zambia to work for a Christian organization; they divorced in 1972. His religious faith is central to his work, and he has continued to do antiracist work on behalf of Christian organizations.

In the early 1970s the National Front Party, a neofascist party, selected Leicester as their national headquarters and became a central force in Leicester's political life. Describing the high visibility and political potency of the National Front at that time, Brian recalled, "They got within either three or six votes of getting elected [to the Leicester City Council]. . . . I finally convinced my political colleagues that they'd got to fight them. . . . And so we had this big cross-party alliance against the fascists. It was called Unity Against Racialism and that was a whole year campaign [leading] to the county council elections." Although Brian was not a "demo man," viewing demonstrations and marches as ineffective, he felt that something public had to be done to show that there was white opposition to the National Front. For that reason he helped to organize a march in the late 1970s against the fascists:

> The local communists who I was working with in antiracist . . . common causes said, "Given the way the National Front is building up its strength, we ought to have a march through Highfields to show solidarity with the black people in Highfields." And I said, "Yeah, they're probably right. We ought to have a solidarity march." . . . There were two groups involved: the International Marxist Group . . . and the International Socialist Workers Party . . . and the communists were quite moderate by comparison with this lot.

In Brian's view there had been no civic leadership in dealing with racism. Instead the leadership had simply hoped that the National Front would go away, "like a bad smell." It was then, in his late thirties, that Brian decided to run for a seat on the city council. This is also around the time he met his current wife, Annette. Brian expressed sensitivity and awareness of the demands that his antiracist commitments placed on Annette during the early years of their relationship: "There were some things which, I think, were a little bit difficult because she found that meeting a man who'd got a social conscience had its price. . . . I was standing for city council at the time. And she came out with me and she did the canvassing with me." Describing how he met his second wife, Annette, a native of Trinidad, in 1972, Brian situated his relationship in the context of his antiracist work and his commitment to politics:

I was still following on this commitment I'd made in 1960 to working in race relations, so I'd gone to a multiracial school [to teach]. I'd
bought a house on the edge of Highfields . . . and began getting involved in community politics and joined the Labour Party. . . . I started
going to this church [because I knew the vicar] and he used to have
musical evenings. And one of the local single mums was a girl called
Joan. . . . And Joan said to me one day, "I've got this friend who wants
to come to this musical evening. Would you mind going and fetching
her? She's got a son but she's on her own." . . . And I went around to
collect this young woman. . . . And this gorgeous black woman was
standing at the door, and I thought, "Oh!" And that was it. . . . I took
her back home that night. And we sat there dinking coffee and we
chatted. I talked about Trinidad. . . . I talked about Calypso. . . . She
didn't know a damn thing about what I was talking about because she
had a missionary education.

Annette had learned nothing about the history or culture of Trinidad.
This all changed after they started dating. Brian explains: "In a sense she
realized that she ought to know more about these things and it was very
embarrassing having this bloody white bloke [explaining Trinidadian history to her] since she was a Trinidadian. So she went down to the library
and got a book on the history of Trinidad." In this case, it was Brian who
became an "agent of epiphany" for his black wife.[3] Annette came to realize that she shared more in common with Brian, a white man, than with
her former husband, a black Jamaican who was not interested in racism
or race politics.

Brian and Annette have been married since 1975. They live in a four-
bedroom Georgian home that is nearly three hundred years old in the
village of South Croxton, nine miles outside of Leicester, with a fruit
orchard and a half-acre garden. Historically this small village of eighty
homes was a farming community, but now houses professionals who
commute to Leicester for work. The only business in town is a pub. Brian
adopted Annette's son, and together they had a second son. Their sons
have also followed the path of transracial family formation: their older
son married a white woman, and their younger son, a professional dancer
in London, has a white girlfriend whom I met.

At the age of fifty Brian retired from full-time teaching and established his own business as a consultant and antiracist trainer. His train-

ings and position as a consultant for the Episcopalian Church make him unique among the white fathers interviewed. He described one of the exercises he assigns to antiracist workshop participants:

> I do an exercise, which can take like half the morning, and longer, where we have a set of cards with racist remarks on, and we invite them to play if they want to. If not, they can sit and discuss them. We pair them off and I make the racist remark and you challenge it. But the technique we try to get them to do is *not* to end up defending their racism or antiracism, but getting that person to think twice about what they're saying. The idea is to keep asking, "What do you mean by that?"

How did Brian became a white antiracist, and how did he differ from the other white men in this study? Like other white men in his age cohort, Brian lived through a series of race riots, witnessed the collapse of the British Empire, and had to negotiate the meaning of his whiteness. What distinguishes him from the other white men and women in this study are his decisions to commit himself to organizing against racism in all aspects of his life and to raise two black sons. His relationship with Annette is unusual in that he did not depend on her to educate him. Instead, as best friends, they worked as a team on antiracist educational training projects. Three periods in Brian's life were central to his commitment to organized antiracism: the three years that he spent in London working on behalf of international students at a youth hostel (1963–66), the period he spent in Zambia with his first wife (1966–69), and the time he spent in Leicester organizing against the antifascist activities of the National Front Party (1973–79). It was during these three periods that he shifted his racial consciousness and developed his racial literacy, which is evident from the fact that he clearly chose to be involved in organized antiracist politics.

Brian and Annette had the highest degree of racial literacy of any of the couples interviewed, which is not surprising given the fact that they both teach antiracism workshops and racism-awareness training. Brian acquired racial literacy prior to his relationship with Annette, so having an interracial romantic relationship did not alter his consciousness. Instead he has served as an agent of change for the people he trains and loves, including his wife.

Annette Piper: Unlearning a Colonial Education

Annette Piper, an only child, was born in 1940 in Port of Spain, Trinidad. When she was five years old her father died, leaving her mother to struggle financially. A bright girl, she earned a scholarship to a grammar school and the government paid part of her fees. She passed her A-levels, but lacking the funds to pay for a university education in Trinidad she applied to a nurse's course in England and was immediately accepted.[4] Shortly after she arrived in England she married her first husband.

Annette grew increasingly discontented in her first marriage over issues of race and racism:

> It became quite clear to me that here [in England] racism was an area of life that—if I was going to stay in this country for any number of years—that I would have to not ignore. And that if I ignored it, it would be at my peril. . . . And that no longer could I see England as the mother country, which is what it was to me. In Trinidad . . . we were led to believe that this was the mother country, so I'd assumed that [I] would be accepted with open arms and unconditional love and acceptance, only to find that it really wasn't like that at all. . . . I tried to get my first husband involved in those issues. I actually tried, but like so many black men in this country . . . he didn't want to know. He just didn't see [racism] as an issue, and he rather felt that my stand was an aggressive stance—which it wasn't. I think perhaps that's one of the reasons why the marriage didn't survive, because I think he found me quite challenging to live with. . . . He was keen to have a child, so the child was planned. But I also felt that he lacked the awareness and responsibility that was necessary to help this child get through his life in a very difficult society. . . . I sort of set out to educate myself about issues because the history that I was taught at school saw blacks in a very negative light really. . . . We sort of looked at the history of Africa, but it was always negative aspects with people running around with spears and with very little clothing on. . . . I wasn't taught black history. It was history from a European perspective, which was essentially [derogatory] to blacks. I just found it ironic that I had to come to Brian to become aware of those issues really.

When Annette met Brian, she was the single mother of a nine-year-old son. She had been divorced for several years and had no plans to remarry. She supported her son and herself as a qualified nurse trained in general and psychiatric nursing. One of her closest friends, a white single mother, introduced her to Brian. And it was Brian, an English white man, who began to teach her about Caribbean history and politics, colonialism, and racism. Annette underwent a reeducation project, first going to the library and reading books to which she had not been exposed as a child. Although she was not racially literate when she met Brian, their relationship became a turning point in her racial consciousness.

In striking contrast to Dorothy Francis, who struggled with guilt and anxiety over whether to commit to her husband because of his whiteness, Annette expressed no fears about being rejected by the black community. Her decision to marry Brian was a simple one, and free of the struggle that other black women reported:

> My relationship with my first husband was . . . based on a conscious decision to marry a black male, and that was a more conscious decision than it was when I married Brian. . . . But my marriage to [my first husband], it was one of the most conscious decisions I'd ever made. And ultimately it didn't turn out to be the best decision because even though he was black and Jamaican, he just didn't understand the issues [of racism] at all. He'd never read the newspapers. He just would never become involved in [antiracist] organizations. He just didn't want to know. So when I met Brian and we became friends and eventually set up home together, there wasn't any big problem because so many of [Brian's] friends were black anyway. And he was so involved in so many black situations, a lot of situations where he may well have been the only white person, and he felt comfortable with that. So I think a lot of people just accepted the relationship.

Unlike other similarly situated black women, Annette did not have to invest labor in either educating Brian or integrating him into her social or political network. They were already friends and, most important, they shared political as well as multicultural values. Annette did not perceive Brian's whiteness as a barrier because they had already been working together on political campaigns and were integrated into the same antiracist networks. She did not view herself as having to make any cultural adjustments. Their lives were not segregated by race or gender. Her lack of anxiety and her confidence in her decision were based on Brian's demonstrated political commitments and his immersion in a black social network that he had developed prior to his relationship with her. In contrast to Kevin, Brian did not need to undergo a reeducation project. Because he had already educated himself, Annette did not have to invest emotional and intellectual labor in helping him understand the racism she faced. He possessed the highest degree of racial literacy of the fourteen white men I interviewed.[5]

Conclusion: Agents of Epiphany

Between 1998 and 2003 Karyn McKinney (2005), an American sociologist, collected the racial autobiographies of white university students between the ages of eighteen and twenty-one in four American universities, one northern and three southern. McKinney found that "the majority of young whites perceive and construct whiteness as a liability" and concluded, "Whiteness is a *prompted identity*; that is, most respondents insist that they have not thought in depth about whiteness until asked to do so by the writing guide" (20). McKinney also found that American blacks play a central role as "agents of epiphany" in the lives of those whites who become conscious of their whiteness and learn to see everyday racism: "Most turning points and epiphanies . . . occur as a result of interactions with others whom I call *agents of epiphany*. In stories of whiteness, the usual agents of epiphany are African Americans. An agent of epiphany is usually a friend, classmate, or occasionally a teacher. Less often agents of epiphany are other whites" (25).

Although some white English people I interviewed engaged in what Frankenberg called race-evasive discourses, contrary to McKinney's findings whiteness was not a prompted identity for white members of British interracial families in my study, even prior to their transracial relationships. Living in a postcolonial, postindustrial, and class-stratified society in which whiteness and Englishness have lost some of their value, their whiteness is visible to them, even though their interpretations of its meaning and its value vary. More than half of the working-class whites in this study grew up in multiethnic communities and had attended schools with black, Asian, and Indian children. Their class-inflected version of whiteness became visible to them at an early age, and their position in the British class system facilitated their ability to analyze the ways their lives were structured by late capitalism and postindustrialism, unlike the white Americans McKinney studied.

The white men I discuss in this chapter occupy four different positions, based on their degree of racial literacy and their awareness of racism: professional antiracist (Brian); racially conscious and aware of racism, but leaves this work to his black partner (Kevin); racially literate, an active coparent, and no longer involved in organizing politics (Stephen); and not actively involved in race politics or parenting (Derek). In addition to their position on the spectrum of racial literacy, they also represent four lifestyles: artist or musician (Stephen and Derek), activist (Brian), affiliate (Derek and Kevin), and agent of epiphany (Brian). Agents of epiphany, as used in this study, prompt those around them to rethink the meanings of race, racism, and antiracism, and thereby to change how they live their lives. Brian's work as an activist positions him as a change agent. Derek and Stephen are both artists. Although they differ in their degrees of racial consciousness, both are immersed in black social networks, which makes them what I call "affiliates" (or honorary blacks). Derek was one of only two whites in a network of thirty black deejays and musicians who managed the black music scene in his youth. Stephen is a graphic artist, although he was no longer employed in this area when he became part of this study. Kevin was neither an artist nor an activist, but as his wife's affiliate he became partially immersed in black social networks.

A university education and participation in antifascist or antiracist political activities directly impacted how these couples managed racism and the degree to which there was a gender gap in their perceptions of everyday racism. Their experiences of interracial intimacy differed in two key ways. First, white men, in contrast to white women, were not exiled from their families or culturally defined as sexually deviant or immoral. This can be explained partly by the fact that the white men in this study were at a different point in their lives than the white women. Half of the white men I interviewed did not meet their future black wives as teenagers but as mature men who had already established themselves. The white men were more likely than their female contemporaries to establish their interracial relationship after a divorce and a failed marriage to a white woman (Brian and Kevin). The white men (two-thirds of this study) who established their first marriage with black women typically met their future wives in black nightclubs, black churches, or black social venues. Thus, like Derek and Stephen, they were more likely to be immersed in black friendship networks prior to dating and marriage. As a group, these white men were less likely to be disciplined by parents, peers, or the public for their relationships with black women, which supports the arguments made by blacks that these relationships were an extension of gender hierarchies and the exercise of white masculine privilege. In other words, white men were given license to establish relationships with women of any racial or ethnic background, and although marriage with a white woman might be idealized, the men who rejected this ideal did not encounter the same forms of social ostracism, exile, or abuse that white women experienced. Stephen was exceptional in that his embrace of Rastafarianism placed him on the margins of both white and black middle-class communities.

White men married to black women vary not only in their awareness of racism and their analysis of their whiteness, but in the degree to which they serve as a resource for their black wives. Brian possesses the highest degree of racial literacy of the men I studied, and acting as an agent of epiphany was a tremendous resource for his black wife. Kevin provided emotional support to his wife, but he does not appear to understand the legacies of British colonialism and the ways his whiteness might be a liability for her. Derek's role is more complicated. Although, in contrast to Kevin and Brian, he immersed himself in a black social network at a very early age, he developed neither an interest in nor a deep understanding of the ways racism structures his life or his wife's experiences. As a man immersed in a black male social and cultural network, Derek closely resembles Annette's first husband, a black Jamaican who was not interested in issues of race or racism, but only in black culture. Derek's indifference to race and racism illustrates what I found among one-fourth of the white parents in this study. Finally, Stephen, like Derek, lives the life of a cultural insider among black men. However, Stephen reads black history, writes and produces black-centered art, and is integrated into a black male network, and thus has acquired a politically sophisticated and nuanced understanding of racism and of the meaning of his whiteness. Stephen was the most visible and highly stigmatized white father; in addition to his low income, he is religiously and politically marginalized. Unlike Brian, he is not active in an organized or mainstream antiracist organization, and as a Rastafarian he is culturally on the far edges of the black and white communities.

Brian and Stephen, although they were born twenty-five years apart, are both racially literate and as youth were involved in antiracist political activism. They differ in their class origins and current class positions and thus in the resources available to them. Brian, who is of mixed-class origins but who grew up in a working-class community, became an upper-middle-class Christian living in a small prosperous suburban village, while Stephen, who is from a solidly middle-class Christian family, experienced downward mobility when he became a Rastafarian living very close to poverty. Thus Stephen lives beyond both the white working-class and the middle-class experience.

Derek never mentioned religion and does not organize his life around politics, religion, or racism awareness, nor does he exhibit racial literacy. Like Brian and Stephen, however, virtually all of his close male friends are black. He is immersed in a black male social world through his love of music. Kevin, although he seems to have more white male friends than black, is comfortable around blacks and has acquired some degree of racial literacy from his wife. Thus Kevin comes closest to the white university students who McKinney described as having turning points. Kevin's turning point was his struggle with his wife over how she interpreted his whiteness. Before this he had never thought about the meaning of his whiteness from a black perspective. In contrast, both Stephen and Derek had lived what can best be called off-white lives prior to their marriages. Derek was socially rejected by his white male peers at an early age and moved into black social networks as a teenager, while Stephen became politically active with antifascist groups.

Among the white British men I interviewed whiteness is not a prompted identity. Instead these men, particularly those who grew up in working-class communities, view themselves as possessing some variant of ethnic culture. They live in a multicultural milieu and do not view their rejected whiteness as a culturally empty category. Moreover, unlike the findings of white American scholars (McKinney 2005; Gallagher 2003a, 2003b), only a handful of the whites in my study say that their whiteness is a liability. In fact, while some of their black relatives perceive whiteness as a liability, two-thirds of the whites believe their whiteness is a resource and a benefit for their children of multiracial heritage in terms of dealing with racism.

Recent work by British scholars have provided analyses of how whiteness and white identities are being reimagined, revised, and reconstructed in postcolonial Britain (Byrne 2006; Knowles 2006; Nayak 1997, 2003; Ware 1997). If we are to understand how ordinary white people negotiate race and racism in postimperial and postcolonial national contexts, we need more studies by sociologists, anthropologists, and geographers in different regions of Britain. Half of the working-class whites in my study grew up in multiethnic communities; one-third reported having friendships with or dating blacks at a young age. They did not grow up in communities that were silent about race or racism. White members of black–white transracial families thus do not have the privilege of not thinking about their whiteness. They are forced to see the racial contours and structures that affect their lives, although they respond to this in a wide range of ways.

CONSTRICTED EYES AND RACIAL VISIONS

Writing of her transformation in the late 1970s from a respectable, married wife and mother of two children living with her family in a town in eastern North Carolina to the lesbian partner of a Jewish woman, Minnie Bruce Pratt describes how she became aware of the limits of her perception and knowledge as a white woman. She had been raised not to see racial histories, racial inequalities, and racialized violence in her community. Looking back after she lost custody of her children and reinvented herself, Pratt explained the conditions under which she acquired a different racial and political vision, one that enabled her to see what had previously been invisible to her, and to form antiracist alliances with Jewish women, black women, and other women of color: "I learned a new way of looking at the world that is more accurate, complex, multilayered, multidimensional, more truthful. . . . I feel the *need* to look differently because I've learned that what is presented to me as an accurate view of the world is frequently a lie . . . so I gain truth when I expand my constricted eyes, an eye that has only let in what I have been taught to see" (1988, 34).

These "constricted eyes" provide a metaphor for the experiences of the white transracial parents in this book. What distinguished white women and men who identified racism as a serious problem and actively prepared their children to cope with racism from those who could not, was the ability to perceive various forms of routine racism. Some parents expanded their vision and learned to see "everyday racism" and came to believe that race (and racism) structured social and economic opportunities and that their children, in spite of their white English or Irish parentage,

FIGURE 60 Naomi and her mother, Glenda Terry.

would encounter similar, if not the same forms of racism as black children. These are the parents who had acquired racial literacy.

There are several patterns that distinguish the white members of transracial families who acquired forms of racial literacy from those who did not: (1) the racial and ethnic composition of their friendship networks (as children and adults); (2) informal education from friendship networks, political affiliations, and experience in antiracist political groups; (3) exposure to overt white racism and immersion in multicultural communities as children; (4) relationships with black women; and (5) the racial consciousness of their children's black father or their domestic partner. White parents, like black parents, can learn to decode, recognize, evaluate, and counter the racist climate in their communities. Acquiring racial literacy involved ongoing labor and was not an automatic consequence of being a member of a transracial family. It was a demanding process that required transracial parents to shift their perspective and to learn a number of significant new skills.

Among the white women who were racially literate, two-thirds had raised their children as single mothers or had never married their children's father. They were typically *more* socially integrated into black community networks than their married counterparts. With the exception of Chelsea Carrington, who grew up in a white middle-class rural community, women of working-class origins were overrepresented among the racially literate. What explains their racial literacy when compared to married women is that most of the latter were in what is best characterized as traditional or conventional heterosexual marriages in which patriarchal gender regimes placed the burden of domestic labor, including cooking and child care, on the women. If their black husband or domestic partner did not take the time to discuss race with them or to teach them explicitly about his experiences with race or racism, these transracial mothers ended up struggling alone with the varieties of everyday racism they and their children encountered. In many cases they experienced more social isolation than their unmarried friends raising children in inner-city and more multiethnic communities. Although I had initially assumed that the married women might have more racial knowledge because of their black partners, this turned out not to be the case. Being married was typically associated with higher levels of social isolation and less flexibility in one's schedule. The married women caring for young children and adolescents tended to spend less time with their girlfriends, attended fewer social events, and had fewer opportunities to cultivate friendships with women or men who were not family members or childhood acquaintances.

By contrast, the racially literate single women who had grown up in multiracial urban communities were immersed in strong female networks of support that included black women, South Asian women, and white women. For example, Chelsea Carrington and Allesandra Richards both identified their closest friends as African Caribbean, and they went on vacations together. Chelsea in particular had a broad network of support that included black men and women (including youth workers such as Gerry Burke) who organized activities in which her daughter participated after school. She and her black friends also went on vacations together. Women like Chelsea who were educated and held professional jobs but chose to remain in inner-city urban communities because of their ethnic diversity typically had more sources of social capital and support than their middle-class married peers living in suburban or more prosperous urban neighborhoods. Their location in diverse residential communities exposed them and their children to more black people and gave them potentially more opportunities to establish relationships with blacks. Living in multiethnic black and Asian communities that were described as impoverished and considered ghetto communities by public officials also gave them access to forms of cultural support, such as the African Caribbean Centre, which operated the Saturday school and was within walking distance from their homes (e.g., Chelsea, Helena Mitchell, Sonya Smyth and Casey Clarke; see chapters 1, 2, 4 and 5).

Middle-class white women married to black professional men, such as Danielle Johnson (chapter 3) and Sue Farrell (chapter 2), had to work harder to develop these same social relationships, unless they held jobs that brought them into contact with black colleagues. They also lived in predominantly white middle-class communities where they drove, rather than taking public transportation or walking to do their weekly shopping. Their ownership of private transportation also restricted their contact with black working-class people, who were viewed as the source of authorized forms of ethnic and social capital in the black communities. When compared to working-class women, they tended to live more regimented and socially restricted lives, organized around heterosexual marital regimes. This made them more dependent for their racial literacy education upon their husbands, who may or may not have possessed it.

Among the ten black fathers I interviewed, only four possessed racial literacy. This means that in most cases they did not serve as a reliable source of daily support for their white wives in managing racism.

Allesandra (chapter 3), Chelsea (chapters 3 and 4), and Helena (chapter 5) were representative of half of the unmarried white women and who lived in urban inner-city areas where they could more easily organize their lives around single parenthood. (Helena married a Welsh man and gave birth to a son during this research.) These women tended to have other friends (black and white) who were raising children of mixed heritage or were single mothers, and they cultivated multiracial support networks that provided them with multicultural experiences. Helena, for example, took her daughter, Eshe, on holidays with other mothers raising their children of multiracial parentage. Helena also lived in Highfields, a few blocks from Chelsea, a residential community with a large concentration of children of multiracial heritage. Thus she had access to a network of resources at the local school that were developed to support black, Asian, and other children from ethnic backgrounds.

There were comparable ideological divides among and within the transracial families I studied. Husbands differed from wives in their analysis of racism. Sisters and brothers debated the racism of white in-laws and the race awareness of white sisters-in-law. White women varied by class and residential location in their perception and analysis of racism. Those who grew up in middle- and upper-middle-class families, attended upper-middle-class boarding schools, and were raised in class-segregated communities, like Chloe Talbot Kelly (chapter 1), and Andrea MacKenzie (chapter 2), did not develop childhood friendships with blacks or Asians. Thus as children they did not witness overt racism targeted against friends or peers. Their class privilege shielded them and sometimes restricted their ability to recognize forms of routine racism. They did not exhibit the same levels of racial literacy. They utilized their class privilege and other forms of social and cultural capital to protect their children after incidents of racism had occurred, rather than preparing them in advance. This strategy is due, in part, to their belief that, because their children are mixed-race and not black, racism will not be their primary problem.

Other white women, such as Sue Farrell and Peggy Hamilton (chapter 2), recognized that discrimination was directed at them because they had engaged in transgressive relationships with black men. This, however, did not translate to a focus on the racism their children might anticipate. Sue, who lives in a spacious, detached four-bedroom home on an acre of land in a prosperous suburb, had difficulty identifying any racial incidents involving her children. However, her black husband, Dane Farrell, took their eldest son back to Highfields on a regular basis for social events and provided him with martial arts lessons so that he could "defend himself if necessary" and to socially integrate him into black friendship networks.

White women who grew up in working-class families, like Allesandra Richards and Sharon Dawkins, were as conscious and critical of class inequalities and gender hierarchies. Each was able to identify and link her father's structural location to his opposition to interracial marriage and antiblack racism. The racially literate women of working-class background also perceived their children as being vulnerable to the same or similar forms of racial and class discrimination. Their social location in black friendship networks and their strong ties to their black sisters-in-law, mothers-in-law, or girlfriends were central to their acquisition of racial literacy. These relationships also reinforced their view that black mothers, not the white mothers of white children, were their reference group.

Relationships with black women gave these racially literate women access to cultural knowledge and information that helped them to decode racist social interactions. They were more likely to acquire an alternative analytical perspective that facilitated the development of racial literacy. The other group of women who were more likely to develop racial literacy had earned a university degree in sociology and thus acquired black female friends in race relations courses. Ultimately, intimacy with other black women proved just as significant as their relationships with their black husband or partner, if not more so.

Sharon Dawkins, Allesandra Richards, Valerie Wellington, and several black fathers in this study were children of members of the Labour aristocracy during a period of decolonization, deindustrialization, and demographic shifts that occurred as former colonial subjects migrated to Britain's urban centers from Africa (East and West), the Caribbean, and Asia. They grew up in the 1970s and 1980s and attended schools in inner-city and increasingly multiethnic neighborhoods that brought them into direct contact with black African, black Caribbean, and South Asian children. They were more likely to establish friendships with black and Asian children and to date black men as adolescents, which enhanced their consciousness of race and their own whiteness.

Allesandra Richards (chapters 2 and 3) and Brian Piper (chapter 8), for example, grew up in urban white working-class communities, but at the state schools and later at university developed friendships with blacks and Asians who were roommates or classmates. They also witnessed firsthand the racism of their parents, teachers, peers, and other members of their community. In contrast to their parents, they became socially integrated into black networks and did not view racial and ethnic minorities as outside of their social group. They learned these racial lessons at an early age.

Racial literacy is something that white people of all class backgrounds acquired. However, class privilege did not translate into more awareness or the ability to more effectively negotiate race and racism. Women of working-class origin who returned to school as mature students and earned a degree in sociology were more likely to develop a more nuanced analysis of racism. I also found that gendered regimes of domestic labor in transracial households meant that white women were more likely to be expected to engage in race and racism training of their children. They rather than the father—the black parent—were held accountable by other blacks in their families if their children were exposed to routine racism and they did not know how to manage it or respond effectively.

The racial literacy projects detailed in this book do not necessarily cohere into an organized public project that is visible to those outside of the study participants' homes. These projects are a form of *political* labor that has been ignored by sociological analyses of social movements. The experiences of white members of transracial families show how social experiences influence the ways that individuals acquire and manage racial identities, racial logics, and racial and ethnic boundaries. These analyses can illuminate how individuals learn to see or not see larger racial structures and forms of everyday racism as it intersects with class structures, gender regimes, and British nationalism. They can provide sociological insights into the microcultural processes in families as they respond to state racial projects such as those that were called during the Thatcher period as "sus" laws (suspicious persons could be stopped and detained and searched by the police). Sociologists and social activists documented patterns in which the British police tended to treat all young black and Asian men as suspicious. Examples of other state racial projects would include the targeting of ethnic minorities that is known in the United States as "racial profiling."

Comparing the experiences of white women and white men in transracial families highlights how gender intersects with class and capital to structure differences between how white women and men negotiate the meaning of race and racism: women are punished when they form relationships with partners from a different racial or ethnic background; men are not. Black women and black men agreed that white women are more likely than white men to be disciplined and punished for establishing transracial families. Racism rebounds onto these women in varied ways, depending on the forms of capital they possess (see chapter 3).

Sociological studies of race and racism in North America, which have focused primarily on the United States, are deeply divided into two theoretical camps. There is, as David Wellman notes, a "theoretical bifurcation" between the structuralists and the culturalists. According to Wellman, sociologists such as William Julius Wilson have neglected the significance of race and racism: "His exclusive emphasis on economic organization, moreover, allows no theoretical room for exploring cultural or ideological expressions that might be related to and activated by the racial division of labor" ([1977] 1993, 6). Wellman accurately points out that the structuralists ignore questions of hierarchy and racial advantage, while the culturalists focus on "meaning systems" and interpretations of race and ignore how these meanings are linked to structural location.

The discourses, cultural practices, and parental labor of white members of transracial families have been undertheorized in analyses of interracial families, postcolonial Britain, and black British communities. The invisibility of white members of transracial families from analyses of racism and antiracism prevents sociologists from understanding new forms of racism (and antiracism) in postcolonial Europe. While feminists have analyzed the political significance of the family as a unit in which racial training occurs, this intermediate institution (and the labor of mothers and fathers) remains marginal in analyses of social movements and antiracism. This study illuminates the pivotal and paradoxical role that white transracial parents play in black British communities. As members of a racially dominant group, they are assumed to occupy a racially privileged position. Nevertheless their class position, political commitments, cultural style, and domestic life may disadvantage them in ways that are not always visible to their black family members. If they challenge racist attitudes or behaviors when they are participating in exclusively white social fields, their symbolic representation of the black experience can make them targets for racial abuse. By focusing on the racial, gender, and class positions of the white members of these families, I seek to synthesize the concerns of the structuralists and the culturalists. By shifting the analysis to England, this ethnographic study fills a gap in the theoretical and empirical literature devoted to the sociology of race and racism, gender studies, whiteness studies, black British cultural studies, and African diaspora studies.

The acts of everyday antiracism in which white parents engage occur off the picket lines and outside of formal community organizing. The antiracist work and racism-awareness training I uncovered in one-fourth of these families provides children with vocabularies, racial logics, and forms of consciousness that are required for collective organizing and can also lead to political action. In the final analysis, the social reproduction of the black British community may rest on these invisible, mundane forms of everyday labor done at kitchen tables, in hair salons, in living rooms, and in those domestic spaces that are not privileged in macro analyses.

Introduction

1. Between 1947 and 1975 anthropologists and sociologists produced a body of community studies that addressed immigration, assimilation, and race relations. Yet neither white women nor the social processes by which white parents attempt to counter racial hierarchies were the focus of these studies. For examples of earlier studies of black community formation, see Banton 1955; Little 1948; Glass 1961; Collins 1957; Patterson 1963. These studies were framed around an analysis of assimilation rather than antiracism.

2. I employ the term *white* as an elastic and economical way to describe people of diverse European heritage who may or may not embrace white as their primary identity. The white women and men who participated in this study self-identify as British, Irish, English, Scottish, and a combination of the above, as well as white. Although I employ the term throughout this book, I recognize that the people I refer to do not belong to a culturally homogeneous group, and their economic situations, social experiences, and phenotypes varied greatly.

3. In eight families I was able to directly compare the interpretations and discourses of sisters, brothers, and sisters-in-law.

4. See the research of Benson, 1981; Dalmage 2000; Ali 2003; Chito Childs 2005; Hildebrandt 2002.

5. Although Bourdieu was not concerned specifically with racism or racial hierarchies, he nevertheless provided theoretical tools that can be deployed in analyses of interracial intimacy and the cultural reproduction of intraethnic hierarchies in second- and third-generation black European communities.

6. For an exceptional analysis of a white grandmother parenting children of African descent in Detroit, see Hartigan 1997.

7. In a review of the theoretical foundations of the field of whiteness studies, Twine and Gallagher (2008) identify new theoretical and methodological trends in whiteness studies which are "broadening it and deepening its international contours."

8. In *Working-Class White: The Making and Unmaking of Race Relations* (2006) Monica McDermott provides an exemplary model of new American research on whiteness and racial identities. McDermott worked as a clerk at a convenience store to analyze how whites and blacks interact and what this tells us about white identities. In a comparative analysis of the white working-class experience in two American cities, Boston and Atlanta, she shows the significance of locality in understanding the discursive and cultural practices of working-class whites as they interpret and interact with blacks. McDermott identifies the impoverished vocabulary in the United States for discussing class inequality and the ways that *race* stands in for various forms of social and economic exclusion. "*White* is typically conceived in terms of economic and social advantage and residence in predominantly white affluent areas. What, then, becomes of the white racial identity of those whites who are poor or working class and live in an area with a substantial black working-class population? The results are not the standard ways whiteness functions in the U.S." (40).

9. I am building upon the theoretical insights of Michael Omi and Howard Winant (1994), who reconciled two opposing positions on race: the notion that race is a fixed and essential condition that individuals possess and the view that race is a mere illusion. Omi and Winant developed racial formation theory to "disrupt and reframe the rigid and bipolar manner in which they [these opposing positions] are posed and debated, and to transcend the presumably irreconcilable relationship between them" (56). They define racial formation as "a process of historically situated projects in which human bodies and social structures are represented and organized" (56). They argue that racial formation occurs at the micro level and the macro level. Describing the presence of race as a macrosystem, they draw upon the work of Herbert Gintis and Samuel Bowles (1981) to argue, "A social structure may be understood as a series of 'sites.' We conceive of a site as a region of social life with a coherent set of constitutive social relations—the structure of the site. Thus in the advanced capitalist social formation, the liberal democratic states, the capitalist economy, and the patriarchal family may be considered sites in that each may be characterized by a distinct set of 'rules of the game' in practices" (Omi and Winant 1986, 67).

10. In the 1990s North American scholars based primarily in the United States examined whiteness and white identities (Morrison 1991; Roediger 1991; Allen 1994), resurrecting an intellectual project that was initiated at the end

of the nineteenth century by the black American scholar W. E. B. Du Bois in his seminal work *The Philadelphia Negro* ([1899] 1970). The number of scholarly works on whiteness and white identities grew exponentially in Britain, the United States, and South Africa (Frankenberg 1993, 1997; Ware 1997; Cohen 1999; Dyer 1997; Morrison 1991). After two decades we have now entered what Charles Gallagher and I refer to as the "third wave" of whiteness studies (Twine and Gallagher 2008).

11. I am following the British use of the term *Asian*, which includes South Asians with origins in Bangladesh, India, Pakistan, and East Africa and excludes the Chinese and other East Asians. The Chinese were counted as a separate category in the U.K. census in 1991; they constitute 0.3 percent of the local population.

12. It is ranked thirty-fifth in size in Britain.

13. In 2001 a new "mixed race" category was added to the U.K. census. That year the census included the following categories: white and black Caribbean, white and black African, white and Asian, and other mixed. Since this category did not appear on earlier censuses we don't have data that can provide a detailed statistical portrait over time of this population. Nevertheless the population of children growing up in multiracial families has increased dramatically.

14. Pakistanis and Bangladeshis constitute 1.0 percent and 0.4 percent, respectively, of the population.

15. They also argued that even more recent migrants from Somalia have rejected the efforts of the black Caribbean community to form alliances with them and that they have exhibited horizontal racism toward indigenous black British.

16. The National Front reaped electoral rewards in local elections in 1976 and 1977, prior to the period when Margaret Thatcher served as prime minister (1979–91).

17. I initially conceptualized this study as a comparative study of families living in London, Leicester, and Liverpool. However, after conducting my pilot research in London and Leicester, I decided to narrow my focus to Leicester because of its unique history and because it has been understudied by ethnographers. Aside from London it is the local authority with the largest percentage of all ethnic minorities and has one of the largest Asian Indian populations with origins in East Africa (Kenya, Malawi, Tanzania, and Uganda).

18. Esther Addley, "Side by Side," *The Guardian*, 1 January 2001, 6.

19. There is a debate regarding whether Birmingham or Leicester will become England's first city with a nonwhite majority, but this debate remains outside the focus of this study. The term *black* is used here to include Asian Indians, Africans, and African Caribbeans. The broader use of the term to refer to

anyone (except the Chinese) from a former British colony in Africa, South Asia, and the Caribbean used to be standard practice but is becoming less common.

20. Warren Hoge, "British City Defines Diversity and Tolerance," *New York Times*, national edition, 8 February 2001, A1.

21. In the 1960s and 1970s Moat Community College served a predominantly immigrant population from Poland, Ireland, the Caribbean, and West Africa. Asians did not constitute a significant presence among secondary school students until the 1980s. The demographics of this school population have changed: according to school records, in 1999, of the 952 registered students of compulsory age, 604 were Indians, 62 were Pakistanis, 47 were Bangladeshis, 54 were black Africans, 54 were white, and 11 were "black others" (presumed to be mixed-race). Only 10 students were black Caribbeans (born in Britain). With two exceptions, all of the black men in this study who grew up in Leicester were former students at Moat Community College.

22. Stephen Small, whom I met at the University of California, Berkeley, as a graduate student, introduced me to his colleague Julia O'Connell Davidson, a member of the sociology faculty at the University of Leicester. I asked Julia to publicize my research in her classes. She posted announcements and also introduced me to several of her African Caribbean female students, who provided me with my first set of referrals: their white friends or sisters-in-law raising children of African Caribbean parentage.

23. In May 1997 I was interviewed on the BBC local affiliate on *Talking Blues*, a show that targets the black community. I used this as an opportunity to further recruit, but didn't receive many referrals, although several listeners who had already met me called in and gave me their support.

24. I introduced Michael Smyth to the neighborhoods in which I had been living and working and asked him to photograph the sites I had identified as significant in my "racial consciousness" biographical interviews and during participant observation.

25. Following Frankenberg, I asked individuals to describe the racial and ethnic demographics of the spaces they frequented as a child—schools, day care centers, vacation areas, and homes—as well as their friendships, and I used this to probe what they were explicitly taught or told about race as opposed to what they learned from living white lives. I asked them to describe events that they considered racial and to detail the events that led to their pregnancies and marriages, and any responses to their relationships with people of color. During follow-up interviews I gave them an opportunity to reframe what they had said in previous interviews or to revise it based on their having time to reflect upon their life.

26. I sent transcripts to all of the individuals interviewed between 1995 and 1997. I then selected a group from this initial group to reinterview. After they had a chance to review their transcript I asked them if they wanted to challenge, revise, or return to any of the issues that had been discussed.

27. Among one-fourth of the transracial families studied, I found that the white mother possessed racial literacy.

28. There have been a number of insightful and provocative memoirs that analyze the experiences of white mothers raising children with black American men, including the memoirs of Jane Lazarre and Maureen Reddy, analyzed in chapter 4. For a notable exception that addresses the experiences of white mothers in the United States, see the chapters on interracial parenting by Frankenberg (1993).

29. Amanda Lewis identifies several challenges facing scholars of whiteness, including "how to tap into differential ways that whites experience and perform race, and how to recognize the complex ways that racial discourses or 'culture' interact with material realities" (2004, 630).

I. Class Analysis of Interracial Intimacy

1. There were also significant numbers of West Indian troops in Britain during the Second World War.

2. See David Reynolds 1995.

3. In *London's Newcomers: The West Indian Migrants* (1961), based on research conducted between autumn 1958 and spring 1960, Ruth Glass identifies mythologies around interracial sexuality as a major cause of the social pathology that led to the riots.

4. Describing these forms of capital, Bourdieu argues, "These fundamental social powers are . . . firstly economic capital, in various kinds; secondly cultural capital or better, informational capital, again in its different kinds; and thirdly two forms of capital that are very strongly correlated, social capital, which consists of resources based on connections and group membership, and symbolic capital, which is the form the different types of capital take once they are perceived and recognized as legitimate" (1997, 3–4).

5. When her son was three years old, Chloe and her husband purchased this house from her parents, who had moved to Leicester after Chloe's father retired from his position as an art master at Rugby, an elite boarding school. Both of her parents lived with Chloe, her husband, and their grandson until their death.

6. Chloe's father, Richard Barrett Talbot Kelly, was born in Liverpool in 1896. He attended Rugby for one year and was called to duty during the Second World War. He became a professional soldier and did tours of duty in India

after the Great War. He later became the art master at Rugby, although he had only been painting part time while a soldier.

7. Chloe's paternal grandfather, a native of Liverpool, left the cotton trade to become an artist during the 1880s. Every winter he took the family to Egypt, where he painted, and then held art exhibitions of his paintings, selling virtually all of his work. He was among the first white men to enter the recently excavated Egyptian tombs in the 1920s during the height of British imperialism.

8. For an analysis of this film see Cripps 1993, chapter 2. *The Birth of a Nation*, originally titled *The Clansman*, a film by D. W. Griffith, premiered in 1915, the fiftieth anniversary of the end of the Civil War. This film was considered spectacular and technically innovative. It demonized recently freed black slaves and presented the Ku Klux Klan as a heroic organization that would defend white womanhood. During a time when black men were regularly lynched in the South, it depicted a black man being tried for raping a white woman, found guilty, and executed by the Klan. It was the highest-grossing box office film before *Gone With the Wind*. It mobilized the National Association for the Advancement of Colored People and became a battleground between white supremacists and organized antiracists in the black community.

9. Unfortunately the United Kingdom did not collect national statistics on interracial marriages during this period, so we don't know how representative these relationships were.

2. Disciplining Dissidents

1. Feminist scholars working in the area of critical race studies have examined certain forms of discipline and racialized regimes of punishment inflicted upon mothers who are unwed, involved in interracial relationships, poor, lesbian, or accused of criminal activity.

2. See Rich 1990, chapter 6.

3. Braunstone is an estate on the west side of Leicester, located approximately three miles from the city center and railway station. It is the most deprived area in the East Midlands. See New Deal Task Force 1999.

4. By the time I completed this study, Valerie and Conrad had celebrated twenty-two years of marriage and had become grandparents.

5. This center set up a lending library of children's and young adult books and provided classes and leisure activities for girls from poor, working-class, and low-income communities. Nelista Cuffy, an African Caribbean woman who had been involved with the center, gave me access to her archive, which included copies of the organization's internal reports. I learned from read-

ing these reports that after intense internecine political conflicts among the leadership, Chelsea remained the only white woman serving on the executive committee. I was told by several black women who had served on this committee that they respected the work that Chelsea had done on behalf of the African Caribbean and Asian community. Chelsea, a modest and unassuming woman, never discussed these conflicts directly with me, but black women activists in the local community always mentioned her with affection.

6. Several of the women I interviewed asked me for letters of support, in the hopes that a letter from an American sociologist would strengthen their case for relocation. I helped one woman hire a solicitor to represent her in proceedings.

7. I was told that this term is the emotional and political equivalent of the term *nigger* when used by nonblacks in the United States.

8. These resources include access to food (e.g., hot breakfasts), supplies that could be purchased at lower cost, and friendship networks.

3. The Concept of Racial Literacy

1. They were intended for a nonscholarly audience and include Maureen Reddy's *Crossing the Color Line: Race, Parenting and Culture* (1996), Jane Lazarre's *Beyond the Whiteness of Whiteness: Memoir of a White Mother of Black Sons* (1996), and Hettie Jones's *How I Became Hettie Jones* (1990). Hettie Jones is the former wife of LeRoi Jones, now Amiri Baraka, and the mother of Lisa Jones, formerly a black columnist for *The Village Voice*.

2. See "Identity: Skin, Blood, Heart" (1984), the classic essay by Minnie Bruce Pratt, a feminist whose sexual position as a lesbian in the American South led to her ability to see racism. She provides a detailed and nuanced analysis of the contingent nature of whiteness for southern women who choose to establish relationships with people other than white heterosexual men. Describing the shifts in perception that she experienced after she left her husband and came out as a lesbian and the partner of a Jewish woman in North Carolina, she analyzes her whiteness in terms of what she was taught not to see: the histories and experiences of blacks and Native Americans and their exclusion.

3. A notable exception to this is the work of critical race feminists such as Becky Thompson (2001).

4. I frequently heard this term used as a form of self-identification and by parents and grandparents of children born into multiracial families. The term was employed most often by working-class blacks and whites in this community and among older people who have not been socialized to use the

terms introduced in more recent years by the government, such as *mixed race*, *dual heritage*, and *black other*.

5. At the age of eleven she failed one of her exams, so she was sent to a secondary modern school rather than a grammar school. When Barbara was a child in the early 1960s, children who attended secondary modern schools were viewed as low achievers. The curriculum they were offered was not designed to prepare them for entrance into a university. Grammar schools, in contrast, were subsidized fee-paying schools that prepared children for a tertiary education.

4. Racial Literacy in Practice

1. Vikram Dodd, "Women Win Payout for Soldier's Abuse," *The Guardian*, 16 September 2000.

2. Women like Sue did not have the option of checking a "mixed-race" box until the census of 2001, and may have appeared on the census of 1991 as either a "black other" or simply an "other."

3. There have been a number of insightful and provocative memoirs that offer analyses of the experiences of white mothers raising children with black American men in the United States, including the work by Jane Lazarre and Maureen Reddy, analyzed in chapter 4. For a notable exception that addresses the experiences of single white mothers in the United States, see the chapters on interracial parenting in Frankenberg 1993.

4. "Racism Is a Problem in Our Schools," *Leicester Mercury*, 13 January 1998, 5.

5. Interview conducted by the author.

6. *African Caribbean* is a term that many young people consider more acceptable than the terms *Afro-Caribbean* or *West Indian*, which appear in older research. Many people over forty-five use the latter terms in self-identification. However, for the purposes of my research, the term *African Caribbean* is problematic because it lacks precision and does not carefully distinguish between individuals who are immigrants from Africa, individuals born in Britain of Caribbean heritage, or Caribbean-born blacks of African ancestry who have no personal knowledge of or living relatives from Africa.

7. The term *white* is employed here to include a range of ethnicities, including Irish, German, Polish, and Arabic people who may not necessarily self-identify as white or embrace whiteness as their primary identity.

8. See the Educational Subcommittee report, "Ethnic Monitoring of Pupils' Educational Attainment," Leicester City Council, 29 September 1998. In this chapter I am drawing on data collected during field research conducted in 1995–97 and structured interviews conducted with ninety-six parents and their family members.

9. In 1977 the Select Committee on Race Relations and Immigration in the United Kingdom published a reported titled "The West Indian Community." The report urgently recommended that "the government institute a high level of independent inquiry into the causes of underachievement of children of West Indian origin in maintained schools and the remedial action required." Two years later, the government established a committee of inquiry to further investigate the issue. The resulting report, also known as the Rampton Report because it was conducted under the chairmanship of Anthony Rampton, was titled *West Indian Children in Our Schools: Interim Report of the Committee of Inquiry into the Education of Children from Ethnic Minority Groups* (London: HMSO, 1981). It was presented to Parliament by the secretary of state for education and science in June 1981. The committee's evaluation of the books and teaching materials called attention to the effects on British schoolchildren of negative and derogatory images of African and African-descent people in school textbooks.

10. The National Front also became the focus for antiracist political mobilization as orchestrated by the Anti-Nazi League and Rock Against Racism. See Solomos [1993] 2003, 190.

11. See Massey and Denton (1993) for an analysis of residential segregation by race and Susan Smith (1989) for an analysis of the British case.

12. In Leicester several of the women who have chaired and administered ACE and who regularly teach at the Saturday school are qualified teachers who earned their degrees and are committed community activists. As in other supplementary schools there is no formal syllabus and the focus of the lesson plans varies considerably depending upon the interests and areas of specialization of the volunteer teacher who leads that week's session.

13. Six of the twenty students who attended in 1997 were mixed-race. The population of the Saturday school fluctuates between twenty and forty. Aisha, the eldest daughter of Sharon and Everal Dawkins, whose photograph appears in chapter 6, cited the retention of the preteens and teenagers as a major problem.

5. Written on the Body

1. Chris Hocker and Sakina Spruell, "Bad Hair Days: African American Firms Losing Control of the Ethnic Haircare Industry," *Black Enterprise*, November 2000; Shawn Taylor, "Big Players Woo Ethnic Market," *Chicago Tribune*, 10 January 10, 2002.

2. In 1964 Edward and Bettian Gardner founded their company in the basement of their home. Testing their products on their children's hair, they refined the products until they had a commercially viable formula. Soft Sheen com-

peted directly with Johnson Products and became the second largest manufacture of "ethnic" hair care in the world. Johnson Products, also located on the South Side of Chicago, had already established itself as the world's largest producer of hair care products targeting black consumers (M. Wilson 2004).

3. This store is within walking distance of about one-quarter of the families that participated in my study, but even blacks who live more than ten miles away shop there. Black men who have moved out of the community and now live in what they term "posh" and upscale suburban neighborhoods return to this store to purchase the dry goods, canned goods, and fresh vegetables that they need to produce what they call West Indian, African Caribbean, or simply black meals.

6. Archives of Interracial Intimacies

1. See the Norton centennial edition of *The Souls of Black Folks* by W. E. B. Du Bois ([1903] 2003). In this critical edition, which Henry Louis Gates Jr. and Terri Hume Oliver edited, the black-and-white photographs that originally illustrated Du Bois's article were reprinted and included.

2. For a discussion of the use of the visual in sociology and anthropology, see Chaplin 1994, chapter 5.

3. One exception is the journal *Contexts*, established in 2002 and financed by the American Sociological Association. This journal regularly publishes photo-essays.

4. During the nine years that I conducted research for this project Sharon regularly invited me to her home to share meals, accompany her on family errands, and attend social events with her closest friends and business meetings with her business partner.

5. Sharon and Everal gave their permission to publish their real names along with the photographs, with the understanding that the photographs would be used to accompany academic publications that reported my research findings. I also provided Sharon with copies of photographs taken by Michael Smyth of her and her family, for her private use.

6. Michael Smyth had accompanied me to Sharon's home on two previous occasions in 2000 and 2003 to shoot photographs of her family.

7. White Like Who?

1. This is the equivalent of what are called O-levels (Ordinary levels) in the British system. You have to pass three A-levels (Advanced levels) to qualify for university entrance.

2. He worked a series of factory jobs, first in a paint factory and then a paper factory, before taking the test for a job in the post office. Shortly after ar-

riving in London he met Chloe Talbot Kelly, a fourth-generation artist (see chapter 3).

3. Netifnet is one of the twenty black women I interviewed who are members of black–white extended families. Half of the black women I interviewed were married to white men and raising children with them, and thus they provided a comparative perspective on the management of race and racism. In most cases I also interviewed their white husbands.

4. I was unable to discuss this issue with Joyce's parents because her mother was on an extended vacation in Guyana when I tried to schedule an interview with her. According to Joyce, both of her parents accepted Danielle and criticized her when she initially rejected Danielle as a family member.

5. In my conversations with Danielle and Adam, Danielle did express more concern about the issue. She seemed to invest more energy thinking about the constant impact of race on her son.

6. *Off-black* refers to a range of identity labels and racialized hybrid positions. It is used to manage the ambiguity and ambivalence around the gap between family perceptions of race and blackness.

8. Gender Gaps in Interracial Intimacy

1. One reason for this could be that the men in this sample all began their relationships in their late twenties or older, so they were not teenagers and most were not living at home under parental supervision.

2. In 1993 Dorothy took Kevin to Jamaica to meet her relatives.

3. Brian and Annette's experience can provide insights into how white men can become what Karen McKinney (2005) calls "agents of epiphany," that is, individuals who enable one to see forms of racism that were previously not visible.

4. She had already earned a Cambridge High Certificate, which is equivalent to a degree from a top college in England (high school in the U.S. context).

5. It is important to note that Brian is not representative; his active involvement for four decades in antiracist work distinguishes him from all of the other white fathers and most of the white mothers. Nevertheless one-fifth of the white women I interviewed reported participation in some antiracist activity, and some had been very active (e.g., Chelsea Carrington and Barbara McBride in chapters 3 and 4).

REFERENCES

Adkins, Lisa, and Beverley Skeggs, eds. 2004. *Feminism after Bourdieu*. Oxford: Blackwell.

Alexander, Claire. 1996. *The Art of Being Black: The Creation of Black British Youth Identities*. Oxford: Oxford University Press.

———. 2000. *The Asian Gang: Ethnicity, Identity, Masculinity*. Oxford: Berg.

Alexander, Claire, and Caroline Knowles. 2004. *Making Race Matter: Bodies, Space and Identity*. London: Palgrave.

Ali, Suki. 2003. *Mixed-Race, Post-Race: Gender, New Ethnicities and Cultural Practices*. Oxford: Berg.

Alibhai-Brown, Yasmin. 2000. *Who Do We Think We Are: Imagining the New Britain*. London: Penguin Books.

———. 2001. *Mixed Feelings: The Complex Lives of Mixed-Race Britons*. London: Women's Press.

Allen, Theodore W. 1994. *The Invention of the White Race*, Vol. 1: *Racial Oppression and Social Control*. London: Verso.

Anderson, Elijah. 1990. *Streetwise: Race, Class, and Change in an Urban Community*. Chicago: University of Chicago Press.

Anthias, Floya, and Nira Yuval-Davis. 1993. *Racialized Boundaries: Race, Nation, Gender, Colour and Class and the Anti-racist Struggle*. London: Routledge.

Back, Les. 1996. *New Ethnicities and Urban Culture: Racisms and Multiculture in Young Lives*. London: University College London Press.

———. 1997. "Nazism and the Call of the Jitterbug." *Dance in the City*, ed. by Helen Thomas. London: Macmillan.

Bakare-Yusuf, Bibi. 1997. "Raregrooves and Raregroovers: A Matter of Taste, Difference and Identity." *Black British Feminism: A Reader*, ed. by Heidi Safia Mirza. London: Routledge.

Banks, Ingrid. 1998. *Hair Matters: Beauty, Power and Black Women's Consciousness*. New York: New York University Press.

Banks, Marcus. 2001. *Visual Methods in Social Research*. London: Sage.

Banton, Michael. 1955. *The Coloured Quarter: Negro Immigrants in an English City*. London: Jonathan Cape.

————. 1960. *White and Coloured: The Behaviour of British People towards Coloured Immigrants*. New Brunswick, N.J.: Rutgers University Press.

Barker, Martin. 1981. *The New Racism*. London: Junction Books.

Barth, Fredrik. 1969. *Ethnic Groups and Boundaries: The Social Organization of Culture Difference*. Boston: Little, Brown.

Becker, Howard. 1995. "Visual Sociology, Documentary Photography, and Photo-journalism: It's (Almost) All a Matter of Context." *Visual Sociology* 10, nos. 1–2, 1–15.

Benson, Susan. 1981. *Ambiguous Ethnicity: Interracial Families In London*. Cambridge, England: Cambridge University Press.

————. 1996. "Asians Have Culture, West Indians Have Problems: Discourses of Race and Ethnicity in and out of Anthropology." *Culture, Identity and Politics*, ed. by Terence Ranger, Yunas Samad, and Ossie Stuart. Aldershot: Avebury Press.

Benyon, John, Bola Dauda, John Garland, Stephen Lyle, and the Afrikan Caribbean Support Group. 1996. *African Caribbean People in Leicestershire: Afrikan Caribbean Support Group Research Project—The Final Report*. Leicestershire: Scarman Centre for the Study of Public Order at University of Leicester.

Bhabha, Homi. 1994. *Locations of Culture*. New York: Routledge.

Blauner, Robert. 1972. *Racial Oppression in America*. New York. Harper and Row.

————. 1989. *Black Lives, White Lives: Three Decades of Race Relations*. Berkeley: University of California Press.

Blee, Kathleen. 1999. "White on White: Interviewing Women in U.S. White Supremacist Groups." *Racing Research, Researching Race: Methodological Dilemmas in Critical Race Studies*, ed. by France Winddance Twine and Jonathan Warren. New York: New York University Press.

————. 2002. *Inside Organized Racism: Women in the Hate Movement*. Berkeley: University of California Press.

Bonnett, Alastair. 1993. "Forever White? Challenges and Alternatives to a 'Racial' Monolith." *New Community* 20, no. 1, 173–80.

————. 1996. "Anti-Racism and the Critique of 'White' Identities." *New Community: Journal of the Commission for Racial Equality* 22, no. 1, 97–110.

————. 1998a. "How Did the British Working Class Become White?: The Symbolic Re(formation) of Racialized Capitalism." *Journal of Historical Sociology* 11, no. 3, 316–40.

————. 1998b. "Who Was White? The Disappearance of Non-European White Identities and the Formation of European Racial Whiteness." *Ethnic and Racial Studies* 21, no. 6, 1029–55.

————. 2000a. *Anti-Racism*. London: Routledge.

————. 2000b. *White Identities: Historical and International Perspectives*: Harlow: Prentice-Hall.

Bordo. Susan. 1993. *Unbearable Weight: Feminism, Western Culture, and the Body*. Berkeley: University of California Press.

Bourdieu, Pierre. 1984. *Distinction: A Social Critique of the Judgement of Taste*. Translated by Richard Nice. Cambridge, Mass.: Harvard University Press.

————. 1997. "The Forms of Capital." *Education: Culture, Economy, and Society*, ed. by A. H. Haley, Hugh Lauder, Phillip Brown, and Amy Stuart Wells. Oxford: Oxford University Press.

Bourdieu, Pierre, and Loic Wacquant. 1992. *An Invitation to Reflexive Sociology*. Chicago: University of Chicago Press.

Bowles, Samuel, and Herbert Gintis. 1977. *Schooling in Capitalist America: Educational Reform and the Contradictions of Economic Life*. New York: Basic Books.

Brodkin, Karen. 1998. *How Jews Became White Folks and What This Says about Race in America*. New Brunswick, N.J.: Rutgers University Press.

Brothers in Trouble. 1995. Directed by Udayan Prasad. Written by Robert Buckler and Abdullah Hussein. First Run Features. 102 minutes.

Brown, Jacqueline Nassy. 2005. *Setting Anchor, Dropping Sail: Geographies of Race in Black Liverpool*. Princeton: Princeton University Press.

Brumberg, Joan Jacob. 1997. *The Body Project: An Intimate History of American Girls*. New York: Vintage Books.

Bulmer, Martin, and John Solomos. 1999. *Racism*. Oxford: Oxford University Press.

Bunster, Ximena. 1977. "Talking Pictures: Field Method and Visual Mode." *Signs: Journal of Women in Culture and Society* 3, no. 1, 193–278.

Bush, Melanie. 2004. *Breaking the Code of Good Intentions: Everyday Forms of Whiteness*. Lanham, Md.: Rowman and Littlefield.

Butler, Judith. 1993. *Bodies that Matter: On the Discursive Limits of "Sex."* New York: Routledge.

Byrne, Bridget. 2006. *White Lives: The Interplay of Race, Class and Gender in Everyday Life*. London: Routledge.

Campt, Tina. 2005. *Other Germans: Black Germans and the Politics of Race, Gender, and Memory in the Third Reich*. Ann Arbor: University of Michigan Press.

Carmichael, Cathy. 1993. "Sleeping with the 'Enemy': The Isolation and Marginalization of White Women with Black Partners and/or Children." Ph.D. diss., University of Lancaster.

Carmichael, Stokely, and Charles Hamilton. 1967. *Black Power: The Politics of Liberation in America*. New York: Vintage.

Carter, Prudence. 2003. "'Black' Cultural Capital, Status Positioning and Schooling Conflicts for Low-Income African American Youth.' *Social Problems* 50, no. 1, 136–55.

———. 2005. *Keeping It Real: School Success beyond Black and White*. Oxford: Oxford University Press.

Cashmore, Ellis, and Eugene McLaughlin, eds. 1991. *Out of Order? Policing Black People*. London: Routledge.

Cell, John W. 1982. *The Highest Stage of White Supremacy: The Origins of Segregation in South Africa and the American South*. Cambridge: Cambridge University Press.

Centre for Contemporary Cultural Studies, ed. 1982. *The Empire Strikes Back: Race and Racism in 70s Britain*. London: Hutchinson.

Chaplin, Elizabeth. 1994. *Sociology and Visual Representation*. London: Routledge.

Chevannes, Mel, and Paul Reeves. 1987. "The Black Voluntary School Movement: Definition, Context and Prospects." *Racial Inequality in Education*, ed. by Barry Troyna. London: Tavistock.

Chito Childs, Erica. 2005. *Navigating Interracial Borders: Black-White Couples and Their Social Worlds*. New Brunswick, N.J.: Rutgers University Press.

Clifford, James, and George Marcus. 1986. *Writing Culture: The Politics and Poetics of Ethnography*. Berkeley: University of California Press.

Cohen, Phil. 1998. *Rethinking the Youth Question: Education, Labour and Cultural Studies*. Durham, N.C.: Duke University Press.

Collier, John, Jr., and Malcolm Collier. 1986. *Visual Anthropology: Photography as a Research Method*. Albuquerque: University of New Mexico Press.

Collins, Patricia Hill. 1986. "Learning from the Outsider Within: The Social Significance of Black Feminist Thought." *Social Problems* 33, no. 6, S14–S32.

———. 1990. *Black Feminist Thought: Knowledge, Consciousness, and the Politics of Empowerment*. London: Harper Collins Academic.

———. 1994. "Shifting the Center: Race, Class, and Feminist Theorizing about Motherhood." *Mothering: Ideology, Experience and Agency*, ed. by Evelyn Nakano Glenn, Grace Chang, and Lynn Forcey. New York: Routledge.

Collins, Sydney. 1957. *Coloured Minorities in Britain: Studies in British Race Relations on African, West Indian and Asiatic Immigrants*. London: Lutterworth Press.

Commission for Racial Equality. 1987. Reprint. 1991. *Living in Terror: A Report on Racial Violence and Harassment in Housing*. London: CRE.

———. 1995. *Annual Report of the Commission for Racial Equality*. London: CRE.

———. 1996. *Annual Report of the Commission for Racial Equality*. London: CRE.

———. 1997. *Annual Report of the Commission for Racial Equality*. London: CRE.

———. 1998. *Annual Report of the Commission for Racial Equality*. London: CRE.

———. 1999–2000. *Annual Report of the Commission for Racial Equality*. London: CRE.

Craig, Maxine Leeds. 2000. *Ain't I a Beauty Queen*. Cambridge: Cambridge University Press.

———. 2006. "Race, Beauty, and the Tangled Knot of a Guilty Pleasure." *Feminist Theory* 7, no. 2, 159–77.

Cripps, Thomas. 1993. *Slow Fade to Black: The Negro in American Film, 1900-1942*. Oxford: Oxford University Press.

Dalmage, Heather. 2000. *Tripping on the Color Line: Black-White Multiracial Families in a Racially Divided World*. New Brunswick, N.J.: Rutgers University Press.

Daniel, William. 1968. *Racial Discrimination in England*. Baltimore: Penguin Books.

Daniels, Jesse. 1997. *White Lies: Race, Class, Gender and Sexuality in White Supremacist Discourse*. New York: Routledge.

Davis, F. James. 1991. *Who Is Black? One Nation's Definition*. State College: Pennsylvania State University Press.

Daye, Sharon J. 1994. *Middle-Class Blacks in Britain: A Racial Fraction of a Class Group of a Class Fraction of a Racial Group?* New York: St. Martin's Press.

Donovan, Brian. 2003. "The Sexual Basis of Racial Formation: Anti-vice Activism and the Creation of the Twentieth-century 'Color Line.'" *Ethnic and Racial Studies* 26, no. 4, 707–27.

Douglas, K. B. 1988. "Impressions: African American First-year Students' Perceptions of a Predominantly White University." *Journal of Negro Education* 67, no. 4, 416–31.

Drake, St. Clair, and Horace Cayton. 1954. *Black Metropolis: A Study of Negro Life in a Northern City*. New York: Harcourt, Brace.

Dublin, Thomas. 1998. *When the Mines Closed: Stories of Struggle in Hard Times*. Photographs by George Harvan. Ithaca, N.Y.: Cornell University Press.

DuBois, W. E. B. [1903] 2003. *The Souls of Black Folks*. Centenary edition. Edited by Henry Louis Gates Jr. and Terri Hume Oliver. New York: Norton.

———. 1920. *Darkwater*. New York: Humanity Books.

———. [1935] 1976. *Black Reconstruction in America*. Introduction by Herbert Aptheker. Millwood, N.Y.: Kraus-Thomson Organization.

Duneier, Mitchell. 1999. *Sidewalk, with Photographs by Ovie Carter*. New York: Farrar, Straus and Giroux.

Durrheim, Kevin. 2005. "Socio-spatial Practice and Racial Representations in a Changing South Africa." *South African Journal of Psychology* 35, 444–59.

Duster, Troy. 2001. "The 'Morphing' Properties of Whiteness." *The Making and Unmaking of Whiteness*, ed. by Bridget Brander Rasmussen, Eric Klinenberg, Irene Nexica, and Matt Wray. Durham, N.C.: Duke University Press.

Dyer, Richard. 1997. *White*. New York: Routledge.

Enloe, Cynthia. 2000. *Maneuvers: The International Politics of Militarizing Women's Lives*. Berkeley: University of California Press.

Essed, Philomena. 1991. *Understanding Everyday Racism: Towards an Interdisciplinary Theory*. Newbury Park, Calif.: Sage.

Feagin, Joe, and Karyn D. McKinney. 2003. *The Many Costs of Racism*. Lanham, Md.: Rowman and Littlefield.

Feagin, Joe, and Eileen O'Brien. 2003. *White Men on Race: Power, Privilege, and the Shaping of Cultural Consciousness*. Boston: Beacon Press.

Feagin, Joe R., and Melvin T. Sikes. 1994. *Living with Racism: The Black Middle-Class Experience*. Boston: Beacon Press.

Feagin, Joe, and Hernan Vera. 1995. *White Racism: The Basics*. New York: Routledge.

Foner, Nancy. 1977. "The Jamaicans: Cultural and Social Change among Migrants in Britain." *Between Two Cultures: Migrants and Minorities in Britain*, ed. by James Watson. Oxford: Basil Blackwell.

———. 2005. *In a New Land: A Comparative View of Immigration*. New York: New York University Press.

Foucault, Michel. 1979. *Discipline and Punishment: The Birth of the Prison*. Translated by Alan Sheridan. New York: Vintage Books.

Frankenberg, Ruth. 1993. *White Women, Race Matters: The Social Construction of Whiteness*. Minneapolis: University of Minnesota Press.

———. 1997. *Displacing Whiteness: Essays in Social and Cultural Criticism*. Durham, N.C.: Duke University Press.

———. 2001. "On Unsteady Ground: Crafting and Engaging in the Critical Study of Whiteness." *Researching Race and Racism*, ed. by Martin Bulmer and John Solomos. London: Routledge.

Fredrickson, George M. 1981. *White Supremacy: A Comparative Study in American and South African History*. New York: Oxford University Press.

Gallagher, Charles A. 2003a. "Color-Blind Privilege: The Social and Political Functions of Erasing the Color Line in Post-war America." *Race, Gender, and Class* 10, no. 4, 22–37.

———. 2003b. "Playing the White Ethnic Card: Using Ethnic Identity to Deny Contemporary Racism." *White Out: The Continuing Significance of Racism*, ed. by Ashley "Woody" Doane and Eduardo Bonilla-Silva. New York: Routledge.

Garner, Steve. 2006. "The Uses of Whiteness: What Sociologists Studying Europe Can Draw from North American Work on Whiteness." *Sociology* 40, no. 2, 257–75.

———. 2007. *Whiteness: An Introduction*. London: Routledge.

Gillborn, David, and Caroline Gipps. 1996. *Recent Research on the Achievements of Ethnic Minority Pupils*. London: HMSO.

Gilroy, Paul. 1987. *There Ain't No Black in the Union Jack*. Chicago: University of Chicago Press.

———. 1990. "Cultural Studies and Ethnic Absolutism." *Cultural Studies*, ed. by Lawrence Grossberg, Cary Nelson, and Paula Treichler. New York: Routledge.

————. 1992. "One Nation under a Groove: The Cultural Politics of 'Race' and Racism in Britain." *Anatomy of Racism*, ed. by David Theo Goldberg. Minneapolis: University of Minnesota Press.

————. 1993a. *The Black Atlantic: Modernity and Double Consciousness*. Cambridge, Mass.: Harvard University Press.

————. 1993b. *Small Acts: Thoughts on the Politics of Black Cultures*. London: Serpent's Tail.

Glass, Ruth. 1961. *London's Newcomers: The West Indian Migrants*. Cambridge, Mass.: Harvard University Press.

Glenn, Evelyn Nakano. 1994. "Social Constructions of Mothering: A Thematic Overview." *Mothering: Ideology, Experience and Agency*, ed. by Evelyn Nakano Glenn, Grace Chang, and Linda Rennie Forcy. New York: Routledge.

Glenn, Evelyn Nakano, Grace Chang, and Linda Rennie Forcey, eds. 1994. *Mothering: Ideology, Experience, and Agency*. New York: Routledge.

Goffman, Erving. 1959. *The Presentation of Self in Everyday Life*. New York: Anchor Books.

————. [1963] 1986. *Stigma: Notes on the Management of Spoiled Identity*. New York: Simon and Schuster.

Gold, Stephen. 1986. "Ethnic Boundaries and Ethnic Entrepreneurship: A Photo-Elicitation Study." *Visual Sociology* 6, no. 2, 9–22.

Gomez, Laura. 1997. *Misconceiving Mothers: Legislators, Prosecutors, and the Politics of Prenatal Drug Exposure*. Philadelphia: Temple University Press.

Gramsci, Antonio. 1971. *Selections from the Prison Notebooks*. Edited and translated by Quintin Hoare and George Nowell Smith. New York: International Publishers.

Griffin, John. 1960. *Black Like Me*. New York: Signet.

Hall, Stuart. 1991. "The Local and the Global: Globalization and Ethnicity." *Culture, Globalization, and the World System*, ed. by Anthony D. King. Minneapolis: University of Minnesota Press.

————. 1992. "New Ethnicities." *Race, Culture and Difference*, ed. by J. Donald and Ali Rattansi. London: Sage.

————. 1994. "Who Needs 'Identity'?" *Questions of Cultural Identity*, ed. by Stuart Hall and P. Dugay. London: Sage.

————. 1995. "Negotiating Caribbean Identities." *New Left Review* 209. January/February.

Haney-Lopez, Ian. 1996. *White by Law: The Legal Construction of Race*. New York: New York University Press.

Harper, Douglas. 1984. "Meaning and Work: A Study in Photo-Elicitation." *Journal of Visual Sociology* 2, no. 1, 20–43.

Harrington, C., and I. Lindt. 1998. "The Use of Reflexive Photography in the

Study of the Freshman Year Experience." *Annual Conference of the Indiana Association for Institutional Research*, ED 4294–73.

Harris, Cheryl. 1993. "Whiteness as Property." *Harvard Law Review* 106, no. 8, 1709–91.

Harris, Clive. 1988. "Images of Blacks in Britain: 1930–1960." *Race and Social Policy*, ed. by S. Allen and M. Macey. London: Economic and Social Research Council.

———. 1993. "Post-war Migration and the Industrial Reserve Army." *Inside Babylon: The Caribbean Diaspora in Britain*, ed. by Winston James and Clive Harris. London: Verso.

Harris, David, and Jeremiah Joseph Sim. 2002. "Who Is Multiracial? The Fluidity of Racial Identity among U.S. Adolescents." *American Sociological Review* 67, no. 4, 614–27.

Hartigan, John, Jr. 1997. "Locating White Detroit." *Dis-Placing Whiteness: Essays in Social and Cultural Criticism*, ed. by Ruth Frankenberg. Durham, N.C.: Duke University Press.

———. 1999. *Racial Situations: Class Predicaments of Whiteness in Detroit*. Princeton: Princeton University Press.

Hartsock, Nancy C. M. 1983. "The Feminist Standpoint: Developing the Ground for a Specifically Feminist Historical Materialism." *Discovering Reality*, ed. by Sherril B. Hintikka and Sandra Harding. New York: Springer.

Henderson, Judith. 1960. "A Sociological Report." *Coloured Immigrants in Britain*, ed. by Institute of Race Relations. London: Oxford University Press.

Hewitt, Roger. 1986. *White Talk, Black Talk: Inter-racial Friendship and Communication amongst Adolescents*. Cambridge: Cambridge University Press.

Hickman, Mary. 1996. "Racism and Identity: Issues for the Irish in Britain." *Culture, Identity and Politics*, ed. by Terence Ranger, Yunas Samad, and Ossie Stuart. Aldershot: Avebury.

Hildebrandt, Melanie. 2002. "The Construction of Racial Intermarriage: A Comparison of the Effects of Gender, Race and Class and Black Ethnicity in the Lives of Black/White Couples." Ph.D. diss., Columbia University.

Hoggart, Richard. 1958. *The Uses of Literacy*. Harmondsworth, England: Penguin Books.

hooks, bell. 1997. "Whiteness in the Black Imagination." *Displacing Whiteness: Essays in Social and Cultural Criticism*, ed. by Ruth Frankenberg. Durham, N.C.: Duke University Press.

Ifekwunigwe, Jayne. 1997. "Diaspora's Daughters, Africa's Orphans: On Lineage, Authenticity and 'Mixed Race' Identity." *Black British Feminism: A Reader*, ed. by Heidiz Safia Mirza. London: Routledge.

Ignatiev, Noel. 1995. *How the Irish Became White*. New York: Routledge.

Ikemoto, Lisa. 1999. "Lessons from the *Titanic*: Start with the People in Steerage,

Women and Children First." *Mother Troubles: Rethinking Contemporary Maternal Dilemmas*, ed. by Julia Hanigsberg and Sara Ruddick. Boston: Beacon Press.

Jacobson, Matthew Frye. 1998. *Whiteness of a Different Color: European Immigrants and the Alchemy of Race*. Cambridge, Mass.: Harvard University Press.

James, Winston. 1993. "Migration, Racism and Identity Formation: The Caribbean Experience in Britain." *Inside Babylon: The Caribbean Diaspora in Britain*, ed. by Winston James and Clive Harris. London: Verso.

James, Winston, and Clive Harris, eds. 1993. *Inside Babylon: The Caribbean Diaspora in Britain*. London: Verso.

Jeater, Diana. 1992. "Roast Beef and Reggae Music." *New Formations* 18, 107–21.

Jones, Hettie. 1990. *How I Became Hettie Jones*. New York: E. P. Dutton.

Kenny, Lorraine Delia. 2000. *Daughters of Suburbia: Growing Up White, Middle-Class, and Female*. New Brunswick, N.J.: Rutgers University Press.

Knowles, Caroline. 2003. *Race and Social Analysis*. London: Sage.

———. 2006. "Seeing Race through the Lens." Photographs by Douglas Harper. "Writing Race," special issue of *Ethnic and Racial Studies* 29, no. 3, 512–29.

Knowles, Caroline, and Douglas Harper. 2010. *Hong Kong: Migrant Lives, Landscapes, and Journeys*. Chicago: University of Chicago Press.

Korgen, Kathleen Odell. 1998. *From Black to Biracial: Transforming Racial Identity among Americans*. Westport, Conn.: Praeger.

Lamont, Michele. 1999. "Introduction: Beyond Taking Culture Seriously." *The Cultural Territories of Race: Black and White Boundaries*, ed. by Michelle Lamont. Chicago: University of Chicago Press.

———. 2000. *The Dignity of Working Men: Morality and the Boundaries of Race, Class, and Immigration*. Cambridge, Mass.: Harvard University Press.

Lamont, Michele, and V. Molnar. 2002. "The Study of Boundaries in the Social Sciences." *Annual Review of Sociology* 28, 167–95.

Lawrence, Daniel. 1974. *Black Migrants, White Natives: A Study of Race Relations in Nottingham*. London: Cambridge University Press.

Lawrence, Errol. 1982. "Just Plain Common Sense: The 'Roots' of Racism." *The Empire Strikes Back: Race and Racism in 70s Britain*, ed. by Centre for Contemporary Cultural Studies. London: Hutchinson.

Lazarre, Jane. 1996. *Beyond the Whiteness of Whiteness: Memoir of a White Mother of Black Sons*. Durham, N.C.: Duke University Press.

Leicester City Council. 1993. *Highfields Review: A Report of Statutory Service Provision and Community Perceived Need in Service Delivery*. Leicestershire: Leicester City Council.

———. 1996. *Leicester Key Facts: Ethnic Population*. Leicestershire: Leicester City Council.

Lewis, Amanda. 2003. "What Group? Studying Whites and Whiteness in the Era of 'Color-blindness.'" *Sociological Theory* 22, no. 4, 623–48.

Lewis, Amanda. 2003. *Race in the Schoolyard: Negotiating the Color Line in Classrooms and Communities*. New Brunswick, N.J.: Rutgers University Press.

Lipsitz, George. 1998. *The Possessive Investment in Whiteness: How White People Benefit from Identity Politics*. Philadelphia: Temple University Press.

Little, Kenneth. 1948. *Negroes in Britain: A Study of Race Relations in English Society*. London: Kegan Paul and Trench.

Lopez, Ian F. Haney. 1996. *White by Law: The Legal Construction of Race*. New York: New York University Press.

Luke, Carmen. 1994. "White Women in Interracial Families: Reflections on Hybridization, Feminine Identities, and Racialized Identities." *Feminist Issues* 14, no. 2, 49–72.

Luke, Carmen, and Allan Luke. 1998. "Interracial Families: Difference within Difference." *Ethnic and Racial Studies* 21, no. 4, 728–54.

MacPherson, William. 1999. *The Stephen Lawrence Inquiry: Report on an Inquiry by Sir Williams MacPherson of CLUNY, Advised by Tom Cook*. Presented by the Secretary of State for the Home Department by Command of Her Majesty. London: HMSO.

Marrett, Valerie. 1989. *Immigrants Settling in the City*. London: Leicester University Press.

Massey, Douglas, and Nancy Denton. 1993. *American Apartheid: Segregation and the Making of the Underclass*. Cambridge, Mass.: Harvard University Press.

McBride, James. 1997. *The Color of Water: A Black Man's Tribute to His White Mother*. New York: Riverhead Books.

McDermott, Monica. 2006. *Working-Class White: The Making and Unmaking of Race Relations*. Berkeley: University of California Press.

McDowell, S. F. 1971. "Black-White Intermarriage in the United States." *International Journal of the Family* 1, 57.

McIntosh, Peggy. 2004. "White Privilege: Unpacking the Invisible Knapsack." *Race, Class and Gender: An Anthology*, ed. by Margaret Anderson and Patricia Hill Collins. 5th ed. Beverley, Mass: Wadsworth Publishing Company.

McKinney, Karyn. 2005. *Being White: Stories of Race and Racism*. New York: Routledge.

McNamara, Robert P., Maria Tempenis, and Beth Walton. 1999. *Crossing the Line: Interracial Couples in the South*. Westport, Conn.: Greenwood Press.

Mercer, Kobena. 1994. *Welcome to the Jungle: New Positions in Black Cultural Studies*. New York: Routledge.

Merton, Robert K. 1941. "Intermarriage and the Social Structure: Fact and Theory." *Psychiatry* 4, 361–74.

Miles, Robert, and Malcolm Brown. 2003. *Racism*. 2nd ed. London: Routledge.

Mills, Charles Wright. 1959. *The Sociological Imagination*. London: Oxford University Press.

Mirza, Heidi Safia, ed. 1997. *Black British Feminism: A Reader*. London: Routledge.

Mirza, Heidi and Diane Reay. 2000. "Spaces and Places of Black Education Desire: Rethinking Black Supplementary Schools as a New Social Movement." *Sociology* 34 no. 3, 477–99.

Model, Suzanne, and Gene Fisher. 2002. "Unions between Blacks and Whites: England and the U.S. Compared." *Ethnic and Racial Studies* 25, no. 5, 728–54.

Modell, J. A., and C. Brodsky. 1994. "Envisioning Homestead: Using Photographs in Interviewing." *Interactive Oral History Interviewing*, ed. by Jon Prosser. Hinsdale, N.J.: Erlbaum.

Modood, Tariq, Richard Berthoud, Jane Lakey, James Nazroo, Satnam Virdee, and Sharon Beishon. 1997. *Ethnic Minorities in Britain: Diversity and Disadvantage*. London: Policy Studies Institute.

Mohr, John, and Paul DiMaggio. 1995. "The Intergenerational Transmission of Cultural Capital." *Research in Social Stratification and Mobility* 14, 167–99.

Moon, Dreama. 1999. "White Enculturation and Bourgeois Ideology: The Discursive Production of 'Good (White) Girls.'" *Whiteness: The Communication of Social Identity*, ed. by Thomas Nakayama and Judith Martin. Thousand Oaks, Calif.: Sage.

Morrison, Toni. 1991. *Playing in the Dark: Whiteness in the Literary Imagination*. New York: Vintage.

Morsy, Soheir A. 1994. "Beyond the Honorary 'White' Classification of Egyptians." *Race*, ed. by Steven Gregory and Roger Sanjek. New Brunswick, N.J.: Rutgers University Press.

Mumford, Kevin. 1997. *Interzones: Black/White Sex Districts in Chicago and New York in the Early Twentieth Century*. New York: Columbia University Press.

Nagel, Joane. 2000. "Ethnicity and Sexuality." *Annual Review of Sociology* 26, 107–33.

———. 2003. *Race, Ethnicity and Sexuality: Intimate Intersections, Forbidden Frontiers*. New York: Oxford University Press.

Nava, Mica. 2007. *Visceral Cosmopolitanism: Gender, Culture and the Normalization of Difference*. Oxford: Berg.

Nayak, Anoop. 1997. "Tales from the Darkside: Negotiating Whiteness in School Arenas." *International Studies in Sociology of Education* 7, no. 1, 57–80.

———. 2003. *Race, Place and Globalization: Youth Cultures in a Changing World*. Oxford: Berg.

New Deal Task Force. 1999. *Delivery Plan: A New Deal for Braunstone*. Braunstone, Leicester: New Deal Centre.

Nobles, Denise. 2005. "Remembering Bodies, Healing Histories: The Emotional Politics of Everyday Freedom." *Making Race Matter: Bodies, Space and Identity*. Hampshire, England: Palgrave MacMillan.

Office for National Statistics. 2003. *Census 2001: National Report for England and*

Wales. Laid before Parliament Pursuant to Section 4(1) Census Act of 1920. London: TSO.

————. 2004. *Census 2001: Key Statistics for Urban Areas in the Midlands.* London: TSO.

Omi, Michael, and Howard Winant. 1986. *Racial Formations in the United States.* New York: Routledge and Kegan Paul.

Ossman, Susan. 2002. *Three Faces of Beauty: Casablanca, Paris, Cairo.* Durham, N.C.: Duke University Press.

Parker, David, and Miri Song. 2001. *Rethinking "Mixed Race."* London: Pluto Press.

Patterson, Sheila. 1963. *Dark Strangers: A Sociological Study of the Absorption of a Recent West Indian Migrant Group in Brixton, South London.* Bloomington: Indiana University Press.

Perry, Pamela. 2002. *Shades of White: White Kids and Racial Identities in High School.* Durham, N.C.: Duke University Press.

Phoenix, Anne. 1997. "I'm White! So What? The Construction of Whiteness for Young Londoners." *Off White: Readings in Race, Power, and Society*, ed. by Michelle Fine. New York: Routledge.

Pilkington, Edward. 1988. *Beyond the Mother Country: West Indians and the Notting Hill Riots.* London: I. B. Tauris.

Pink, Sarah. 2001. *Doing Visual Ethnography.* London: Sage.

Porterfield, Ernest. 1976. *Black and White Mixed Marriages: An Ethnographic Study of Black-White Families.* Chicago: Nelson-Hall.

Pratt, Minnie Bruce. 1984. "Identity: Skin, Blood, Heart." *Yours in Struggle: Three Feminist Perspectives on Anti-Semitism and Racism*, ed. by Elly Bulkin, Minnie Bruce Pratt, and Barbara Smith. Brooklyn: Long Haul Press.

————. 1991. *Rebellion: Essays 1980-1991.* New York: Firebrand Press.

Prosser, Jon. 1998. "The Status of Image-based Research." *Image Based Research: A Sourcebook for Qualitative Researchers*, ed. by Jon Prosser. London: Routledge.

Ranger, Terence, Yunas Samad, and Ossie Stuart. 1996. *Culture, Identity and Politics: Ethnic Minorities in Britain.* Aldershot: Avebury Press.

Reay, Diane. 2000. "A useful Extension of Bourdieu's Conceptual Framework? Emotional Capital as a Way of Understanding Mothers' Involvement in Their Children's Education." *Sociological Review* 48 no. 4, 568–84.

————. 2005. "Beyond Consciousness? The Psychic Landscape of Social Class." *Sociology* 39, no. 5, 911–28.

————. 2007. "A Darker Shade of Pale? Whiteness, the Middle Classes, and Multi-ethnic Schooling." *Sociology* 41, no. 6, 1041–59.

Reddy, Maureen. 1994. *Crossing the Color Line: Race, Parenting, and Culture.* New Brunswick, N.J.: Rutgers University Press.

Reeves, Frank. 1983. *British Racial Discourse: A Study of British Political Discourse.* London: Cambridge University Press.

Reynolds, Daniel. 1995. *Rich Relations: The American Occupation of Britain, 1942-1945*. London: Harper Collins.

Reynolds, Tracey. 2006. "Families, Social Capital, and Caribbean People's Diasporic Identities in Britain." *Ethnic and Racial Studies* 29, no. 6, 1087–1103.

Rich, Paul. 1990. *Race and Empire in British Politics*. 2nd ed. Cambridge: Cambridge University Press.

Richmond, Anthony. 1955. *The Colour Problem: A Study of Racial Relations*. Harmondsworth, England: Penguin.

Roberts, Dorothy. 1995. "Punishing Drug Addicts Who Have Babies: Women of Color, Equality, and the Right to Privacy." *Critical Race Theory: The Key Writings that Formed the Movement*, ed. by Kimberle Crenshaw, Neil Gotanda, Gary Peller, and Kendall Thomas. New York: New Press.

———. 1997. *Killing the Black Body: Race, Reproduction, and the Meaning of Liberty*. New York: Pantheon.

———. 1999. "Mothers Who Fail to Protect Their Children: Accounting for Private and Public Responsibility." *Mother Troubles: Rethinking Contemporary Maternal Dilemmas*, ed. by Julia Hanigsberg and Sara Ruddick. Boston: Beacon Press.

Rockquemore, Kerry Ann, and David L. Brunsma. 2002. *Beyond Black: Biracial Identity in America*. Thousand Oaks, Calif.: Sage.

Roediger, David. 1991. *The Wages of Whiteness: Race and the Making of the American Working Class*. New York: Verso.

Roediger, David, ed. 1998. *Black on White: Black Writers on What It Means to Be White*. New York: Schocken.

Romano, Renee. 1998. "Immoral Conduct: White Women, Racial Transgressions, and Custody Disputes." *"Bad" Mothers: The Politics of Blame in Twentieth-Century America*, ed. by Mollay Ladd-Taylor and Lauri Umansky. New York: New York University Press.

Rothman, Barbara Katz. 2005. *Weaving a Family: Untangling Race and Adoption*. Boston: Beacon Press.

Ruddick, Sarah. 1989. *Maternal Thinking: Towards a Politics of Peace*. Boston: Beacon Press.

Saeed, Amir, Neil Blain, and Douglas Forbes. 1999. "New Ethnic and National Questions in Scotland: Post-British Identities among Glasgow Pakistani Teenagers." *Ethnic and Racial Studies* 22, no. 5, 821–44.

Scarman, Lord. 1981. *The Scarman Report: The Brixton Disorders, 10-12 April 1981*. London: HMSO.

Schwartz, Dona. 1989. "Visual Ethnography: Using Photographs in Qualitative Research." *Qualitative Sociology* 12, no. 1, 119–54.

Secrets and Lies. 1996. Written and directed by Mike Leigh. Twentieth-Century Fox.

Segrest, Mab. 1994. *Memoir of a Race Traitor*. Boston: South End Press.

Sennett, Richard, and Jonathan Cobb. 1972. *The Hidden Injuries of Class*. New York: Norton.

Shillingford, Joia. 2005. "Hair-care Firms Wise Up to Ethnic Pound." BBC *Business News*, 2 May, online.

Silverman, Robert Mark. 1998. "The Effects of Racism and Racial Discrimination on Minority Business Development: The Case of Black Manufacturers in Chicago's Ethnic Beauty Aids Industry." *Journal of Social History* 31, no. 3, 571–97.

Skeggs, Beverly. 1994. "Situating the Production of Feminist Ethnography." *Researching Women's Lives from a Feminist Perspective*, ed. by Mary Maynard and Jane Purvis. London: Taylor and Francis.

———. 1997. *Formations of Class and Gender: Becoming Respectable*. London: Sage.

Small, Stephen. 1994. *Racialised Barriers: The Black Experience in the United States and England in the 1980s*. London: Routledge.

Smith, David. 1977. *Racial Disadvantage in Britain: The PEP (Political and Economic Planning) Report*. Middlesex, England: Penguin.

Smith, Graham. 1987. *When Jim Crow Met John Bull: Black American Soldiers in World War II Britain*. London: I. B. Tauris.

Smith, Shawn Michelle. 1999. *American Archives: Gender, Race, and Class in Visual Culture*. Princeton: Princeton University Press.

Smith, Susan. 1989. *The Politics of "Race" and Residence: Citizenship, Segregation and White Supremacy in Britain*. Cambridge: Polity Press.

Solinger, Rickie. 1992. *Wake Up Little Susie: Single Pregnancy and Race before Roe v. Wade*. New York: Routledge.

Solomos, John. 1988. *Black Youth, Racism and the State*. Cambridge: Cambridge University Press.

———. [1989] 2003. *Race and Racism in Britain*. 3rd ed. Hampshire: Palgrave.

Solomos, John, and Les Back. 1994. "Conceptualising Racisms: Social Theory, Politics and Research." *Sociology* 28, no. 1, 143–61.

———. 1996. *Racism and Society*. London: Macmillan.

Solomos, John, Bob Findlay, Simon Jones, and Paul Gilroy. 1982. "The Organic Crisis of British Capitalism and Race: The Experience of the Seventies." *The Empire Strikes Back: Race and Racism in 70s Britain*, ed. by Centre for Contemporary Cultural Studies. London: Hutchinson.

Song, Miri. 1993. *Choosing Ethnic Identity*. Cambridge: Polity Press.

Spensky, Martine. 1992. "Producers of Legitimacy: Homes for Unmarried Mothers in the 1950s." *Regulating Womanhood: Historical Essays on Marriage, Motherhood and Sexuality*, ed. by Carol Smart. London: Routledge.

Sprague, Stephen F. [1978] 2002. "How I See the Yoruba See Themselves." *The*

Anthropology of Media, ed. by Kelly Askew and Richard Wilk. London: Wiley-Blackwell.

Stacey, Judith. 2004. "Cruising to Familyland: Gay Hypergamy and Rainbow Kinship." *Current Sociology* 52, no. 2, 181–97.

———. 2005. "The Families of Man: Gay Male Intimacy and Kinship in a Global Metropolis." *Signs: Journal of Women in Culture and Society* 30, no. 3, 1911–35.

Stasz, Clarence. 1979. "The Early History of Sociology." *Images of Information: Still Photograph in the Social Sciences*, ed. by J. Wagener. Beverly Hills, Calif.: Sage.

Steyn, Melissa. 2001. *Whiteness Just Isn't What It Used to Be: White Identity in a Changing South Africa*. Albany: State University of New York Press.

Stoler, Ann Laura. 1999. "Making Empire Respectable: The Politics of Race and Sexual Morality in Twentieth-Century Colonial Cultures." *American Ethnologist* 16, 634–59.

———. 2002. *Carnal Knowledge and Imperial Power: Race and the Intimate in Colonial Rule*. Berkeley: University of California Press.

Storrs, Debbie. 1999. "Whiteness as Stigma: Essential Identity Work by Mixed-Race Women." *Symbolic Interaction* 22, 187–212.

Swidler, Ann. 2001. *Talk of Love: How Culture Matters*. Chicago: University of Chicago Press.

Tabili, Laura. 1994. "The Construction of Racial Difference in Twentieth Century Britain: The Special Restriction (Coloured Alien Seamen) Order, 1925." *Journal of British Studies* 33, no. 1, 54–98.

———. 1996. "Women of a Very Low Type: Crossing Racial Boundaries in Late Imperial Britain." *Gender and Class in Modern Europe*, ed. by Laura Frader and Sonya Rose. Ithaca, N.Y.: Cornell University Press.

Tatum, Beverly. 1997. *Why Are All the Black Kids Sitting Together in the Cafeteria? And Other Conversations about Race*. New York: Basic Books.

Telles, Edward. 1993. "Racial Distance and Region in Marriage: The Case of Marriage among Color Groups." *Latin American Research Review* 28, 141–62.

Thompson, Becky. 2001. *A Promise and a Way of Life: White Antiracist Activism*. Minneapolis: University of Minnesota Press.

Thompson, Cooper, Emmett Schaefer, and Harry Brod. 2003. *White Men Challenging Racism: 35 Personal Stories*. Durham, N.C.: Duke University Press.

Tizard, Barbara, and Anne Phoenix. 1993. *Black, White or Mixed Race? Race and Racism in the Lives of Young People of Mixed Parentage*. London: Routledge.

Twine, France Winddance. 1997a. "Brown Skinned White Girls: Class, Culture and the Construction of Whiteness in Suburban Communities." *Displacing Whiteness: Essays in Social and Cultural Criticism*, ed. by Ruth Frankenberg. Durham, N.C.: Duke University Press.

———. 1997b. *Racism in a Racial Democracy: The Maintenance of White Supremacy in Brazil*. New Brunswick, N.J.: Rutgers University Press.

———. 1999. "Bearing Blackness in Britain: The Meaning of Racial Difference for White Birth Mothers of African-Descent Children." *Social Identities: Journal of Race, Nation and Culture* 5, no. 2, 185–210.

Twine, France Winddance, and Charles Gallagher. 2008. "The Future of Whiteness: A Map of the 'Third Wave.'" "Whiteness and White Identities," special issue of *Ethnic and Racial Studies* 31, no. 1, 1–24.

Twine, France Winddance, and Amy Steinbugler. 2006. "The Gap between 'Whites' and 'Whiteness': Interracial Intimacy and Racial Literacy." *DuBois Review: Social Science Research on Race* 3, no. 2, 341–63.

Twine, France Winddance, Jonathan Warren, and Francisco Ferrandiz. 1992. *Just Black? Multiracial Identity*. Video. New York: Filmmakers Library.

Van Ausdale, Debra, and Joe Feagin. 2001. *The First R: How Children Learn Race and Racism*. Lanham, Md.: Rowman and Littlefield.

Ward, Janie Victoria. 1996. "Raising Resisters: The Role of Truth Telling in the Psychological Development of African American Girls." *Urban Girls: Resisting Stereotypes, Creating Identities*, ed. by Bonnie Ross and Niobe Way. New York: New York University Press.

Ware, Vron. 1992. Beyond the Pale: White Women, Racism and History. London: Verso Press.

———. 1997. "Island Racism: Gender, Place, and White Power." *Dis-placing Whiteness: Essays in Social and Cultural Criticism*, ed. by Ruth Frankenberg. Durham, N.C.: Duke University Press.

Washington, Joseph R. 1970. *Marriage in Black and White*. Boston: Beacon Press.

Weekes, Debbie. 1997. "Shades of Blackness: Young Black Female Constructions of Beauty." *Black British Feminism: A Reader*, ed. by Heidi Safia Mirza. London: Routledge.

Weiss, Lois. 2004. *Class Reunion: The Remaking of the American White Working Class*. New York: Routledge.

Wellman, David. [1977] 1993. *Portraits of White Racism*. 2nd ed. Cambridge: Cambridge University Press.

Williams, Patricia. 1995. *The Rooster's Egg: On the Persistence of Prejudice*. Cambridge, Mass.: Harvard University Press.

Wilson, Anne. 1981. "In Between: The Mother in the Interracial Family." *New Community: Journal of the Commission for Racial Inequality* 9, no. 2, 208–15.

———. 1989. *Mixed Race Children: A Study of Identity*. London: Allen and Unwin.

Wilson, Mark. 2004. "Cosmetics and Hair Care Products." *Encyclopedia of Chicago History*, Newberry Library, www.encyclopedia.chicagohistory.org.

Winant, Howard. 1997. "Behind Blue Eyes: Whiteness and Contemporary U.S. Racial Politics." *New Left Review* 225, 73–87.

———. 1998. "Racism Today: Continuity and Change in the Post Civil Rights United States." *Ethnic and Racial Studies* 24, no. 4, 755–66.

———. 2000. "Race and Race Theory." *Annual Review of Sociology* 26, 169–85.

———. 2004. *The World Is a Ghetto: Race and Democracy Since World War II.* New York: Basic Books.

Young, Michael, and Peter Wilmott. [1957] 1986. *Family and Kinship in East London.* London: Penguin Books.

INDEX

Page numbers in italics refer to illustrations.

Black Americans (*continued*)
33–34; racism resistance in families and, 121–22

Black British: census category for, 15–17; double standard and, 201; economics and sexuality of, 202; interracial intimacy statistics on, 117; race studies and, 6–7, 36–37; racial literacy and, 261; representations of, 34–35; as term, 27, 140

Black British feminism, 146–147, 167, 169

Black ethnicity, 147, 149. *See also* Blackness

Black feminist theory (North American), 10, 12, 112; forms of discipline and, 62–64, 137–38

Blackness: culinary skills and, 163–67, 169; definitions of, 17–18; European vs. American, 18, 32; hair care and, 150, 152, 154–57; honorary, 2, 69–70, 72, 92, 194, 213, 227, 252; locality and, 112, 131; one-drop rule of, 135, 139–43; sexuality and, 218–20; social production of, 117

Black–white domestic partnerships. *See* Interracial families; Transracial families

Black, White or Mixed Race? (Tizard and Phoenix), 121

Body and ethnic capital, 146–47

Bourdieu, Pierre, 8; on capital types, 37, 149; on culture and food, 158; ethnic capital and, 147–49

Bragg, Kenneth, 116–17

Braunstone Housing Estate (Leicester), *82*, 83–84; Household Survey (1999) and, 71

British Asians, 13–18, 20. *See also* East African–Asian diaspora

British feminists, 10–12

British National Party, 20, 128

Brothers in Trouble (film), 69

Brown, Jacquelyn Nassy, 6

Brown, Owen, *221*

"Brown baby" crisis, 33

Burke, Gerry, *74*, 260

Burke, Mandy, *74*

Capital. *See* Economic capital; Ethnic capital; Social capital; Symbolic capital

Caribbean populations. *See* African Caribbean populations

Caribbean Supermarket (Leicester), 158–62, *159*, *160*

Carpenter, David, 214–16

Carpenter, Simone, 72–73, 214–16

Carrington, Chelsea, 80–81; class origins of, 259; everyday racism and, 104–5; friendships of, 104, 260, 261; portrait of, 102–7; racial literacy of, 105–7, 114; socialization by, 140–43

Censorship, military, 31

Chaplin, Elizabeth, 174

Chase, Adam, 93, 95, 209–11, 243

Chastity, code of, 219

Childcare and legal system, 64

Church of England Monthly Review, 65

Clarke, Casey, *63*

Class: inflected whiteness and, 251; interracial distinctions and, 203–6; marginalization and, 191; postwar Britain and, 37–38; racism and, 92, 101

Collins, Patricia Hill, 10, 62, 112, 137

Color-blindness, 105, 239–40

Commission for Racial Equality (CRE), 83

Critical race theory, 8, 9–12, 61, 117, 144, 146

Cuffy, Nelista, *130*, 136

MacKenzie, Andrea, 78–80, 261
Marrett, Valerie, 18–20
Marriages, mixed. *See* Interracial families; Transracial families
Masjid Umar mosque (Leicester), 42
Maternal empowerment, 62
McBride, Barbara: on class, 107–8; portrait of, 107–11; on racial ideologies, 109; racial literacy of, 109–10, 114
McDermott, Monica, 268n8
McKinney, Karyn, 251, 254
Memoir of a Race Traitor (Segrest), 91
Memoirs, 89–92
Mercer, Kobena, 156
Mercury (Leicester newspaper), 118–19
Micropolitical sites, 4
Mills, C. Wright, 109, 114
Mitchell, Eshe, *148*, 152–56, *153*, *155*, 261
Mitchell, Helena, 152–56, *153*, 261
Mixed marriages. *See* Interracial families; Transracial families
Mixed-race populations, 14, 140
Mixed-race studies, 3
Moat Community College (Leicester), 22
Modood, Tariq, 15, 129–31
Moonen, Justine, 133–35, *134*, 163–65
Moonen, Sasqua, 133–35, *134*
Mothers. *See* White transracial mothers
Moult, Julia, *172*, 177, *185*, 186
Moult, Raymond Charles, *172*, 177, *185*, 186
Murray, Natasha, 122–25
Music, black, 236

Nagel, Joanne, 58
Nash, Katrina, 70–71, 213

National Front Party, 12, 20, 128, 246, 248
Nava, Mica, 31–32, 34
Nayak, Anoop, 146
Negro, use of term, 32
New Racism, 2
New York Times, 22
Noble, Denise, 146–47, 167
Nottingham, 15, 116; race riots in, 35–36, 199
Notting Hill (London) race riots, 35–36, 108

Office for Standards in Education, 120
Omi, Michael, 268n9
One-drop rule, 135, 139–43
O'Riley, Anita, 152, *153*
Ossman, Susan, 157
Otherness, as attractive, 31–32, 57
Outsiders within concept, 137–38

Parental rejection. *See* Family rejection
PEP. *See* Political and Economic Planning
Phoenix, Ann, 121
Photography: documentary vs. photojournalism, 176; meaning and transformation in, 188; negotiating race and, 192–94; visual sociology and, 174–76. *See also* Family photographs
Picture Post (newspaper), 31
Pilkington, Edward, 35
Pink, Sarah, 188
Piper, Annette, *245*; marriage of, 246–48, 249–50; on race, 249–50
Piper, Brian, *245*; as antiracist professional, 128–29, 244–48, 252; background of, 128, 244, 253–54; class origins of, 263; marriage of, 246–48,

France Winddance Twine is a professor of sociology at the University of California, Santa Barbara. She is the author of *Racism in a Racial Democracy: The Maintenance of White Supremacy in Brazil* (1998) and *Outsourcing the Womb: Race, Class, and Gestational Surrogacy in a Global Market* (forthcoming, 2011) and the editor (with Kathleen Blee) of *Feminism and Antiracism: International Struggles for Justice* (2001).

Library of Congress Cataloging-in-Publication Data
Twine, France Winddance
A white side of black Britain : interracial intimacy and racial literacy / France Winddance Twine ; photographs by Michael Smyth.
p. cm.
Includes bibliographical references and index.
ISBN 978-0-8223-4900-6 (cloth : alk. paper)
ISBN 978-0-8223-4876-4 (pbk. : alk. paper)
1. Racism—England—East Midlands. 2. East Midlands (England)—Race relations. 3. Interracial marriage—England—East Midlands. 4. Racially mixed children—England—East Midlands. 5. Anti-racism—England—East Midlands. I. Title.
DA125.A1T95 2010
305.8'05960210425—dc22   2010025680

South Boston Educational Complex
95 G St.
S. Boston, MA 02127